Praise for *The Way of Jesus*

"Jonathan Campbell provides us with a guidebook to authenticity—
a way to follow Jesus that encourages us to be whole and centered.
While many have left the church in search of Jesus, Campbell
gives legitimate hope that all who wander are not lost."

—Rt. Rev. Ray Lévesque, founder, New
Gatherings; director, First Nations
Learning Center

"Since we met Jonathan and Jennifer Campbell as a whole family, we were impressed to see how they were ready to follow Jesus
without compromise. You will be encouraged and learn from their
experiences by reading this book!"

—Daniel and Cornelia Hari, authors,
Healing Like Jesus, Luzern,
Switzerland

"Jonathan Campbell has courageously followed a call to imagine
and practice a way of Christian life in the midst of a North American church that too quickly sells itself out to the latest trends or
images of success. One may not agree with all of his conclusions
or descriptions, but he needs to be listened to because he was willing to go on a radical journey of pilgrimage and discovery. In that
journey, he reconnected with the centrality of Jesus and redis-
covered the need to listen to others before imagining what God
may be up to in our neighborhoods and in the reforming of Christian life in Western culture."

—Alan J. Roxburgh, president, Missional
Leadership Institute; author,
*The Missionary Congregation,
Leadership, and Liminality*

"Jonathan and Jennifer Campbell carry within them a unique mix of something old and something new, which enables them to speak about the journey of life with a fresh perspective. Read this and you will venture with them to discover truth beyond the trappings."

—Brett Johnson, author, *Convergence*;
founder, The Institute for Innovation,
Integration, and Impact

"A cosmic gypsy experience, a pilgrimage paced by light speed and amoebic slowness in the same eternal moment, discovering that eternity is always, always now. The Campbells have encouraged me by their courageous love of Jesus, by framing some edges I had not quite seen."

—Marsha Gilliland, manager,
Intel Corporation

The Way of Jesus

A Journey of Freedom for Pilgrims and Wanderers

Jonathan S. Campbell
with Jennifer Campbell

Foreword by Brian D. McLaren

A Leadership Network Publication

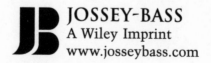

JOSSEY-BASS
A Wiley Imprint
www.josseybass.com

Published by Jossey-Bass
A Wiley Imprint
989 Market Street, San Francisco, CA 94103–1741   www.josseybass.com

All Scripture quotations, unless noted otherwise, are from *The Holy Bible, New Living Translation*
(NIV). Copyright 1996, Tyndale Charitable Trust. All rights reserved.

Excerpt by Thomas Merton, from THE COLLECTED POEMS OF THOMAS MERTON, copyright
© 1949 by Our Lady or Gethsemani Monastery. Reprinted by permission of New Directions
Publishing Corp. Reproduced by permission of Pollinger Limited and the proprietor.

Excerpt from "The Way It Is" copyright © 1998 by the Estate of William Stafford. Reprinted from
The Way It Is: New & Selected Poems with the permission of Graywolf Press, Saint Paul, Minnesota.

Library of Congress Cataloging-in-Publication Data

   Campbell, Jonathan Stuart.
     The way of Jesus: a journey of freedom for pilgrims and wanderers / Jonathan Campbell,
  with Jennifer Campbell; foreword by Brian D. McLaren.—1st ed.
      p. cm.
   Includes bibliographical references.
   ISBN-10: 0–7879–7683–0 (alk. paper)
   ISBN-13: 978–0–7879–7683–5 (alk. paper)
   1. Christian life. 2. Campbell, Jonathan Stuart. I. Campbell, Jennifer, 1965- II. Title.
  BV4501.3.C357 2005
  248.4—dc22   2005007790

Printed in the United States of America
FIRST EDITION
HB Printing 10 9 8 7 6 5 4 3 2 1

Leadership Network Titles

Shaped by God's Heart: The Passion and Practices of Missional Churches, by Milfred Minatrea

The Ascent of a Leader: How Ordinary Relationships Develop Extraordinary Character and Influence, by Bill Thrall, Bruce McNicol, and Ken McElrath

The Elephant in the Boardroom: Speaking the Unspoken About Pastoral Transitions, by Carolyn Weese and J. Russell Crabtree

Contents

About Leadership Network

Since 1984, Leadership Network has fostered church innovation and growth by diligently pursuing its far-reaching mission statement: to identify, connect, and help high-capacity Christian leaders multiply their impact.

Although Leadership Network's techniques adapt and change as the church faces new opportunities and challenges, the organization's work follows a consistent and proven pattern.

Leadership Network brings together entrepreneurial leaders who are focused on similar ministry initiatives. The ensuing collaboration—often across denominational lines—creates a strong base from which individual leaders can better analyze and refine their own strategies. Peer-to-peer interaction, dialogue, and sharing inevitably accelerate participants' innovation and ideas. Leadership Network further enhances this process through developing and distributing highly targeted ministry tools and resources, including audio and video programs, special reports, e-publications, and online downloads.

With Leadership Network's assistance, today's Christian leaders are energized, equipped, inspired, and better able to multiply their own dynamic Kingdom-building initiatives.

Launched in 1996 in conjunction with Jossey-Bass (a Wiley imprint), Leadership Network Publications present thoroughly researched and innovative concepts from leading thinkers, practitioners, and pioneering churches. The series collectively draws from a range of disciplines, with individual titles offering perspective on one or more of five primary areas:

1. Enabling effective leadership

2. Encouraging life-changing service

3. Building authentic community

4. Creating Kingdom-centered impact

5. Engaging cultural and demographic realities

For additional information on the mission or activities of Leadership Network, please contact:

Leadership Network
2501 Cedar Springs, Suite 200
Dallas, TX 75201
(800) 765-5323
client.care@leadnet.org

Foreword

I am for the church in all its diversity. I am for churches that meet in cathedrals, meeting houses, chapels, homes, storefronts, parks, and pubs—churches with and without names, churches with and without formal structures or written liturgies, and churches with and without longevity. I sincerely love and see beauty in all expressions of Christian faith. When authentic disciples are being formed, how can we choose any option over celebrating the diversity of our faith's many embodiments? That's why I believe we need them all, and the healthier they are the more effectively they equip people "for love and good deeds" and the better for everyone. Of course I also believe that all forms of church are subject to distortion. Any form of church can become dysfunctional. There are no foolproof forms for being and doing church since we humans achieve nearly infinite ingenuity in finding new ways of being foolish.

Meanwhile, the secret is getting out: in spite of the great strengths and proven virtues of the organized church, many Christians are leaving it these days and finding their lives, including their spiritual lives, improve (at least temporarily) as a result. As Jonathan and Jennifer Campbell say later in the book you have just begun reading, many are leaving church not because they have lost their faith but rather because they want to save it. Jonathan and Jennifer Campbell know what they are talking about because they lived those statistics: they worked within the organized church and then walked away. But they are not discouraged or overly cynical. They believe "the decline of institutionalized religions is setting the stage for spiritual revival."

If the Campbells were to suggest in these pages that their path away from institutional Christianity into what they call more organic forms of church is the only good path, their overstatement could be excused because at least they would be serving as informants to the rest of us, revealing what it is about organized religion that has become an insurmountable stumbling block to so many and what it is they are seeking instead. Whether or not you consider yourself a defender, reformer, or preserver of institutional Christianity, you will be able to learn much in the pages that follow from Jonathan and Jennifer Campbell's sincere, articulate, and put-your-money-where-your-mouth-is example and experience.

Jonathan and Jennifer Campbell's voices resonate with the voices of thousands of young Christian leaders I've met in the last ten years. In some ways, they are saying things that people were saying when I was just coming of age as a new disciple in the early 1970s—people like Ray Stedman, Chuck Smith, and the Jesus Movement. The fact that now, thirty years later, these things still need to be said tells us at least three things:

1. The radical, countercultural message of the Jesus Movement was not sufficiently understood or embraced thirty years ago although it may have been co-opted and "bought" on a more superficial level.
2. The problems that it was addressing have not gone away.
3. Something or Someone still stirs in the hearts of Christians today and will not let them be satisfied with the status quo.

We humans are generally too quick to judge (and to make overly general statements as I've just done). In recent months I have heard people talk about the Jesus Movement as a clear and obvious failure, but maybe that judgment is premature. Maybe what we call the Jesus Movement was simply the first wave of a rising tide that is still coming in. Maybe Jonathan Campbell and thousands of young leaders like him represent the next wave. Maybe their refusal to just go along with the program is not a sign of rebellion but of vision—the kind of vision young men and old men alike are supposed to see and dream in the age of the Spirit.

Maybe some of the people who quickly write off these emerging voices as young, naïve, and idealistic will themselves be written off—not because they're wrong in their judgment but because they're making judgments in the first place. After all, people without wild dreams and high ideals don't have much of anywhere to go, and it's hard to follow anyone who's not going anywhere, you know?

What might happen if bright, idealistic people like Jonathan and Jennifer Campbell succeed? What if there really were a wave of people who began practicing what Dietrich Bonhoeffer called a "religion-less Christianity," where church liturgy, property, polity, (and politics?) were eclipsed by community, charity, fidelity, and integrity in daily discipleship? Would anyone be so sour or jaded as to complain about that?

"Well," you might be thinking, "can't we have both? Can't we integrate the latter with the former?" It's possible to remain cautiously hopeful, but it won't happen unless people listen to voices like the Campbells', and learn from them.

In the meantime, they blaze a trail many others will follow. That less-traveled path will appeal to those who can't bear the thought of spending decades trying to bring about structural renewal in cold-molasses-institutional settings, especially when there are neighbors to meet and love, neighborhoods to transform, and movements of Christ followers to launch and lead. It will appeal to those for whom staying in the institutional forms of church (whether mainline, evangelical, or charismatic) is not an option; for them, the only options are walk away from the faith entirely or seek to live—in simple yet costly ways—the Way of Jesus.

My hope is that the tide will rise and lift all our boats—the big ocean liners, the middle-sized yachts and tugs, and the scores of little kayaks and rafts and rowboats and canoes. My hope is that we will move ahead together in the Way of Jesus. Don't be surprised if it's the little guys who are leading us, since Jesus told us to expect the unexpected.

Laurel, Maryland   Brian D. McLaren
June 2005

Preface: Beginnings

The journey of a thousand miles begins with one step.
—*Lao Tzu (c. 570–490* B.C.*), Chinese philosopher*

Pilgrims are poets who create by taking journeys.
—*Richard R. Niebuhr, American theologian*

The best of journeys never go as planned. It's the surprises and detours that make life interesting. We all know that life is rarely safe, linear, and predictable.

Just days after graduating college I joined the many coeds who converge upon Europe with only a backpack and EurRail pass. I was free—free of deadlines and responsibilities, free to explore. I saw many beautiful sites and historical places, but the real journey was the inward one. My eyes and heart were wide open to experience new perspectives on life, cultures, and God.

After several weeks on my own, the romance and freedom of travel suddenly paled one drizzly evening in Luzern, Switzerland. These feelings peaked as I chewed my stale baguette and goat cheese under the awnings of a musty hostel crowded with weary travelers irritated by the cramped conditions and rain. I caught the bug of their discontentment and spiraled down. I wanted a traveling companion.

Really, I wanted Jennifer, my best friend and future bride.

In the theatre of my mind, I replayed the scene of my parting with Jennifer three weeks earlier at Chester Station, just outside Wales. While she toured northern England with her brother and sister, I was to continue on my own and wouldn't see her for another two months until we were to meet in Los Angeles.

The rain cleared by the next morning. I boarded a train for Zürich and settled into a compartment I hoped to have for myself. So I did what I could to look unwelcoming, with my backpack filling the seat next to me and my feet propped up on the seat across. Occasionally I'd raise my gaze to see if someone was walking down the hall looking for a seat. On one such glance I recognized a familiar face. My future brother-in-law, Charlie, was walking past my compartment. I knew Jennifer was somewhere in Europe; but the same village, the same day, the same train, and same car? After the initial shock, I stuck my head out the door and yelled down the hall, "Charlie?"

Charlie's eyes opened wide and his mouth dropped open. "Jonathan! What are you doing here?"

"I'm eating breakfast on my way to Zürich. Hungry?" as I offered Charlie some of my leftovers.

"Oh, man . . . we've got to surprise Jennifer. . . . She's just boarding on the next car with Cindy!" We quickly came up with a scheme. Charlie will direct Jennifer to a "free" compartment. I'll sit there, scraggly beard, hat cocked over my face, leaning against the wall. He zips out and I take my position.

Moments later, Jennifer did a double-take before realizing that this Euro-bum was actually her Euro-chum! I caught Jennifer before she staggered backward in shock. We embraced with the joy and wonder of running into each other in the middle of Europe!

Jennifer and I journeyed together from that point on. We traveled the Austrian Alps, and then took the Orient Express to Budapest where we spent a weekend. We caught a barge down the Rhine River in Germany, and finished our journey with a sobering tour of the concentration camp at Dachau before we flew back home to California. Those few weeks in Europe traveling together planted seeds within us that continue to bear fruit today and were the beginning of our life and journey together.

I tell this story because the metaphor of life as a journey has become so powerful for us. Life is meant to be a journey. And the purpose of a journey, in contrast to a trip, is to embody the experience—to learn from it, grow, and enjoy it. I haven't always seen life this way nor appreciated it as such. But I'm learning to embrace life as "journey" instead of life as a series of trips or some set of tasks to accomplish.

I hardly call the nine and a half hour flight from Seattle to Heathrow a journey. But trekking the Olympic Mountains with my son and a few friends—now, that is a journey. It is characterized with the highs and lows of the trail, the blisters from an ill-fitted boot or bites from attacking mosquitoes, as well as by the treasures of an alpine sunset or beauty of a hidden stream tumbling down through ferns and trees.

A trip can be taken on paved roads, but a journey cannot. The grueling lessons of life are revealed not so much in the predictable and well-worn ways, but through the unknown back roads. Typically the most memorable experiences I have when traveling are not what I plan or expect, but the detours and crises along the way like getting lost while leading my first backpacking expedition in the Sierra Nevada Mountains or hitch-hiking with my family after our van broke down on a desolate South African highway. Though the back roads may take more time, the journey is well worth it.

Venturing into the wilderness we begin to see new vistas and come to new understandings of self, our surroundings, and Spirit. For every pilgrim knows the purpose of a wilderness journey is not to get from one end of the trail to the other, but to experience the landscape, adapting and enjoying whatever we encounter on the way.

On the edge of medieval maps, cartographers inscribed the Latin phrase *terra incognita* or "unknown territory." The doomsayers said that if you ventured too far you'd fall off the edge of the earth. But that didn't keep the explorers from venturing into uncharted waters or unknown territory. The Spirit is still calling us into *terra incognita*. God's objective is always to get us to go beyond what we know!

Trips Begin and End, But Journeys Unfold and Unveil

> An adventure is, by its nature, a thing that comes to us. It is a thing that chooses us, not a thing that we choose.
>
> —*Gilbert K. Chesterton (1874–1936),*
> *philosopher and author,* Heretics

All journeys are spiritual. They are also paradoxical. Embodying the experience often brings pain that eventually transforms into joy. Jennifer and I find this to be true at the spiritual core of our very being. We're sharing our story of adventuring on the Way of Jesus—both our difficulties and our delights. As Jen and I look ahead, we can't always see the full picture of what God is doing or where he is leading us. But when we take the time to pause and reflect on life, we begin to see his loving presence at work in our lives.

It reminds us of the simple tapestry I brought back from a small mountain village in the Philippines. It's difficult to make out the picture from the knots and frays of thread on the backside. And it would be equally difficult to see the whole as the tapestry is woven, hour by hour, and day by day. But as we give up our myopic vision and illusions of control, we can begin to appreciate the wisdom of the Master Weaver, who brings in different threads of color and texture that don't make any sense at the time. Is that dark thread really necessary? We might ask, why the rough yarn? Why not a soft silk thread? The temptation in our lives—both in good times and in bad—is to try to take back control and attempt to tidy up what we can see on the backside of the tapestry.

Though we may not always recognize it, our hearts' desire is to trust not in our ways, but in the strength of our God. We find encouragement in a psalm King David wrote centuries ago, "Happy are those who are strong in the Lord, who set their minds on a pilgrimage . . ." (Psalm 84:5). Daily we are faced with the decision to trust the Creator of our lives or to take control for ourselves. Such trust in a wise and loving God is not the invalidation of self, but instead requires the setting aside of self-rule. We've discovered, in one of many God-drawn paradoxes, the transformation and fulfillment of self without selfishness as we journey in Jesus. "The Way It Is" by William Stafford, a Pacific Northwest poet, captures the spirit of our life's journey:

> *There's a thread you follow.*
> *It goes among things that change.*
> *But it doesn't change.*
> *People wonder about what you are pursuing.*
> *You have to explain about the thread.*
> *But it is hard for others to see.*
> *While you hold it you can't get lost.*
> *Tragedies happen; people get hurt*
> *or die; and you suffer and get old.*
> *Nothing you do can stop time's unfolding.*
> *You don't ever let go of the thread.*

In our journey of the past fifteen years, Jennifer and I have joined with others to (re)discover and (re)embody the gospel of Jesus. This book comes out of our journey and is for the many who have become weary of religion of any sort, regardless of their involvement as participant, dabbler, leader, or skeptic. Like some of our friends, you may have questions about the relevance of Jesus or you may be in a process of breaking out of religion, or have already broken out but can't allow yourself to give up on your own spiritual identity, or maybe you long for deeper connection with Creation and your Creator.

Our life is still in process but we are certain of one thing: Jesus is powerfully real. To know Jesus is not an event, a ritual, creed, or

a religion. This book points toward a way of living a holistic spirituality from the core of being—to the very connections that define
our humanity. It is written for those, like us, who are yearning for
Spirit and spirituality, for depth and meaning in life, for belonging
and community. We are spiritual pilgrims, religious refugees, searching for a place to live and to belong. We are moved by our spiritual
longings, and we just intuitively know there has to be another way
of being and doing religion and spirituality.

This is our "travelogue" of what we have experienced and discovered in our journey of learning to live outside the "system"
of organized religion. As the great Oxford professor and writer
C. S. Lewis said, "We read to know that we are not alone." We
write to know that we are not alone. Our journey informs our writing and our writing brings clarity to our journey.

This book is about the journey Jennifer and I have been on thus
far and it is about the journey we invite you to consider. We join
with those of old who have drawn their strength from God and set
their hearts on pilgrimage. It is a journey of trust and adventure.
And as with any journey, there are times of great thrill and equally
huge disappointment, joy and sadness, fast-paced movement and
agonizing waiting, shortcuts and detours. Our journey has been
marked by conversations and questions we have engaged in with
people along the trail. We invite you to share in the stories of fellow pilgrims and some of our observations that have helped guide
our journey.

In a way, this book is a journal of our thoughts from the road, a
road we are still on. We do not claim to have answers because we
have completed the journey. Rather, we write as ones still on pilgrimage, still processing the adventure as it unfolds. We resonate
with Paul, an apostle of the first century church, when he writes a
letter to his fellow disciples:

> I'm not saying that I have this all together, that I have it made. But I
> am well on my way, reaching out for Christ, who has so wondrously
> reached out for me. Friends, don't get me wrong: By no means do I

count myself an expert in all of this, but I've got my eye on the goal, where God is beckoning us onward—to Jesus. I'm off and running, and I'm not turning back [Philippians 3:13–14, *The Message*[1]].

An Invitation

I shall not find Christ at the end of the journey
unless he accompanies me along the way.
—*Esther De Waal, English author,*
Celtic Way of Prayer

The Way of Jesus is about adventuring with him toward freedom, in every sphere of life. It is a journey into relationship where we simply live in Jesus, where his life flows from within us "as springs of living water." As we taste of this new life, we will not settle for anything less than moving in the flow of his Spirit.

So we invite you to join the adventure as a fellow pilgrim. May this book be a navigational guide to help you chart a course for experiencing a deep and fulfilling spirituality in the life and Way of Jesus. We hope you will be encouraged on your spiritual pilgrimage to

- Experience the love and reality of Jesus
- Gain courage to journey and not to settle for anything less than fullness in Jesus
- Be on guard against pitfalls that will hinder your freedom in Jesus
- Experience the love, power, and truth of Jesus in community
- Join with others to experience and embody the Way of Jesus in and across cultures

Our goal is to (re)discover the "ancient paths" that will enable us to experience Jesus in a way that is indigenous to both our culture and our hearts. So the important thing is not what is *on* these pages, but *the Life lived out through us* in our friendships, families, communities, and world. And it's not so much a matter of *what* we believe, but really *who* we believe in, *how* we believe, and who we believe *with*. We cannot fully understand this way of life outside of personal experience, nor outside of vital community. This Way of Jesus is inherently spiritual and relational. It is spiritual in that Jesus is the Center and it is the Holy Spirit who breathes life into us. It is relational because the reality and fullness of Jesus Christ is experienced in community, not only individually. We resonate with this passage from a letter written to a group of young Jesus followers by John, one of the original twelve disciples of Jesus:

> From the very first day, we were there, taking it all in—we heard it with our own ears, saw it with our own eyes, verified it with our own hands. The Word of Life appeared right before our eyes; we saw it happen! And now we're telling you in most sober prose that what we witnessed was, incredibly, this: The infinite Life of God himself took shape before us. We saw it, we heard it, and now we're telling you so you can experience it along with us, this experience of communion with the Father and his Son, Jesus Christ. Our motive for writing is simply this: We want you to enjoy this, too. Your joy will double our joy! [I John 1:1–4, *The Message*].

This is an experiential path. It is a journey of life, of traveling the unknown and beautiful and sometimes stark backroads of moving from freedom to freedom! It is *not* intended to give all the answers, to present a model, or set out a program. We will share some core observations that have emerged from our journey. So, be like the Bereans described in Acts 17 who didn't believe everything they heard from the apostles Paul and Silas, but discerned together as a community in light of the Scriptures and the Spirit among them.

We encourage you to read with your eyes open to the vital relationships around you—with self, the Spirit, your community, and the world. We encourage you to join with others in discussing this book together. You may wish to preview the questions at the end of each chapter, then go back and read the chapter. Invite the Holy Spirit to guide you in all truth and understanding. Check everything to the fullness of Word and Spirit and community.

May this book open your eyes to new ways of seeing reality, experiencing Jesus, and engaging with others on a spiritual journey.

> *May the Son of God be at the outset of my journey,*
> *May the Son of God be in surety to aid me;*
> *May the Son of God make clear my way,*
> *May the Son of God be at the end of my seeking.*
>
> —Celtic prayer, *Carmina Gadelica* III[2]

To our children,
Lauren, David, Rachael, and Nathanael,
our first and most daring sojourners of the Way.

Soli Deo Gloria!

The Way of Jesus

Part One

PERSPECTIVES

These hard times are small potatoes compared to the coming
   good times, the lavish celebration prepared for us.
There's far more here than meets the eye.
The things we see now are here today, gone tomorrow.
But the things we can't see now will last forever. . . .
It's what we trust in but don't yet see that keeps us going.
                    —*Apostle Paul, to the church at Corinth,*
            II Corinthians 14:17–18; 5:17, The Message

1

THE JOURNEY
IS THE GIFT

Happy are those who are strong in the Lord,
who set their minds on a pilgrimage.
—*King David of Israel (ninth century* B.C.*), Psalm 84:5*

Pilgrimage involves committing to a way.

I came to a major crossroads in my own journey one night around midnight. It was a cold fall evening during my junior year at the University of California at Davis. I wrestled with the Spirit of God that night—or should I say, the Spirit wrestled me. Like many brought up in a Christian home, I had to come to terms with my own beliefs and convictions. A heart-based pilgrimage can't be inherited, and, anyway, I wasn't one to believe something just because I was told to. I figured if Jesus is truly God and I am not—as the Bible proclaims—then he is worthy of my complete trust or none at all. So I struggled with what it meant to trust God with my life—*all* of it. I decided I would either trust and follow him[1] or just live on my own.

After several hours of praying through tears, I was finally able to voice a wholehearted promise to Jesus: "I trust you, Jesus. My answer to you is an eternal yes. I will be who you want me to be, I will do what you want me to do, I will say what you want me to say, I will go where you want me to go. I am yours, Lord Jesus." I simply believed Jesus was far more able than I to lead my life.

The moment I surrendered, the angst subsided and a tangible peace flooded my heart and mind. I gave up my blueprint for life in order to follow the Spirit. I had no more decisions to make about overall direction, because my spirit had settled on Jesus Christ as my ultimate Spiritual Director. I knew I just wanted to live from a place of intimacy with Jesus, not from others' expectations (or even my own). I hungered to hear the voice of Jesus and to discern his ways and walk in them. That night proved to be a spiritual marker that has set me on a course that would shape my life, marriage, and friendships.

A Companion on the Journey

Two people can accomplish more than twice as much
as one. . . .
If one person falls, the other can reach out and help. . . .
A person standing alone can be attacked and defeated,
but two can stand back-to-back and conquer.
for a triple-braided cord is not easily broken.

—*Ecclesiastes 4:9–12*

At about that time, I met Jennifer at a spiritual retreat in the Sierra Nevada Mountains. From our first meeting during an initial snowball fight, we continued nearly daily conversations back at the UC Davis dorm cafeteria. As weeks went by, we found ourselves talking long after the rest of our friends were gone and the grill was closed. It probably helped that neither of us was interested in dating anyone at the time, so we weren't trying to impress each other. We struggled with the same life questions. Our hearts both longed to experience life led by the Spirit, enjoy real community, and make a difference in the world. Those early days of our friendship were marked by a genuine openness and searching. We stayed up late many nights, wrestling with how to surrender our lives to Jesus. As much as our hearts yearned for a deeper spiritual reality that would transform every area and moment of our lives—a passionate, reckless abandon—we struggled with what this would mean.

Little did we know at the time that we were setting our bearings to navigate life together. But those critical, deep conversations altered our paths forever and set us apart from a conventional way of living. They demanded sacrifice and surrender of our selves before God. Jennifer remembers wrestling with not wanting to lay down her desire for spontaneity and adventure in life. At the time, she thought a deeper spiritual reality meant conforming to the daily rigors of pious (and boring) life. She now looks back and laughs at how foolish that perception was! Our lives are anything but rigorously religious, but they are deeply spiritual, highly adventuresome, and (frequently enough) punctuated with major challenges that bring us closer to God and one another as a family.

Eventually, our united desire for God influenced how we viewed our relationship with each other. Although we kept insisting we were "just friends," as we grew closer in friendship we began to talk about marriage. We soon realized we were considering much more than whether we loved each other, enjoyed spending time together, or had common interests and passions. We agonized over whether we should even get married. *Would our marriage dilute our spiritual passion? Would we be better together than apart?*

We finally came to the point of laying down our relationship. One night we prayed about whether to get married. Jennifer asked God to help us clearly know whether we were to continue. The Spirit spoke to each of us, saying basically, "I've already told you; what more do you want?" Like so many before us in the Bible and in history, we insisted on questioning God, asking for more signs, but God made it clear to us that night. Our hearts were united, and we had the blessing of our families and countless friends.

Twists on the Way

> Keeping to the main road is easy, but people love to be sidetracked.
>
> —*Lao Tzu (c. 570–490 B.C.), Chinese philosopher*

Our tapestry changed even before we married. Just as I was about to go to graduate school in organizational psychology, a growing church in the foothills of Northern California invited me to serve as associate pastor. This was the same church at which I had worked as a youth director the previous summer. Jennifer and I both sensed God leading us on this path.

So in the fall of 1987, just six months before we married, I began ministering at the church. Soon I was speaking at conferences, writing religious curricula, and leading mission projects overseas. The church even paid me to take time to commute two days a week to San Francisco to earn my Master's degree at seminary. I was on the fast track to prototypical success as defined for professional church pastors. Everything was going well, and even better after our wedding. We enjoyed the congregation, and our church grew rapidly. We bought our first home and helped design the new church building on the growing edge of the city. It was a good life. We were doing all the seemingly right things for continued success. But the more we did, the more restless we became.

I had it made, at least from a career perspective. It took me a while to realize I was being groomed to pastor a large church. As I was rising up the church corporate ladder, my soul was disintegrating in spiritual decline—even though I didn't know it at the time. Little by little, I was being pulled apart, slowly conforming to ways that I have since come to realize were unnatural to who I was. What began as serving Jesus and people slowly turned into serving the needs of an organization. It was a subtle but significant shift.

For instance, I no longer felt the freedom or had the time to pursue certain relationships that I was drawn to. Instead, I felt tied to maintaining and propping up "key" relationships within the church. And regardless of how I was feeling, or the spiritual condition of my heart at the time, I was still expected to fulfill my duties and responsibilities.

In a way, I was extracted out of living a life in the real world and inserted into an artificial Christian subculture. As well as I was doing in the world of ministry, I still had a constant nagging in my soul, a feeling that my spiritual life was slowly withering away. In contrast to the spiritual vitality of my college years, my seemingly successful professional church life felt stagnant. As the church grew numerically, I grew increasingly more disenchanted. With so much time spent on administrative meetings and organizational logistics, we had little room to nurture friendships. We were expending more time and energy on preparing for next Sunday or the next event than in being present and listening to the Spirit. The church budget reflected little concern for the real needs within our community, and no regard for social justice, environmental stewardship, or the world's poor.

Jennifer and I kept asking ourselves, *Do we really want to give our lives to this? Are we willing to spend the rest of our lives building the organization of the church? What difference is all this making in society?* In college, we'd given our lives to Jesus to follow him and serve him wherever he would lead. But somehow, in the course of events, it seemed as though we were serving the church more than Jesus. Our life in Jesus and our position in church blurred. The needs of the organization outweighed the Spirit of God moving in our hearts. We wondered, *How did we lose our way with Jesus? And how can we recover it?*

From Pastor to Planter

In the midst of my growing spiritual crisis, the senior pastor left our church for a denominational job, so I was asked to serve as the primary pastor while the church searched for a replacement. Even without a permanent senior pastor, the number of people at the church continued to grow. But, as is typical when there is no senior leader, the church's finances were unstable. As I sat in the next quarterly business meeting, my heart sank as I watched what was happening. Buildings and budgets replaced the focus on Christ and community. The deep cuts wiped out any funds for our ministries to the outside community, to children and overseas mission, while the mortgage payment and salaries remained untouched. Midway through the business meeting, I came very close to making a motion to sell the building, so we could be free to move as the Spirit would lead us. Why, I thought, are we paying professionals to do what the people of God should be doing anyway? Why do we need a professional pastor? Why do we need a building to be a church, especially when it's only used a few hours on two days a week? What do buildings and salaries have to do with being the Body of Christ? Are we moved more by money or by the Spirit of God?

As Jennifer and I asked these questions, we came to realize we could no longer perpetuate such a system. We were not as free as we thought we were. We had to get out. But how? We explored options: start a business, move overseas, start a new church free of religious trappings.

Eventually, we sensed God's leading to plant a new church in an urban area. Our aim was to follow the example of Jesus and gather a community of people who simply wanted to live out the Way of Jesus in relationship with one another. So in 1992 we sold our home and moved to Southern California to establish a church in the fast-growing area of Riverside.

As we will share later, the next seven years would prove transformational in *every* aspect of our lives. Some of those we journeyed with called this our season of "deconstruction and discovery" since we questioned *everything* about our faith, our church, and our very lives.

During that period, we experienced simple community, centered in Jesus and lived out with our friends and neighbors. The original church we started multiplied several times over. Its generations crossed over many cultural barriers that are typical in Southern California. This network caught the attention of people in power, who, for better or for worse, keep looking for the "next big move" for growing churches. And so I was discovered. I began to teach seminary. I traveled throughout the United States and overseas, teaching on New Testament spirituality, church planting, and cross-cultural leadership.

In my day job, I worked as a church-starting consultant for one of the largest evangelical denominations in North America. I coached and consulted with hundreds of church leaders and seminary students who were preparing for careers in the church.

Then, at night and on weekends, our family gathered with others to worship and pray freely. We met simply as friends and families in one another's homes. We were a microcosm of the metropolis, a diversity of ages, social strata, and cultures. We began to see ourselves as pilgrims, journeying together to discover the Way of Jesus. We experienced authentic community, united by our common love for Jesus. We laid down our pretenses of having it all together and became real with one another. We experienced the Spirit of Christ in action as we shared our lives with each other, loving one another in practical, everyday ways. We saw men become role models for fatherless boys. We paid for a college student's auto engine to be rebuilt so she could get to work. We painted houses. We played in the parks. We cared for one another's children. We listened to each other, we cried with one another, we gave to one another. Simply put, we learned to live together in the Way of Jesus.

We were pilgrims exploring alternative paths in Jesus, which often conflicted with what I was being paid to do all week long.

As a church planter strategist, I was paid to consult with churches and leaders who were usually asking how to plant or grow a church. But the questions most on our minds were "What does it mean to be a disciple of Jesus?" and "How do we make more disciples?"

Those I consulted with were concerned with raising money for a new building, salary increases for the staff, or a better sound system. Our community asked, "Where should we give our money away since we don't have to spend it on real estate, salaries, or a sound system?" So once again I found myself living a double life. The disparity between what I was living on my own time and what I was doing at work began to take its toll on me.

In my day job, there were also political factors to dance around, because there were positions and money to preserve or gain. My clients asked questions of demographics and marketing strategies, primarily to achieve quantitative growth. Meanwhile, people in our community of Jesus were discovering qualitative ways to get to know our neighbors and serve their real needs, whether it was helping them get a job, shoveling compost into their backyard, or listening to them cry over their marriage.

The more we experienced the life-changing dynamic that loving one another can have, the more we became convinced that the Body of Christ was far more than, and much different from, what we see on a typical Sunday in church. The Body of Christ is simply enjoying communion with Jesus, enjoying community with one another, and moving together as his Spirit leads.

> If you cannot bear to live in everlasting dissonance between your beliefs and your life, thinking one thing and doing another, get out of the medieval whited sepulchers, and face your fears. I know very well it is not easy.
>
> –Leo Tolstoy (1828-1910), Russian novelist and reformer

In short, the discussions by day were about church and all the logistics to make church structures happen, while at night and on the weekends we were asking, "How do we live out our intimacy with Jesus?" and "How do we live out the life of Jesus among our family, neighbors, coworkers, and friends?" As time went on, the chasm between the two environments widened. I could no longer continue furthering the American church system. As this conviction grew, I knew I had to get out. It wasn't because I had ever had a bad church experience in growing up or on the staff of a church or mission organization. But I had always suspected, and now I knew, that there was something more. I had growing convictions of *what* the Body of Christ *was not* and new experiences in which I was discovering *who* the Body of Christ *is*.

For a while, I thought formal church institutions could be renewed. I thought I could make a difference by working inside them. I thought wrong. As traditionally focused churches grow, they take on a life of their own; so much energy is needed to keep the services and programs moving each week that less and less time is spent listening together to what the Spirit is saying.

Jennifer's and my experience in seeking to bring about change in an institution can be likened to planting a garden. Before planting, you must weed and remove plants that can compete with the roots of the new seeds. There must be enough room for plants to receive the sunlight and air needed to grow to their full size. So it is with our spiritual lives; if there are too many competing agendas and authorities telling us what to do, we do not have the space we need to freely experience Christ in our midst.

We've known many people whose heart's desire was to move freely in the Spirit, but they felt their church leadership and structure required them to conform to the church program. Others have tried to add new convictions about listening to Jesus and following him to all their previously held convictions. It just doesn't work. We cannot fully experience Jesus if we accept any other competing authority. Jesus plus religion equals something less than what Jesus intended.

Risking All to Return to the Root

Not all who wander are lost.
—J.R.R. Tolkien (1892–1973), author, Lord of the Rings

The seeds of change began to grow in the spring of 1999, after I returned from a trip to the Philippines with Hseih and Ben, two young leaders from our community. Having trained hundreds of indigenous leaders to be free of Western methods, controls, and resources, I realized that we needed to do even more of the same work in our own context. Around the same time, several of my friends and colleagues challenged me to practice what I'd been preaching: set an example by giving up my profession, and lead a life that others could emulate.

Being a church planter strategist for a large denomination was not something that many could follow. I was convinced that any indigenous movement following the Way of Jesus in the West was not going to be led by religious professionals. Instead, it would be embodied by diverse and ordinary people. When Jesus was with his disciples, he not only lived a life they could model but said, "Greater things will you do." In fact, it was obvious to all that the early followers of Jesus "were ordinary men who had had no special training" (Acts 4:13). I wanted to lead a life that others could look at and say, "Hey, I can do that." I wrestled with the question, "Am I living this way of life because I am paid to live it?" *How could I teach others to be free of Western methods, institutional controls, and financial dependencies when I myself was not fully free from these things? How could I teach something I was not fully living?*

In May 1999, Jennifer and I both sensed the Spirit impressing us that it was time to get out of the system. As a family, we made the radical decision to leave the safety of everything we had known. After completing my Ph.D., I gave up religion *and* my profession and all that went with it. I would have no church strategist job, no seminary teaching, no conference speaking, no international engagements. And no financial security! We gave up everything that supported us

Jesus plus religion equals something less than what Jesus intended.

externally: position, stable pay, a respectable profession, our spiritual community, and a life lived close to family and friends.

I'll never forget the reaction of the team of leaders in our spiritual community when we told them how we sensed God was leading our family. Ben responded with, "It's about time!" He knew that we had been wrestling within our hearts as we sought to discern what it would mean for us to follow Jesus with full integrity to our convictions, and to be about his work alone. He knew our desire to live a life about which we could say, "Follow our example as we follow Christ." The rest of the team and the broader spiritual community also heartily agreed and sent us off, with prayer and enough money to pay for the moving van.

When I told fellow ministry colleagues what I was doing, more often than not, they had only two responses. First, they couldn't believe that I would give up financial security and a prestigious position. But second, most of them also expressed envy; they wished they could get out of their church-related jobs. They confessed sharing some of the same inner conflict but didn't feel they could afford to face it. The comforts and security of ministry outweighed their desire to follow the leading of the Spirit within their heart. One senior denominational leader simply said, "I admire your courage. I know many who want to leave but won't because of finances or family obligations."

Some Rewards of Risk

To risk is to lose one's foothold for a while; not to risk is to lose one's self forever.
—*Søren Kierkegaard (1813–1855),*
Danish philosopher, Writings

That spring, we moved with our four children to the Pacific Northwest to start a new life. With no guarantee of income, we bought a fixer-upper home on Bainbridge Island, a thirty-five-minute ferry ride from Seattle. On evenings and weekends, we worked at making our house livable, since our kitchen consisted of a microwave and toaster oven on the living room floor, a refrigerator on the front porch, and a faucet out the back of the house. This was a challenge, especially since our four children were all under six years old. But by the fall, we had made ourselves a home.

For the next two years, I was baptized into the business world as I built a small media-technology company with a friend I had known from California. In a matter of months, our little company moved from the basement of my partner's house to loft offices in Seattle's Pioneer Square, growing from two employees to ten, and shifting from small dot-com gigs to contracts with Fortune 100 companies. I found a new place in business, and an income too. My entrepreneurial gifting began to emerge in Seattle's growing business climate.

When we moved to the Island, we didn't know anyone. We learned how to be a family again apart from the many demands that had clamored for our attention in the fast-paced life of Southern California. We had no expectations to fulfill. This was truly a new start. We built new friendships. More than anywhere we have ever lived or visited, we feel at home in the Northwest. We appreciate the strong sense of connection with the land and the fresh openness about spirituality.

Over the next few years we didn't "do" Christianity. Our focus was not on leaving the church or Christianity, but on moving closer to Jesus. Jennifer and I knew that my transition out of professional ministry and into business would be big. We just didn't realize how big. The process was a paradox, both liberating and painful. It was a time of stripping and shedding religious baggage, a lot of which we didn't even know we were carrying. As we moved outside the box of religion, we came into a whole new perspective on life, family, and spirituality.

⬥ Reflection and Discussion ⬥

In ancient Sanskrit, the word for chess player is the same as that for pilgrim. This implies thoughtful consideration rather than aimless wandering. Take a few minutes to reflect on your spiritual pilgrimage.

- Where are you? Are you satisfied with your progress on the pilgrim path?
- What is your next move? Can you identify anything that may be hindering your progress?
- As you look at the journey before you, what are your greatest hopes, fears, and challenges?

2

AN ALTERNATIVE REALITY

You only see what you know.

—*African proverb*

We do not see things as they are but as we are.

—*Jewish proverb*

I seem to have been born with an inherent desire for understanding. Being bent on asking root questions has been a mixed blessing, especially within educational and religious institutions where questions are not valued as much as regurgitating the supposed correct answers. I'm not rebellious; I just don't conform well. Since my years at university, I've been exploring and questioning the reality that I have been given.

After nearly a decade in professional ministry roles, I began a Ph.D. program in intercultural studies. I explored how global cultural shifts affect our worldview and approach to religion, spirituality, organization, and leadership in the West. I had a host of gnawing questions that were not being addressed in the West: Why is there such a difference between the Jesus of the New Testament and the common church today? How did Christianity become a Western religion when Jesus was actually from the East? Is Jesus really the originator of church as we know it today? How long would Jesus last if he showed up at a typical church? What happened to the revolutionary, antireligious gospel that spread through the first century like wildfire?

The more I looked to Jesus in light of the New Testament, the more I saw the growing chasm between the life of Jesus and Americanized Christianity. As I traveled overseas and witnessed the striking difference between churches in the West and those in the developing world, I wondered: *Is it just me?* Am I being rebellious or heretical? Why do the Christ-centered spiritual movements in the East and developing world seem so much more vibrant than the church in the West? I found an inverse correlation between material possessions and spiritual vitality; the poorer the people and the less they relied on things money could buy, the more vibrant their spirituality. The more a group relied on dedicated buildings, professional clergy, sophisticated programs, and other religious accessories, the less spiritually alive they were. In the area of religion, *less is more*.

> There is an age when one teaches what one knows. But there follows another when one teaches what one does not know. It comes, maybe now, the age of another experience: that of unlearning. . . .
>
> —Roland Barthes (1915–1980), French philosopher

So, I set out on a quest to ask root questions—to explore the spiritual, theological, historical, biblical, and cultural perspectives on what we've come to know as the Western Church, or Christianity. Jennifer and I experimented with a variety of religious expressions in the rich diversity of greater Los Angeles and in our overseas travels. We came to see a cluster of related truths: we are all blind to some degree, reality is never as it seems, and each of us has been both shaped and bound by culture.

As I finished my dissertation, my doctoral work turned out to be an apologetic for me to find my way out of the religious system where I had spent my entire adult working life (for those who have seen *The Matrix*: I took the red pill of reality). Having been unplugged just over six years now, I have been undergoing a type of religious detoxification. Not only did I have to get out of religion; religion had to get out of me.

Breaking Out of Cultural Blindness

Have you ever noticed something new, only to find out that it is not new at all? It has been there the whole time; you just didn't see it.

This cultural blindness is an effect demonstrated in *The Truman Show,* the critically acclaimed movie in which Truman Burbank (played by Jim Carey) is a happy, carefree insurance salesman who lives in the idyllic coastal town of Seahaven. He's married to a beautiful nurse and loves to hang out and drink beer with his best friend, Marlon. Despite his complacent happiness, Truman begins to notice peculiar occurrences—especially ones that repeat every day. In this safe and predictable environment, he begins to question everything.

Truman doesn't realize everyone he knows is an actor playing a part on a TV show, created and directed by Christof (Ed Harris). Christof's complete control and manipulation of Truman's life ensures that the audience will continue watching. As Truman becomes more suspicious of what is really occurring, Christof does all he can to prevent his prized star from discovering the truth. But after much toil, Truman finally breaks free. At the end of the movie, a reporter asks Christof why Truman had never discovered the true nature of his world. Christof replies, "We accept the reality of the world with which we are presented. It's as simple as that."

I can identify with Christof's principle. When I was growing up, playing with my childhood friends in the foothills of Mount Diablo in Northern California, we pretended to be soldiers fighting for freedom, or pioneers taming the Western frontier. Life was an adventure and a discovery! Then I grew up. My sense of adventure faded as I went to school and started a career. The future seemed to roll out in a predictable way. Eventually I'd retire, learn to play golf, enjoy my grandchildren, take a few trips, and finally I'd die. Life was safe and predictable. Everything around school, church, and work seemed to reinforce this.

Like Truman, I also had to break free. Before I could embark on a journey of rediscovery, I first had to free myself of the thoughts and structures that blinded me from seeing a bigger reality. Eventually I had to make a choice: hold on to the safety of religion or jump out into the dangerous and unknown life of walking with Jesus.

This book is about nonreligious expressions of spirituality, but we want to be clear that our intention is not to criticize any religious group, whether Eastern or Western. As the apostle James comments simply, "Pure and lasting religion in the sight of God our Father means that we must care for orphans and widows in their troubles, and refuse to let the world corrupt us" (James 1:27). There is much spiritual and social good that comes from formal religion, but like any human invention religion has inherent limitations. This book is not against anything; rather, it looks beyond religious structures and cultural barriers to the powerful simplicity of Jesus.

Illusions are the truths we believe until we know better.

–From a story on the September 11 attacks, *Time,* Sept. 2003

As we shall see, there is another reality besides the Western Christian worldview. The changing global spirituality is screaming for the West to undergo a systemic paradigm shift that goes to the root of our identity and how we live and relate together as spiritual beings—one that sets us free from the many assumptions of cultural Christianity and of the modern agenda. This is not about Christianity or church as we know it, but about the reality of Jesus being lived in our lives and in a community that brings life and freedom.

Journeying Beyond

> Traveler, there are no roads. Roads are made
> by walking.
>
> —*Spanish proverb*

As I look back on my life, I can see I've set out on three paths to find meaning and fulfillment. I've tried the "American way" of humanism with a strong dose of individualism, rationalism, and materialism, where I dreamed dreams, worked hard, and found some success. I immersed myself in Christianity—even mastering its dogma and serving the sacred institutions of the Western Church. In more recent years, I have experimented with Eastern philosophies and their reflective practices. But well into each path, I found myself in a similar place: alone in a crowd, questioning the structures, and thirstier than when I began.

Now our family is finding another way, one that transcends these paths, beyond East or West. It is a deep spirituality that is centered in Jesus and permeates all we are and do. It draws spiritual sojourners from Western and non-Western backgrounds, religious and nonreligious. Over the past several years, we have seen this way of life embodied in a variety of cultures, from Seattle to Austin; from Cape Town to Shanghai; from the Makah Nation of Washington to the Telegu of East India; and across Africa, Asia, Europe, and Latin America.

Wherever Jennifer and I travel, we meet people who also yearn to experience Christ deeply and holistically, to make a difference in society. We've been amazed at the number of those we have met around the world who are on their own journey of deconstruction and discovery, breaking out of the complexities of religion to get back to the powerful simplicity of life in Jesus. They likewise have seen the widening gap between *talking about Jesus* and *walking with Jesus*. It's not that they are against church; they are just making more room in their lives to experience the living reality of Jesus in community with their family and friends.

We are beginning to experience Jesus personally again—as if for the first time. Our spirituality was never to be measured by *what* we believe in or what we do. That's religion! In Jesus, it's about *who we believe in*, *who we are*, and *who we are becoming*. Our beliefs and behavior are being transformed out of our encounter with the living Jesus.

As difficult and uncertain as times have been, we've never looked back. We join with the resolve of our son Nathan's favorite literary character, Reepicheep, the valiant mouse of C. S. Lewis's

Voyage of the Dawn Treader. Just before he left the security of the ship and his friends, Reepicheep voiced his resolve to reach Aslan's country: "My own plans are made. While I can, I sail east in the Dawn Treader. When she fails me, I paddle east in my coracle. When she sinks, I shall swim east with my four paws. And when I can swim no longer, if I have not reached Aslan's country, or shot over the edge of the world in some vast cataract, I shall sink with my nose to the sunrise."[1]

✛ Reflection and Discussion ✛

We all have some idea of Jesus, and that image of Jesus affects how we live. Take a few minutes to explore the questions here. You might wish to exchange your thoughts and feelings with a friend.

- What comes to your mind when you hear the name *Jesus*?
- Who is Jesus for you personally? How did you come to this belief: through your own experience? through those of other people?
- In your experience, how has your spirituality been shaped by cultural influences such as family, friendships, religion, education, government, media, and so on?

3

NAVIGATING THE NEW AGE

I am the Lord, who opened a way through the sea, a
path through the mighty waters. . . .
>—*Isaiah (eighth century* B.C.*),*
>*Hebrew prophet, Isaiah 43:16*[1]

I'd always wanted to surf with my sea kayak, so one afternoon I
set out from the calm sandy inlet of Salt Creek on the Olympic
Peninsula toward the open waters of the Pacific. Paddling swiftly
through the white foam of the surf, I rode my kayak, cutting through
several small swells that suddenly turned into four-foot breakers.
The frigid ocean spray didn't keep me from breaking into a full
sweat. Other kayakers were also being pummeled, but they were in
plastic "wet" kayaks designed to ride and tumble with the surf. In
a flash, I imagined all seventeen feet of my handmade Okoume
wood kayak smashed to pieces on the rocks. Though designed for
the sea, the lightweight wood was no match for the rocks. With
adrenaline pumping, I managed to turn my craft around between
the swells. I caught a wave and made my way back into the calm
mouth of Salt Creek.

I continued paddling upstream aided by the incoming tide. The
ocean current was stronger than the creek. I navigated around drift-
wood and paddled through thick beds of brown seaweed. In just
moments, everything around me was still. No crashing surf. Now I
was drifting up a winding stream bordered by tall grasses. No sooner
had I adjusted to the landscape of marshlands with its sea ducks and

blue herons moving in and out of the tall grasses than I paddled under a low-hanging alder branch.

As if passing through a curtain, I was now in a narrow stream paddling under a canopy of towering cedar, red alders, and big leaf maples. I splashed water on my face to cool down and discovered that there was no salt in it to burn my eyes. I was now gliding along a freshwater stream in the midst of lush forest.

In less than fifteen minutes, I had paddled through three distinct ecosystems, from surf to marshlands to forest.

When did the clear water from the stream prevail over the ocean's salt water pushing up into the plains? Where did the salt water cease and the fresh water begin? In an *ecotone*—a transitional zone where two or more ecosystems merge—clear borders are hard to find as sea water mixes with fresh water, forest meets tundra, and the river merges with the lake. Although it supports a rich diversity of life unique to a particular area, an ecotone can also be very unstable. The dynamic exchange among divergent ecosystems creates a unique environment of continuous change and shifting boundaries. It is much like many of the conditions we are living in today.

Just as there are biological ecotones, we are now living in the midst of a cultural-spiritual ecotone. Jesus' challenge rings as true today as it did two thousand years ago: "You know how to interpret the appearance of the earth and the sky, but you can't interpret these present times" (Luke 12:56). We need his Spirit to navigate this global ecotone.

On the Edge of Aquarius

> God made the heavens by the word of his
> command, and he brought the earth up from the
> water and surrounded it with water.
>
> —*Peter, disciple of Jesus, II Peter 3:5*

We live in a turbulent age. The *zeitgeist*, or spirit of the times, in the West is an ecotone where divergent cultures converge upon each other. With the second millennium now behind us, the cultural shifts are fluid and unpredictable. We no longer live with fixed landscapes, but seascapes where the waters are always moving. Though we can observe cultural currents in motion, there is no certainty where they will lead. We are in a borderless world. Our geographical and conceptual maps are not valid for very long. One way of life is ending and another is beginning.

These shifts in this global ecotone have been emerging for some time. Perhaps some will remember the popular song "Aquarius" from the hippie-era rock musical *Hair*. According to that song and many popular teachers, the Age of Aquarius brings promise of an era of harmony, understanding, sympathy, and peace. Astrologers and New Age philosophers interpret Aquarius, the water bearer, as the time where the water of life will be poured out upon the people. But many who have been hoping for the New Age (referring to the New Age of Aquarius) are becoming weary. The promise of the New Age remains illusive.

We are on the edge of a frontier, somewhere between the known and the unknown, between modern and postmodern, between order and disorder, between control and chaos, between answers and questions. We live in the Aquarian Age. Everything that was fixed is now fluid. Everything, both old and new, is being questioned. But this much we know: we live and work in a time of unparalleled opportunity and unprecedented uncertainty. Anything could happen!

The Chinese pictogram on the next page combines the characters for "danger" and "opportunity" to communicate the idea of "crisis." My friend Stephen, a Chinese businessman, explains: "The Asian concept of crisis is best understood as a turning point—a type of crossroads with potential for being positive or negative. Just as the tide goes out only to return again, so it is with both the good and the bad of life. Crisis is not only part of life; crisis is essential for life. Crisis can spark innovation and transformation in both people and systems and can represent the beginning of new opportunities."

Danger   Opportunity

Chinese Pictogram for *Crisis*

Culture Shifts: Moving from Modern World to Postmodern Worlds

> This time, like all times, is a very good one, if we
> but know what to do with it.
> —*Ralph Waldo Emerson (1803–1882),*
> *American author, poet, and philosopher*

Reality isn't what it used to be (or ever seemed to be). The safe, predictable world of my youth does not exist. Most of the ideals and assumptions that shaped Western society and science in the modern era have been shattered by the political and ecological realities of an endangered planet.[2] We are fast becoming a culture of fear. Whether it's Internet worms, global climate change, new diseases, economic breakdown, or fear of terrorist attacks, human beings never tire of the latest reports that tell us the end is near. Fear sells. Nowhere is safe; no one is trustworthy. Neither church nor school prepared us for such rising social, political, economic, environmental, and religious unrest as we see today. The solutions and structures that once governed people's lives don't seem to work anymore. We're losing faith in the political process, in science, even in human goodness.

What do we trust? Whom do we trust? Our own ability to think and reason? religious leaders? computer firewalls? politicians? military intelligence? Insecurity hangs like a dark cloud over both the present and the future.

In the last forty-odd years, the very core beliefs, values, and institutions of Western culture have been challenged. We feel new cultural sensitivities or moods, lacking clear foundation, emerge beyond our familiar modern sensibilities. In spite of profound scientific and technological advancements of quantum physics, space exploration, and semiconductor technology, there is a progressive loss of confidence in the assumptions of the modern world. Knowledge, progress, and technology do not guarantee a better, safer world.

It's not simply *a* new world we find ourselves in, but rather postmodern *worlds*. What was "Western culture" is fast becoming a multiplicity of streams with currents of beliefs and realities that often run contrary to one another. Whereas modernity was birthed in the West, postmodernity is a global phenomenon with an array of cultural expressions. The global culture shift is forcing fundamental changes in our Western worldview. We no longer have a cohesive system to explain reality, to help us understand and explore the world around us. Everything is becoming fuzzy, pluralistic, and uncertain—accompanied by an increasing degree of social unrest. Adrift in a sea of competing voices, we're unsure where to satisfy the deep questions of life:

Who am I? What are the nature, purpose, and significance of my existence?

Where am I? What are the origin and nature of the reality in which I find myself?

What's wrong? How can I account for the distortion, pain, and brokenness in this reality?

What's the remedy? How can I alleviate this brokenness, if at all?

Trying to understand the zeitgeist and the future we are moving to is like snatching at a shadow. As we grasp for a way to classify these times, many descriptions emerge: post-Enlightenment, postindustrial, post-Christian, deconstructionist, hypermodern, postmaterialism, terminal civilization, postindividual, and kaleidoscope era, to name a few. Regardless of label, these times represent a shift unlike any other in Western civilization. Instead of a new lens, the post-modern shift is a multifaceted prism. It is dynamic, paradoxical, and eclectic. Though impossible to define fully, we can see several major shifts in the attitudes of emerging postmodern cultures. Some of these emerging values are constructive, while others are quite destructive:

• *We're all connected.* With value increasingly placed on unity, wholeness, reconciliation, and healthy community, the West is moving from hierarchies to "holarchies," and from fragmentation to integration. Here, the primacy of the whole suggests that relationships are more fundamental than parts. The whole is *different* from the sum of the parts. Identity is defined not so much by *what* you are as *who* you are connected to. In short, postmodernity is mending truly complementary pairs that modernity tore asunder: individual and community, spiritual and material, public and private.

• *There are multiple truths and realities.* The assumptions and truths of modernity are being questioned, particularly the notion of ultimate authority. People now look for a patchwork of stories rather than one main story (or metanarrative) as a source of meaning—or they even craft their own stories. With little loyalty to their past, some people develop their identity the way they fill their plate at an all-you-can-eat buffet. My friend Tony, for example, takes a bit of his Italian heritage and patches it together with a bit of Celtic values and Buddhist meditation practices. We now have freedom to believe whatever we want to believe, as long as we do not impose those beliefs on others.

• *Everything is being questioned.* Everything is up for grabs. Whether belief systems, morality, ethics, or family, nothing is left untouched. Modernity's romantic view of the future—believing that things are bound to get better through human ingenuity and technological progress—has been eroding in the wake of the Holocaust and Hiroshima. It was driven home on U.S. soil with the attacks of September 11, 2001. We live in an irrational world. We have given up believing that things are going to get better. Progress is unlikely. The future is marked by uncertainty, and loss of hope. We now live in a state of flux and distrust, a culture of doubt and cynicism.

• *Truth is in the eye of the beholder.* Objective truth is beyond the grasp of any one person or group. People are, by definition, limited in their capacity for discerning truth. There are now other ways of knowing besides the limited rational constructs of modernity, among them the emotions, intuition, pleasure, and revelation. No one way is authoritative. Truth is defined by each individual or the community to which he or she belongs ("I believe in what I feel. I believe in what I want to believe."). The truth will never be certain because everyone's reality differs.

• *Choice is no longer a choice, but a right.* Moral values are arbitrary and contingent upon the situation and the changing cultures. This opens the way to hedonism, where sensuality and personal pleasures become the ethical standards: "I have a right to fulfill my desires, and no one has a right to criticize my choices (even if my choices limit the choice or rights of another)." People resent, and even rebel against, whatever limits their personal choices.

• *We long for belonging.* Though individualism remains a defining characteristic of the postmodern West, there are signs of movement to a greater social consciousness. People are feeling the effects of the breakdown of community and family. Many want community but are frustrated with their inability to build healthy relationships. In the aftermath of September 11, New York became the biggest little city in the world. But as with any tragedy, the majority of people reverted back to their familiar ways of independence. The West has ironic and conflicting forms of belonging; at the same time that we are becoming a global village, fierce tribal rivalries threaten local and global peace.

• *There is growing distrust of authority.* Daily news headlines of corruption in the government, corporations, and the religious sector of society feed our growing disillusionment and distrust toward persons and systems of authority. Unprecedented cynicism carries over to any institution traditionally perceived to be authoritative, whether political, educational, financial, or religious. It is not that we are necessarily *anti*authoritarian, but rather *a*-authoritarian (they just don't care). Many also reject the perceived intolerance and narrowness of social conservatives and the Religious Right. They see folks who believe they hold the perfect answers as being arrogant at best, at worst dangerous lunatics or controlling tyrants. People won't trust beyond the perceived care they receive.

• *We're moving from knowledge to experience.* The highest compliment is reserved not for rational smarts, but for real experience. The preoccupation with reality TV, extreme sports, blogs, and anything that cuts through the superficial façade is a manifestation of this shift. People can tell the fake from the genuine. No longer content with confessions and creeds, people want to experience the truth to which the creeds and confessions are pointing. Meaning ultimately emerges from experience. The attitude is that "I don't know what is real, but I can experience reality." The present is the primary reality. Journey is valued over destination, subjective over objective, "walk" over "talk," participant over spectator; what is valued is the risk taker with the ingenuity and guts to go out into the unknown or create a new reality.

> The greatest enemy of knowledge is not ignorance, it is the illusion of knowledge.
>
> —Stephen Hawking, theoretical physicist

• *There are multiple spiritual realities.* More and more people in the West recognize we are living in a new world of plural spiritualities. Ultimate reality is not physical or material but metaphysical and spiritual. More than their modern predecessors, new spiritualities do celebrate tradition, but not the traditions of the West. Dismissed as superstitious and naïve just a few decades ago, premodern and non-Western religions are now enchanting large numbers of people.

We live in a time of chaos and convergence. The philosophical currents we've just briefly explored are pushing and pulling contemporary cultures worldwide. The breakdown of modernity is more than an intellectual or pop-cultural phenomenon. It is intertwined with the emerging global consciousness and its underlying tensions. Old distinctions are muddled or mixed together, like spiritual and secular, left and right, conservative and liberal. Anything can (and eventually will) be juxtaposed with anything else—a global consciousness where numerous, often paradoxical forces converge into an eclectic soup.

Spirit Shifts: From Western Religion to Global Spiritualities

> You can't trust anything; you have to be suspicious
> of everything.
> —N. T. (Tom) Wright, Bishop of Durham, England

The cultural currents we've just surfed are advancing a spiritual revolution in the West. In modernity, the God-oriented worldview of the Middle Ages was displaced by one centered on human reason. Skepticism (as in the scientific worldview) was valued over spirituality. Modernity tried to remove the spiritual or mysterious as a reality of life. At the time, many believed that modernity was going to bring an end to religion—that reason would ultimately triumph over faith. They thought it was the beginning of the end when *Time* magazine ran "God Is Dead" as a cover headline in 1966. Instead, and ironically, yesterday's agnostics are now today's mystics.

The emphases of modernity have left us socially and spiritually bankrupt. But, as postmodernity hits against the rational exteriors of modernity, it exposes our vulnerability and hunger of spirit. It reveals the hole in the soul of the culture and the longing in people for connection and fulfillment that cannot be satisfied with the products and institutions of modern religion. Five hundred years after the Enlightenment, many in the West feel they are in a kind of spiritual darkness. We grapple to find and embrace true enlightenment. There is nothing new in this yearning, for secularism has never proved itself able to eradicate people's inherent need for something beyond the material. All over the Western world, we see a reenchantment with the spiritual and transcendent.

The postmodern transition is cultivating a unique spiritual openness. Over the past several years, we've seen an explosion of interest in all matters metaphysical and spiritual. It's no longer embarrassing to admit to having spiritual interests or feelings. For more and more people both in and outside of religion, it has become acceptable to begin to speak openly about some of the most fundamental spiritual questions. This shift in worldview not only makes recovery of belief possible but also makes belief in God natural and acceptable again.

> The world that has come of age is more godless, and perhaps for that very reason nearer to God, than the world before its coming of age.
> —Dietrich Bonhoeffer (1906-1945), Lutheran pastor, activist against Hitler

When I hear someone say, "I'm spiritual, but not very religious," it points to the trend that many are separating their spiritual life from traditional religious expression. In this distinction lies the seed of the new spirituality. Wade Clark Roof, a professor of religious studies and scholar, calls this a manifestation of the "quest culture." There has been "a qualitative shift from unquestioned belief to a more open, questioning mood, a search for certainty, but also the hope for a more authentic, intrinsically satisfying life."[3]

It's hard to find a branch of Western culture that has not at least been touched by this surging wave of newfound spiritual fervor. Over the past thirty years, millions of Americans have ventured beyond the materialistic promise of the American Dream and the Sunday school religions of their youth in search of deeper spirituality, extraordinary experiences, and a more meaningful way to live. Their search takes many forms: from the Beatles to the Grateful Dead; from Astral Projection to Zen Buddhism; from the many incarnations of Shirley MacLaine to the rising popularity of the Dalai Lama; from *Autobiography of a Yogi* to *The Celestine Prophecy*; from Promise Keepers to Burning Man.

Although many of those who seek spirituality object to institutional religion, they are not necessarily anti-God. Often, they simply react against the modern forms of religion: the human-made systems for understanding God, the lack of genuine community, and what they experience as anemic spirituality. Our friend Meghan shared her story with us, saying in part: "After many years of attending church, feeling absolutely nothing in the supernatural, I began to search outside the church for something beyond the natural. I was confronted with many spiritual experiences within the framework of an indigenous peoples conference. Many shamans and spiritual healers from around the world attended. . . . I was drawn into a place of enchantment. . . . I was hooked on experiencing the supernatural. . . . I put myself at the mercy of the Universe—pursuing whatever spirituality opened up to me. . . ."

For years Meghan wandered spiritually, reading as many books on alternative healing and spirituality as she could find. In the fullness of time, she had a personal encounter with Jesus. She reflects on her (re)awakening: "Over a period of weeks, I was totally released from what I call spiritual seduction and deception. God had allowed me to go on a journey where I came to understand in an experiential way that the spiritual realm is very real, and that not all spiritual revelation is good."

Intrigued with spirituality more than the generations before them, today's spiritual seekers are reluctant to commit to any one religious tradition. In simple terms, they are antireligious and anti-institutional spiritual seekers who may actually be open to fresh expressions of Jesus that are free of modern values and institutional structures.

These new spiritual seekers are no longer looking to the Western church or to secular humanism for fulfillment. Ravenously hungry, they are looking *everywhere else* to satiate their newfound spiritual longings. Though there is no monolithic force or clear boundaries for this spiritual revolution, various streams are converging upon the Western landscape. These new spiritual pilgrims have an eclectic blend of beliefs and practices that span a combination of Eastern, Western, and earth-based spiritualities.

From Western Religious Worldview	To Global Spiritual Worldviews
Religion (Shaped by Christendom)	**Spirituality (Influenced by the East and South)**
Physical reality	Metaphysical realities
Greco-Roman, Eurocentric	Native American, Hebrew, Asian
Traditional institutions	Spiritual relationships
Disenchantment, objectivity	Reenchantment, mystification
Passive participant (settler)	Journey and experience (pilgrim)
Atheism, secular humanism	Panentheism, pantheism
Humanity above nature	Humanity merged with nature
"Is there a God?" and "God is dead"	"Which god (or gods)?" and "We are god"
Evidence, propositional truth	Experience, personal beliefs
Dualism (sacred-secular split)	Holism (unification)
Individualized, private	Interbeing, interconnected, community
Orthodoxy, dogmatism, theology	Paradox, mystery, story
What you believe	How we live (or be + lieve)

The question is no longer "Do you believe in God?" but "Which god (or gods) do you believe in?" for there are many paths that lead to God. Reluctance to commit to any one religious tradition leads to a permanent search for the next new thing—a sort of "serial spirituality." Globalization allows people of world cultures to selectively extract and combine elements they find significant from divergent belief systems spread around the world. Many are like Jennifer's friend Amy, who is twenty-nine and claims "I'm not religious" but regularly reads Buddhist writings and "dabbles in Judaism." One afternoon, she cut a conversation short so she could be on time for her manicure before she went to her palm reader.

But mixing and matching divergent streams does not always lead to spiritual fulfillment. As my friend Hal, who is Jewish and now a "Buddhist at heart," said, "I've been on a very intentional spiritual quest that began with my Jewish heritage and continued through alternative healing practices, Buddhism, and Eastern practices, but I have yet to realize healing or wholeness. . . . I've come to accept that it may not happen on this side." The irony of this new spiritual identity is that many like Hal feel trapped in their spiritual wanderings. The endless search can be tiring. It often leads to a lonely desperation where we still yearn for a spiritual center or unifying truth, for transformational power, and for loving community.

The emerging spirituality of this Aquarian Age expresses a deep search for the transcendent without the Western trappings. In a sense, it is an awakening to a spiritual reality that values integration of divergent beliefs, holistic healing, environmental sensitivity, a simple lifestyle, and attunement to the greater cosmos.

Contrary to the opinion of many Christian leaders, author and professor John Drane of Scotland believes that these searchers are likely to be more open to a radical life-changing encounter with Jesus than many Christians are. He explains: "The New Age agenda has many striking points of contact with the agenda of the Gospel. Concern for personal freedom and maturity, for the environment, for peace and justice, for self-discovery, for a holistic view of life— these are all things that were an integral part of the message of Jesus. The most significant difference between Christian faith and New Age spirituality is not to be found in their social, economic, political, or environmental hopes and aspirations, but in their beliefs about how these goals are likely to be achieved."[4]

This emerging spirituality is not so much about what we do or even what we believe, but rather about a spiritual journey in relationship—who we are, who we believe, who we walk with, and who we are becoming. The Holy Spirit is using culture shifts to burn away the façade of modernity and the religious structures of Christendom. The emerging spirituality might be described as an interactive flow of relationships that explore the mysteries of this life and the Beyond.

This is the emerging story that we are now all living.

Reflection and Discussion

Many believe the West is at the beginning of a spiritual awakening, one that yearns for depth and meaning in life, for belonging and community; one that raises new questions.

- What major cultural or spiritual shifts have the greatest influence on your outlook on life, religion, and spirituality?
- Why are so many Westerners turning toward the East for answers to their spiritual questions?
- What questions are emerging from your heart? from those around you?

4

CULTURAL CHASMS

From the tribe of Issachar . . . all these men
understood the temper of the times and knew the
best course for Israel to take.

—*I Chronicles 12:32*

When Jennifer and I were preparing to start a church in Riverside,
we began to listen more deeply to the Spirit of God *and* the spirit of
the times. We could feel change in the air, but we couldn't define it.
What was the culture saying to us? to the church? How was the
Spirit moving in these times? What was the Spirit saying to us?

Like the tribe of Issachar, we sought to understand what the
Spirit was revealing through the changes in the culture. As we listened, we began to see two cultural chasms widening: between the
church and culture, and between the church and Jesus.

The Church-Culture Chasm

Though I was aware of the widening gap between church and culture, it was not until one Saturday in South Central that I was
struck with its reality. The dust hadn't settled from the L.A. riots
when I met up with a group of community leaders, local residents,
and pastors to spend a day simply to look, listen, and pray for needs
in the community. We divided into about a dozen pairs to drive and
walk sections through the neighborhood and converse with the
people on the streets. What startled me most was not the bars on

the windows (indicating a high crime rate), the trash littering the streets, or other signs of despair. I had, after all, been to some of the worst slums of the developing world. The shock was the number of churches. We counted more than a hundred churches in less than a two-square-mile area! I could stand on one corner and see as many as five church buildings or religious storefronts. How could there be so many churches and yet so little evidence of community health? How is the church affecting culture? Did we really need another church here?

> The relevant church is sowing the seeds of its own irrelevance, and losing its identity to boot.
>
> −Carl Braaten,
> American theologian

For nearly two thousand years, the Christian church has held a monopoly on spirituality in the West, and during this time nurturing the soul was the task of religion. But as the curtain of modernity is pushed aside, postmodernity casts new light on what the church is and does.

Western culture is not as Christian as previously thought. Once at the center of Western culture, Christianity is now being marginalized; it is no longer the primary source of spiritual direction, community, or power. Despite the influence of theologically conservative Christians in the United States, the church is losing its voice. Empty churches and cathedrals throughout Europe give clear indication of Christendom's demise. We see rising numbers of both the "dechurched" (Christians who no longer identify with church) and "postbelievers" (Christians who for whatever reason no longer believe in Christianity) throughout Western cultures. According to recent studies, approximately one-third of born-again believers in America do not attend church.[1] These studies reveal even more about this new spiritual exodus and its growing number of religious refugees:

- There are fewer than half as many churches today as in 1900, in proportion to the population.

- Roughly four thousand churches are started each year in the United States and Canada, while seven thousand close their doors.

- There has been a 92 percent increase in the number of unchurched Americans in the last thirteen years; in 1991 there were thirty-nine million, compared with seventy-five million in 2004.[2]

- The United States now has the fourth largest unchurched population in the world, behind China, India, and Indonesia.

- Eighty-five percent of the traditional ("mainline") Protestant denominations are in serious decline; nearly every city in the United States has falling church attendance. Average attendance decreases annually at a rate of 10–12 percent.

Many Christians are leaving organized religion—regardless of its size or denominational flavor—to explore their spirituality. It's not just nominal Christians (that is, people who are Christian in name only and not in lifestyle) or youth who are leaving church. In his surprising study, Andrew Strom of Australia observed that 94 percent of the Christians in the West who are currently churchless were formerly in positions of leadership, such as deacons, elders, and Sunday school teachers; and 40 percent were once in full-time professional ministry. Many of them said that they left the church not because they had lost their faith but rather to save their faith.[3] For many people who cannot conceive of anything other than traditional

> I consider Western Christianity in its practical working a negation of Christ's Christianity. It is my firm opinion that Europe does not represent the spirit of God or Christianity but the spirit of Satan. And Satan's successes are the greatest when he appears with the name of God on his lips.
>
> —Mohandas Gandhi (1869-1948), peace activist, leader of India's independence

Christianity, this flight from church is unsettling or even frightening. Those most threatened at these times are the ones most intertwined with the structures and ideology of modernity. But this trend seems unstoppable. Western culture and the church will never be the same. The decline of institutionalized religion is setting the stage for spiritual revival.

The Church-Jesus Chasm

He who is near the Church is often far from God.
—*French proverb*

I believe most Western churches are in this marginalized position not because they haven't kept up with the times but because they have not remained in step with Jesus. More and more people see the gap between the vitality they read about in the life of Jesus and the sterility they experience in today's churches. Many are seeing what Mohandas Gandhi saw more than fifty years ago, when he responded to a Christian leader by saying, "I like your Christ, but I don't like your Christians because they are so unlike your Christ." It's not just that most churches are not relevant to culture, but that they have lost their connection with Jesus.

My friend Bob represents a growing number of postbelievers who are still on a spiritual sojourn. Bob and his wife, Mary, have two small children and run a successful design and media studio out of the basement of their home. Bob and his young family are trying to make a spirituality that works for them; they read the latest from Ken Wilber and the Dalai Lama for spiritual food but still long for a spiritual community to call home. Bob has a strong Christian background: he was raised in the mainline Presbyterian denomination and cotaught Sunday school with his mother. He served as a leader in Young Life (a Christian club) as a radical Christian teen, and then he was active in an evangelical charismatic denomination as a young adult after college. The more time Bob spent in churches and Christianized activities, the greater the chasm he saw between the life of Jesus and church. He told me, "Today's church just doesn't look like anything I see in the Gospels. It seems to be a human invention to fulfill some psychological, social, and at times political needs." As we shared our stories together, Bob expressed firmly that he's always liked Jesus but is not sure what to believe about Jesus because Jesus has been co-opted by religious authorities for other agendas.

As we visited one Sunday afternoon at their home, I said to Bob, "Maybe you've thrown the baby Jesus out with the bath water of church."

He paused before he answered: "Yes, I think I have . . . and I miss Jesus. It's just that the church really gets in the way of me experiencing Jesus."

Sincerely spiritual people like Bob and Mary see a growing disconnect between church, which has became a cultural-religious institution, and the simple way of Jesus. Even the popular American psychiatrist M. Scott Peck rightly observes the gap between what most churches profess and what they live out: "It has become apparent to me that the vast majority of churchgoing Christians in America are heretics. The leading—indeed, traditional—heresy of the day I call pseudo-docetism. It is this predominant heresy that intellectually allows the Church to fail to teach its followers to follow Jesus."[4]

Jennifer and I continue to meet more and more people disillusioned with Christianity and religion in general. Contrary to popular opinion, breaking through the illusion

> I don't know anyone less Jesus-like than most Christians.
>
> —Bill Maher,
> political humorist

is not all that bad, especially when it opens us up to new insights and freedoms. It doesn't matter whether they have little experience in church or lots; they don't like what they see. They don't like the emphasis on money. Or the fact that honor is given to someone on the basis of position in the church rather than character. Or the lack of positive social impact outside the walls of the church. They often say "If Jesus is like this, I don't want it" or

"What I see in churches is nothing like Jesus." That's why so many have rejected both Jesus and church: they know church ought to reflect the nature of the Jesus of the Gospels, and they just don't see it. Though their stories vary, the reason is the same. Here's a sampling of what we hear from those around us:

- "I'm not often so comfortable in church. It feels pious and so unlike the Christ that I read about in the Scriptures."—Tony, twenty-one, student
- "The church has been bastardized.⁵ All it's about is money and politics. There's little resemblance between the church of today and the life of Jesus."—Donna, thirty-three, ex-Catholic mother of two
- "Pastors don't live and work in the real world. Their world is church. How can they tell me how to live my life? They don't have to struggle with all I have to . . . and I can't trust them. . . . It's like they are paid to be nice."—Bruce, twenty-seven, insurance adjuster
- "I don't want to go to church. The leaders really don't care about the people. It's all about building a big church with the young and the wealthy."—Ima, eighty-two, women's speaker and former Presbyterian elder
- "The church has [expletive deleted] Jesus. . . . Church isn't anything like Jesus."—Tom, twenty-three, student
- "The church is just too [expletive deleted] commercial. They're always asking for money and trying to sell me stuff."—Bob, sixty-two, semiretired electrical engineer
- "I am spiritual, believe in God, and pray daily, though I don't go to church. Church is an angry place—even politically violent at times."—Paul, forty, entrepreneur and son of Christian pastor
- "I hurt. My husband told me to visit the priest, but I didn't want to. All he will have me do is say 'Hail Mary' many times— that doesn't do anything."—Maria, twenty-seven, Catholic mother of three

- "The primary design of religious institutions is to prevent enlightenment."—Phil, fifty-two, Rolfing practitioner and teacher
- "I don't have to go to church to believe in God . . . I love God, but I hate the church."—Melissa, twenty, daughter of Christian missionaries
- "The form of the church is to make people afraid—if you don't do what they do then you will have to reckon with bad consequences. It's just a story about power. This is to me why people deal with reincarnation. From the structure of the church, it's like a prison. They want to escape."—Ivan, twenty-eight, spiritual seeker from Berlin

Today's ambivalence toward (and sometimes outright attack upon) contemporary churches begins to look very much like Christ's attack on the religious institutions of the first century.[6] Many people see a lack of integrity in church; something is not right. The current expressions of church just do not match with their images of Jesus, whatever their thoughts of him may be. Modern cultures may have been "Christianized" or "Christened" by the religious structures of Christendom, but a majority of people remain untouched by the authentic, life-transforming gospel of Jesus. They don't reject God so much as they do formal religion. At best, churches are seen as archaic religious structures that exist to conserve and control for the sake of themselves, and at worst, they are considered mean-spirited, intolerant political groups.

As we shall see later, this chasm began to develop when Jesus didn't fit the religious expectations of his day. Even the first-century apostles warned against straying from simple devotion to Jesus; but then came the fourth century, when the Roman emperor Constantine made Christianity the official religion of the Empire. That act politically structured the move away from the simple life and teachings of Jesus. Can we ever get back to what this Way was meant to be? If so, how can we recapture the reality of the Way of Jesus as he intended it to be?

✦ Reflection and Discussion ✦

You may want to grab a journal or a good friend and explore these questions:

- What comes to your mind when you hear the word *Christian*? the word *church*? Is there a difference? Why?
- Where do you see the greater gap: between culture and church, or between church and Jesus?
- Do you know anyone who has turned away from his or her religious roots? Why is the person turning away?

Part Two

DISCOVERY

Come, let us return to the Lord! In just a short
time, he will restore us so we can live in his
presence. Oh, that we might know the Lord!
Let us press on to know him! Then he will
respond to us as surely as the arrival of dawn
or the coming of rains in early spring.

—*Hosea 6:1, 3*

5

(RE)DISCOVERING THE ANCIENT-PRESENT PATHS

> The great Christian revolutions come not by the
> discovery of something that was not known before.
> They happen when someone takes radically
> something that was always there.
> —*Helmut Richard Niebuhr (1894–1962),*
> *American theologian and author*

What are we doing here?

Which way do we go?

Who do we listen to?

Jennifer and I were asking these questions and many more during the summer of 1992. Expecting our first child, we moved to the Los Angeles basin to take a job I wasn't qualified for. A large denomination invited me to develop and direct a strategy to start one thousand new churches in the fastest-growing region of the United States. I didn't meet any of their three basic requirements: being a seminary graduate, at least thirty-five years old, and having five new churches under one's belt. I was twenty-seven, hadn't finished seminary, and had never started a church. I was in way over my head. It didn't make any sense. Maybe that's what attracted me—I knew I couldn't do it on my own!

Jennifer and I had been sensing for several months that God was beginning to prepare us to leave the church we had pastored for five years in Northern California. We were waiting and listening to how and when God would lead us next.

Then one Sunday we hosted a guest speaker at our church. L. E. was not your typical denominational guy. In his mid-forties, he had spent most of his adult life in business until he came to a radical encounter with Jesus, started a church in the South, and then became director of church planting for California. He spoke with a freshness we hadn't heard in a long time. His message was simply about relationships—that the essence of the gospel of Jesus is about restoring relationships with God, one another, and the world. Anything else is a distraction. Jennifer and I invited L. E. to our home for lunch, which went late into the evening. Our hearts leapt inside as we shared our stories with each other and prayed for one another.

Just weeks after we met, L. E. invited us to lead an effort to start "new paradigm" churches in Southern California that would have a simple focus on building healthy relationships. He pushed the paperwork through the system and I was approved, despite being grossly underqualified. There was a significant bit that I wouldn't fully appreciate until years later: my job description was to oversee the development of "New Testament" churches—which meant not every local church I worked with needed to be connected to the denominational system. As far as I know, I was the only one in the country with such an open mandate.

> Do not seek to follow in the footsteps of the men of old; seek what they thought.
>
> —Matsuo Bashō (1644–1694), Japanese poet

I was given a salary and, more important, great freedom. This opportunity called forth the pioneer spirit within both Jennifer and me. In every sphere I had strong support, from the local team as well as state, regional, and national leadership. And I was encouraged to take time to explore and experiment. I was even told to make some mistakes. Since I couldn't very well recruit and coach others in something I'd never done, I set out to start a church as a sort of prototype of the churches that would follow.

In those first few months, I read everything I could on church strategy and mission—domestic and foreign, simple and complex. I felt pressure to decide on a plan of action and get started. Which strategy would help achieve the goal of a thousand churches in eight years? Bill Hybel's Seeker-Driven, Rick Warren's Purpose-Driven, Carl George's MetaChurch model, Ralph Neighbor's cell church, something from overseas, or perhaps some exotic new combo? The more I read and interviewed people, the more overwhelmed I became.

More confused than when I began, I was taking a walk in San Francisco one sunny afternoon, reflecting on the daunting task ahead of me and wondering why I had even accepted this impossible job. Then I finally prayed in desperation: "Lord Jesus, I don't know what to do. Which model of church and mission do you want us to follow?"

After a few moments of silence, I sensed a clear answer: "Do you want me, or a model?"

It wasn't the answer I had hoped for. It would have been so much easier if he had given me some specific blueprint to build out or pointed me to some expert I could follow. But at the same time an enormous rush of peace came over me.

Then I sensed the Spirit of Jesus say, "If I show you a model, you will follow it. You will seek to perfect it with the best of intentions. Instead, will you trust me? Follow me . . . I am the Way."

So Jennifer and I began praying together for the Spirit to reveal to us his ways to follow and to direct us to the people he was already preparing us to join with. It was with this prayer that we moved to Southern California with lots of unknowns, but trusting Jesus to make the way clear. One afternoon, while searching for homes in the Orangecrest neighborhood, Jennifer and I saw a house we liked, so we knocked on the door to inquire about the area. A woman opened the door and welcomed us in, offered us ice tea, gave us a tour of her home, and then asked why we were moving to the area. We told her. Janine wasn't a Christian, but she had lots of spiritual questions.

Within a few weeks, we were meeting in Janine and Kyle's home with about a dozen others, from differing ages and walks of life. We even had one couple sell a custom home they had just built in Northern California to join our team. Others—from college students to teachers and from engineers to office administrators—joined with us. We all shared a desire to experience Jesus in simple community and within reach of friends who were open spiritually but didn't want religion.

From the start, we resisted the temptation to remodel or reengineer what we already understood church to be, or to come up with our own idea. Our challenge was to die to our own understandings and let Jesus birth something new within us. We were at a crossroads. One path was wide and well worn by all our previous experiences and the proven church growth programs. We knew where this would take us. On the other side was just an image of Jesus, standing as the portal by which we would come to the ancient paths. We didn't quite know where that venture would lead. Would we strive to reinvent something, or choose to rediscover the ancient-present Way of Jesus?

Our choice of ways was clear, but the process on the ancient path wasn't as easy as we expected. We began meeting together in each other's homes for meals, sharing our stories, reading the Bible, and praying for one another. We expected God to show us his ways and to birth new movements in the greater Los Angeles area. We began asking questions: What is church? Did Jesus even start a church? Why isn't the gospel of Jesus moving as freely in the West as it is in developing countries and places of persecution? Do we not have the same gospel? How is the Spirit leading us to embody the gospel to our neighbors and friends who are open spiritually but have no time or need for religion or church?

One evening I remember asking the group, "Why is it that we don't see any movement like the first-century Jesus movement? We have the gospel in written form, on the Internet, in seminaries, and so many 'Christian' things like books, stores, music, television, radio, T-shirts, and so much other stuff."

Having given fifteen years of her life to serving the poor in Guatemala, Marian answered simply, "It's because with all the stuff, we don't need God. . . . It's not that the gospel is not powerful but that we have replaced the power with so many other things we deem essential for church but that actually weigh it down or dilute its power. Most churches rely on all this stuff that the early Jesus followers never had."

The promise of Jesus that "Upon this rock I will build my church, and all the powers of hell will not conquer it" (Matthew 16:18) became the foundation of our quest. We believed Jesus would build his church, so the question for us became, How then do we let Jesus build his church? Or as a friend of mine put it, "What does it mean to lead a group of people who are supposed to be following someone else?"

We began to embrace Jesus as our guide—not church growth consultants, mission organizations, or even missionaries. We didn't want a church that we could invent or that money could buy. We wanted to experience the presence of Jesus in our lives and our neighborhoods. So we set out to uncover—actually, to recover—the life of Jesus again for ourselves.

We were blessed on this leg of the journey to join with many fellow travelers who were also asking some of the same questions about living a simple life in Jesus. We first met Mike and Shannon while Mike was serving as associate pastor of a wealthy church in the Los Angeles area. It didn't take long to see that they were now at a crossroads similar to the one Jennifer and I had been at when we were pastoring. As couples, we encouraged one another in our journey. Within a few months, Mike gave up the financial securities of a church position to work as a potter and live out his faith among his family, neighbors, and friends.

For the first eighteen months, Mike and his family struggled financially but grew spiritually as they invited people into their home and lives. As a starving artist struggling to launch a viable business, he was constantly tempted with pastor jobs—some with a six-figure salary, great benefit package, and even freedom to set his own hours. One afternoon, I shared over lunch about some of my discouragement over the slow process by which we were seeing new spiritual communities emerge. Mike just smiled. "Relax," he told me. "I'm in it for the thirty-year plan. The Book of Acts covers a period of about thirty years, and it's taken us nearly two thousand years to devolve to where we are now. So I figure it will take some time to recover the vitality of Acts in our lives. I hope not. But if it does, I'm prepared for the long haul."

Now, eight years later and having started a pottery business out of his garage, Mike is influencing hundreds of youths and their families as a part-time art teacher at the local high school, where he also coaches football and basketball. He now has an opportunity to demonstrate the life of Jesus in ways he never could in the professional ministry. Though his spiritual community is smaller, his influence in his city is much greater than he ever imagined.

We have also been blessed with fellow travelers who gently (and sometimes not so gently) pointed out our very Eurocentric views of Jesus, church, and culture. We don't believe we would have ever made significant progress without the friendship and challenge from many parts of the world: Kasareka and his friends offered perspectives from East and West Africa, Petros and Annie from Eastern European, Shahid from a Middle-Eastern viewpoint, and William from an African American experience. Ramon and Theresa introduced us to new foods, friendships, and the views of diverse Latin cultures. Naoto, Song, and Hseih brought Asian viewpoints.

During many lively roundtable discussions, we questioned each other's assumptions and judgments. Though we each had our biases, there was never any doubt that I had the most stuff to work through. But they did also, as they came to realize how much they had been conditioned by modernity and Christendom. We helped each other to strip away the baggage that had been passed down to us from Western culture. At first we started seeing the obvious of what church was *not*: a building, a service, worship, a denomination, a set of programs. The Way of Jesus is not dependent on or confined to any one culture, but moves

> To look at something as though we had never seen it before requires great courage.
>
> —Henri Matisse (1869-1954), French painter and sculptor

and flows through people of diverse cultures. Church is not even about church. It's all about Jesus: Why did he come? What is the Way of Jesus? What does Jesus expect of us?

This ancient path is perfectly illustrated in the life and ministry of Jesus. We see church in its embryonic phase with Jesus and his disciples. Jesus could have left a book of specific instructions or initiated a formal institution before he left. Instead, he gathered a group of people and lived with them. Their identity was not found on a certain day of the week, or a place where they would meet; it was found in *who* they gathered with. Jesus initiated a community whose identity, mission, lifestyle, and power was—and would continue to be—rooted in him. Jesus not only instructed his disciples but also modeled to them what community is and would be. To (re)discover the ancient paths, we need to encounter Jesus.

Ancient-Present Worldview

> People like us, who believe in physics, know that
> the distinction between past, present, and future is
> only a stubbornly persistent illusion.
> —*Albert Einstein (1879–1955),*
> *theoretical physicist and Nobel laureate*

The modern agenda resulted in fragmentation, individualism, alienation, and depersonalization. In its response, the postmodern era is in some ways reflecting a time before *and* after the modern age. As we compare the social and religious climates in which we live today, we see striking similarities between the premodern first century A.D. and the postmodern twenty-first century. Many students of culture see parallels between the Roman world at the time of Christ with today's post-Christian West. The first century offers clues for making the most of the opportunities in the world we now find ourselves in.[1]

Despite the obvious differences, today's Western culture holds much in common with the cultural-spiritual environment of two thousand years ago. Religious pluralism is on the rise, as it was

A Continuum of Worldviews

First century Premodern Pre-Christendom	Modernity Christendom	Twenty-first century Postmodern Post-Christendom
Worldview or Philosophy		
Spiritual	Natural, material	Spiritual-natural
Eastern	Western	Eastern-Western
Primitive, organic	Mechanistic, organized	Ecological, organic
Holistic	Fragmented, analytic	Holist, interbeing
Both-and	Dualism, either-or	Both-and
Cyclical, seasonal	Linear (Newtonian physics)	Spiral, double helix
Metanarrative; Oran Mor	Scientific rationalism	Metanarratives
Society or Community		
Identity in community	Autonomous individual	Individual in community
Global trading (Silk Road)	National economies	Global economy (trade pacts)
Koine Greek as lingua franca	No lingua franca	English as lingua franca
Oral communication	Verbal communication	Visual and virtual communication
Incremental change	Inevitable Progress	Negative ethos, cynicism
Tribe, clan, nation	Hierarchy, top-down	Holarchies, networks
Spirituality		
Enchantment	Disenchantment	Reenchantment
Paganism	Humanism, materialism	Neopaganism
Pluralism	Rationalism	Pluralism
Superstition	Science	Experience
Many gods	No god (atheism)	Many gods, we are god(s)
Martyred church	Civil, mainstream religion	Marginalized church

during the first century. Just as the Roman world had a common language, economy, and transportation, so the global economic and cultural climate of the twenty-first century is increasingly integrated. Our current age has much more in common with the predominant philosophy and spirituality of the first century than modernity ever did. The stage is being set for God to do something dramatic in the digital age, more than any other time since Jesus walked the earth.

Some may also say that our times reflect one of the darkest periods of Jewish history, when the Babylonians defeated the Jews and took them into captivity. How, they wondered, could God care about their plight? How could their beloved Jerusalem be defeated? How could God use wicked invaders to destroy his chosen people? In response, God assured Habakkuk, a Hebrew prophet, that the Babylonians at the height of their power would prevail not because they were righteous but because they were instruments of judgment. In the end, God would demonstrate his righteous character: "For the time will come when all the earth will be filled, as the waters fill the sea, with an awareness of the glory of the Lord" (Habakkuk 2:14). When the Babylonians surrounded Jerusalem, God responded to Habakkuk's cry for help: "Look at the nations and be amazed! Watch and be astounded at what I will do! For I am doing something in your own day, something you wouldn't believe even if someone told you about it" (Habakkuk 1:5).

Is God doing something in our day we would not believe if we were told? It's time to look and listen through the cultural noise and spiritual chaos. What is the Spirit saying in and through the culture shifts? Do the tension and anxiety signal birth pangs of something new emerging? Are we open to the possibility that the Creator is still at work and desires to bring us to a place of rest?

Listen!

A Rising Cultural Anxiety

It was the best of times, it was the worst of times, it was the age of wisdom, it was the age of foolishness, it was the epoch of belief, it was the epoch of incredulity, it was the season of Light, it was the season of Darkness, it was the spring of hope, it was the winter of despair, we had everything before us, we had nothing before us, we were all going direct to Heaven, we were all going direct the other way.

—*Charles Dickens (1812–1870),*
English novelist, A Tale of Two Cities

Dickens's words ring as true today as they did when he wrote his classic novel. Indeed, these are the best of times and the worst of times. They are also the only times we have.

For over a millennium, the culture of church and the church of the culture were all but synonymous. There was almost no distinction between Christendom and the West, modernity and the church. But these structures are now crumbling. Drifting farther from the familiar security of the modern world into the uncharted waters of this new world induces feelings of cultural anxiety that our institutions (notably the Western church) are in no position to alleviate.

While many churches are feeling marginalized by the shifting culture, many still choose not to engage with culture, holding strong to the ways of a bygone era and fighting off threats to their sense of control, even to their very survival.

Many have one foot in the shifting currents of change and one foot in fixed structures of modernity that for generations have served them well. They feel both pulled forward and held back by these forces, producing a restlessness that begs to be attended to. It's no wonder so many feel paralyzed by the hard choices.

The tides of change are rising, and the currents they create are getting stronger. There is a point of decision that will come when we stand with one foot on the stable dock of everything that we have known and the other foot in the boat that's being pulled away by the currents. With the rising fear and anxiety, there seem to be only two options. The first is to "hold your ground": strengthen your grip on the structures of the past. The second is to "trust the universe": jump out on your own and drift on the sea of relativism, hoping the currents will take you safely where you need to go.

I know what it feels like to hold on to the supposed safety of the dock. But at times I have also drifted with the culture, tossed here and there by the prevailing cultural trends, people's expectations, and majority opinions.

Both options are fear-based and stifle our spiritual freedom. The first is motivated by fear of the unknown. It looks for safety in trusting that the authorities and structures will offer security. The other is founded in a fear of being controlled, but we end up giving up our control to the cultural currents. True freedom will never be found in culture or in structures. We need surer ways of navigating in times of cultural-spiritual upheaval.

We believe there is a third option: to catch the wind of the Spirit that blows with and across the currents of culture. Jesus called most of his disciples from the sea; the earliest symbols of Christ were the fish and the boat. An early church father, Clement of Alexandria, described church as a "ship running in the wind."[2] Instead of the false security of the dock or a lone rowboat at the mercy of the currents, we are called to jump into a sailboat powered not by our own efforts but by the winds of the Holy Spirit, one with a strong, heavy keel and a rudder to steer the course. Our role is not to power the vessel, nor to set the course, but to listen and obey. Jesus is our captain. We follow his lead and stay close to the wind of the Holy Spirit, who is blowing across all cultures.

> The sea is dangerous and its storms terrible, but these obstacles have never been sufficient [for one] to remain ashore.
>
> —Ferdinand Magellan (1480-1521), Portuguese explorer, first to circumnavigate the globe

This letting go and jumping into the boat is what we chose when we left the safety net of religion and set out for the Pacific Northwest. Only as we continue to move deeper into Jesus with reckless abandon will we experience the reality of the One who holds heaven and earth together. In Jesus there is peace in the midst of the storms outside us and the storms that are even harder to navigate: those within us. From resting in Jesus as our Center we also gain the courage to share in the sufferings of others, not with a detached sympathy but with a joining in their passion and suffering as Jesus did.

Most of us who venture out feel displaced for a season. We are no longer on the shore, and we are not really anywhere very long, but often out on the wide-open sea. Our hearts are set on the journey, knowing we may never really settle, always being somewhere in between. Jesus prepares us through difficulty and loneliness for the times ahead. It is only by being fully engaged in the world that we will be able to feel the heartbeat of Jesus for people who are losing the secure moorings they have relied on for generations and for those who are drifting with the current of the times. It's like the old sailing proverb: "One does not discover new lands without consenting to lose sight of the shore for a very long time." We won't cross the sea merely by staring at the water. Each of us must choose: either we hold on to the dock or we jump into the boat and let the Spirit lead us across the currents.

We are seeking to listen to the voice of the Spirit stirring within the currents of culture, and to move with the rhythm of Jesus. With our eyes fixed on Jesus, we hoist our sails, waiting for the Holy Spirit to breathe air into them. So we invite you to jump into the boat, raise the sail, and join the adventure. Remember, the journey is the gift.

> *When you go through deep waters and great trouble,*
> *I will be with you.*
> *When you go through rivers of difficulty,*
> *you will not drown!*
>
> —Isaiah (eighth-century Hebrew
> prophet) Isaiah 43:2

Reflection and Discussion

Read the Gospel of John and then reflect on the questions here to discover the Way according to Jesus and his first disciples. Resist the temptation to answer the questions from your own experience or religious tradition. Instead, expect the Holy Spirit to reveal to you fresh understanding from the Gospels. You may also wish to compare and contrast John's account of Jesus with the Gospels of Matthew, Mark, and Luke.

- Who was Jesus? What was his purpose and message? his passion?
- What example did Jesus leave us? What didn't he leave us?
- What did Jesus ask of his disciples?
- How did the views and expectations of Jesus that were held by the disciples change over time?

6

RETURNING TO THE
ANCIENT PATHS

So now the Lord says:
"Stand at the crossroads and look;
ask for the ancient paths,
ask where the good way is, and walk in it,
and you will find rest for your souls."
But you reply, "No, that's not the road we want!"
—*Jeremiah (c. 600 B.C.), Hebrew prophet, Jeremiah 6:16*[1]

Jesus' first encounter with those who would eventually become his twelve disciples set the tone for the rest of his ministry. From his opening invitation ("Come, be my disciples, and I will show you how to fish for people!" Mark 1:17) to his final commission to "go and make disciples of all nations" (Matthew 28:19–20), Jesus made his intention clear. He called them into relationship with *himself*, not to church, religion, or even community. By living in community with Jesus, the first disciples discovered the nature and purpose of their lives. The invitation he gave more than two thousand years ago is the same today: "Come to me."

Since this book is about adventuring on the Way of Jesus, we must delve into more of what that means. We've found one of the best frameworks for understanding the Way comes from Jesus' response to a disciple's question, one we find ourselves asking today.

During their last meal together, Jesus pours out his heart to his closest friends. He begins by washing their feet and foretelling his betrayal. He says he'll be with them only a little while longer and then will depart to a place to which they could not come. Thomas voices his concern on behalf of the others: "We haven't any idea where you are going, so how can we know the way?" Jesus answers, "I am the way, the truth, and the life. No one can come to the Father except through me. If you had known who I am, then you would have known who my Father is. From now on you know him and have seen him!" (John 14:6–7). Jesus' response is accessible enough to those who will listen. In his statement, he encapsulates his life and mission. To embrace Jesus in all his fullness is to know God. The gospel is not an abstract idea or an institutional structure. The gospel is a living reality. Jesus is the *Way*, the *Truth*, and the *Life*.

Jesus as the Way

Jesus is our path or roadway *to* life. This is mirrored by the story Jennifer tells our children of a man who was home warming by his fire while a winter storm raged outside. He was startled when he heard a loud thud. The man looked outside to discover that a bird had flown at the window seeking refuge from the storm. He then looked up to see a flock of birds frantically looking for cover. The man was moved to compassion and went out in the storm to try to help the birds before the storm overcame them. He opened the door to his barn with the hope they would fly in to find cover. But the birds continued flying about, not knowing the refuge that was being provided for them. He then went and spread birdseed on the snow, hoping the trail would lead the birds into safety. Still to no avail. He waved his hands frantically at the birds seeking to bring them to safety. Again, no response. Then he realized that the only way to save these poor birds was to become a bird himself, that he might show them the way to shelter. At that moment, he realized that's what Jesus did. Jesus became one of us that he might show us the way. That's the mystery of his incarnation: Jesus, already being God, chose to take on human flesh. He understands us.

Jesus is also the Way *of* life. Jesus provides a living example of what he expects us to continue to live. Jesus both taught and demonstrated a whole new value system that would need to be exercised in community. Consider the many "one anothers" that we find throughout the New Testament Scriptures (love one another, care for one another, share with one another, pray for one another, serve one another). Healthy community emerges from our shared life in Jesus.

As we journey with Jesus, he is our *Waymaker*, the leader on the road, the guide to the wandering, the teacher of the seekers, and the example to all. Not only has Jesus traveled the road before us; he is our guide and he is our path. Through him we are reconciled to God; we need no other mediator. Jesus invites us to walk with him to the path of freedom, to experience his presence in our midst.

We realize it's becoming common belief that all paths lead to God. No doubt this would be comforting to some people, but it is not the case. We've done enough wilderness backpacking to know how easy it is to lose our bearings. In Washington State, not all trails lead to the summit of Mount Rainier; even some with the same starting point may end in very different places. It's also quite possible to get lost by choosing the wrong path. This is the difference between all religions and experiencing a real relationship with Jesus. All religions may offer pathways, but not all paths lead to freedom. Some lead to bondage or endless wandering.

> To deny believing in Jesus makes him to be a liar. He can't be just a good man. He was too radical for that.
> —C. S. Lewis (1898-1963), Irish-born author

Jesus as the Truth

Wandering in a sea of relativism, we find there *is* truth, and the truth is Jesus. Jesus not only *preached* the good news; he *is* the good news. This truth is not religious dogma, an institution, or even religion. Truth is a person. We gain hold of what is true through grabbing hold of Jesus, the author of truth. In a cultural landscape that shifts increasingly, Jesus is our integrating reality (Colossians 2:17).

Truth is the basis of the Way, and the Way is the embodiment of the truth.

Jesus is our *Liberator*, the truth that sets us free from our spiritual wandering, from religious legalism, from the weight of our separation from God (John 8:31–32). In Luke 4:16–21, we read that Jesus went to the synagogue of his hometown of Nazareth on the Sabbath. The scroll of Isaiah was handed to him, he unrolled to the place that was foretold by the prophet, and proclaimed his mandate:

> *The Spirit of the Lord is upon me,*
> *for he has appointed me*
> *to preach Good News to the poor.*
> *He has sent me to proclaim that captives will be released,*
> *that the blind will see,*
> *that the downtrodden will be freed from their oppressors,*
> *and that the time of the Lord's favor has come.*

Jesus rolled up the scroll, handed it back to the attendant, and sat down. Everyone in the synagogue stared at him intently. Then he said, "This Scripture has come true today before your very eyes!" His incarnation, life, death, and resurrection are all about setting us free. He didn't come to teach us, to judge us, or to set up a new religion. Jesus came to offer us freedom from our individual bondages and the demands of institutional religion.

Jesus as the Life

Through Jesus we experience the life he spoke of many times: "My purpose is to give life in all its fullness."[2] Eternal life is now. To share in the life of Jesus is to experience him both now and forever.[3] Jesus calls the world not to a new religion or even a better life but to a fundamentally new life. "What this means is that those who become Christians become new persons. They are not the same anymore, for the old life is gone. A new life has begun!" (II Corinthians 5:17). To know Jesus is to know life, and this life is like no other.

Jesus came to restore the original design of a pure, unmediated relationship with God. The new life that he gives fulfills our deepest longings. To those walking an Eastern path toward enlightenment in this lifetime (or, failing that, counting perhaps on the next), Jesus is more than just an enlightened one; he is the source and free giver of light itself. To those who are trying to earn their salvation or gain favor with God by living a moral life, Jesus has already done the work. To those who are sampling spiritual beliefs, looking for fulfillment, Jesus meets us in our loneliness and confusion.

Jesus is the Way *to* life and the Way *of* life. He is more than teacher, guru, or bodhisattva. Jesus is the *Lifegiver*, the very embodiment of God who invites us to experience his life. As we believe in Jesus and follow him as the Way, we will hear him as the Truth, and he will give us new Life. This is good news, indeed! In the words of Jean Guyon, a French mystic of the seventeenth century:

> *It is to the Lord Jesus that you abandon yourself.*
> *It is also the Lord whom you will follow as the Way;*
> *it is this Lord that you will hear as the Truth,*
> *and it is from this Lord that you will receive Life.*
> *If you follow Him as the Way, you will hear Him as the Truth,*
> *and He will bring life to you as the Life.*[4]

Jesus and His Disciples

Jennifer was stopped recently by her friend Meg, who asked, "What are you up to these days?"

Jennifer responded, "I'm working on a book with Jonathan."

"What's it about?"

"It's called *The Way of Jesus.*"

"Oh," Meg answered, "you're writing a book about religion."

"Well, not really. You see, the Way of Jesus is not about religion; it's about relationship—relationship with Jesus and one another."

Jennifer continued to share with Meg how the Way of Jesus is more than what is experienced in many supposed religious settings.

If we were to join Jesus as he walked this earth, we would simply live life together: traveling together, enjoying meals, hearing his stories, and witnessing his healing power that gave sight to the blind and even raised the dead. We would be shocked by the boldness by which Jesus confronted the religious establishment. He exposed the human-made rituals and traditions, and he unpeeled the layers that had grown over people's hearts and were keeping them from true communion with God.

Jesus gave his disciples a living image of what genuine spiritual community is and should always be. The same work Jesus began with his twelve disciples is to continue now in the power of the Holy Spirit through his followers, who are the Body of Christ. He promised they would do "even greater things" than he had done.

He left this promise with a band of broken men and women. For his disciples, all their hopes and dreams were shattered on the cross. Peter betrayed him, three times denying that he even knew Jesus, while the rest of the disciples hid in fear. They lost hope. They lost courage. But the testimony of a woman broke through their hopelessness with the shocking news, "He's alive!" The Way came back, and their hope was restored.

After his resurrection, Jesus gave his disciples a direct commission with radical implications: "Peace be with you. As the Father has sent me, so I send you." Then he breathed on them and said to them, "Receive the Holy Spirit. If you forgive anyone's sins, they are forgiven. If you refuse to forgive them, they are unforgiven" (John 20:21–23).

Jesus did not call his disciples to be creative or ingenious or even strategic. He simply expected his disciples to follow the example lived before them.[5] But even after living with him for three years and witnessing his resurrection from the dead, the disciples still couldn't appreciate his Way. They still held onto the long-held expectation that the Messiah would establish an earthly kingdom where they would have political and religious positions. They were still stuck in a religious paradigm. In fact they kept asking him, "Lord, are you going to free Israel now and restore our kingdom?"

(Acts 1:6). *They believed in Jesus, yet they were not transformed.* Jesus told them it wasn't meant for them to know and that they need not worry about the timing of a kingdom on this earth. Instead, he gave them this promise: "But when the Holy Spirit has come upon you, you will receive power and will tell people about me everywhere—in Jerusalem, throughout Judea, in Samaria, and to the ends of the earth" (Acts 1:8).

When Jesus left again, this time ascending directly to heaven, the disciples were perhaps not as frightened as before; but they had no clue of what they were waiting for. What is the Holy Spirit? What did he mean by "we would receive power"? How do we get this power? What do we do? How do we wait?

They didn't know what else to do, so they prayed (always a wise option that exemplifies dependence on the Holy Spirit!). Luke says, "They all met together continually for prayer, along with Mary the mother of Jesus, several other women, and the brothers of Jesus" (Acts 1:14). For ten days, 120 disciples waited in an upper room of a house with prayerful anticipation.

They were not disappointed. As the Holy Spirit was poured out on those women and men, they were anointed with the presence of God; the Spirit of Jesus came upon them. In that dramatic moment, they realized that this was not about an idea or following a man or setting up a political or religious reign. It was the very presence of God with them. Not just any spirit but the Spirit of the triune God was now with them in the upper room. Jesus continued to live among them and in them through the power of the Holy Spirit. This was a radical paradigm shift, for in just three years they'd moved from experiencing God enfleshed in Jesus and dwelling *among* them to the Spirit of God now dwelling *within* them!

Twice the disciples had been left by Jesus, and twice their expectations were shattered. First, he demonstrated his power over life and death through his resurrection. Then, forty days later, Jesus ascended to heaven and soon after the Holy Spirit descended upon them at Pentecost. Through the Holy Spirit, his very presence would remain with them as the source of both their comfort and their power. A new way of living was to emerge from their new Life, the Way of Jesus.

Following Pentecost, the disciples didn't have to figure out what to do. They had been with Jesus.

They lived with him. For three years Jesus walked with his disciples. When he ascended into heaven, he passed the baton to his disciples with the confidence that they would spread the gospel throughout the world. The disciples were expected to continue the ministry of Jesus, in the Way of Jesus. They were given no other option.

The timing for the coming of the Holy Spirit was no coincidence. On the day of Pentecost, an influx of as many as two hundred thousand pilgrims would have been visiting Jerusalem. The territory represented by these people would have included the entire area known as the Near East: from Arabia and Egypt on the south, to Persia on the east, throughout the Mediterranean, and as far west as Rome. This visitation of the Holy Spirit turned Jerusalem upside down; three thousand people became new followers of Jesus in one day. These new believers "met together constantly and shared everything they had. They sold their possessions and shared the proceeds with those in need. They worshiped together at the Temple each day, met in homes for the Lord's Supper, and shared their meals with great joy and generosity—all the while praising God and enjoying the goodwill of all the people. And each day the Lord added to their group those who were being saved" (Acts 2:44–47).

To me who am but black cold charcoal, grant O Lord, that by the fire of Pentecost, I may be set ablaze.

–St. John of Damascus
(c. 676-749)

These new believers were totally transformed and given the power to live out the promises of Jesus. So what did they do? They continued to meet together as they had with Jesus. They raised families, worked their fields, engaged in commerce. They simply lived the life of Jesus wherever they were.

Jesus said, "I have given you an example to follow. Do as I have done to you" (John 13:15). The same life Jesus gave to his first-century disciples is to be continued in the power of the Holy Spirit through his disciples today, who are the Body of Christ.

✛ Reflection and Discussion ✛

Read the Book of Acts and then reflect on the questions to discover the Way of Jesus according to the first-century disciples. Resist the temptation to answer the questions from your own experience or religious tradition. Instead, ask the Holy Spirit to reveal to you fresh insights.

- According to the Book of Acts, how can we experience the reality of Jesus in community?
- Why did the news of Jesus spread so rapidly throughout the Roman Empire, despite intense opposition? What were the major hindrances to the movement?
- Who were the key players in the movement? What did they do? What did they not do?
- What was the role of the Holy Spirit among these first disciples?

7

THE LIVING REALITY
OF THE BODY OF CHRIST

Yes, I see the Church as the Body of Christ. But,
oh! How we have blemished and scarred that body
through social neglect and through fear of being
nonconformists.

—*Martin Luther King Jr. (1929–1968),*
Baptist pastor, civil rights activist

What did the New Testament writers envision when they used the word *church*? How did the early Jesus followers see themselves? If you entered their city and asked directions to church, they might give you a puzzled look before they invited you to their home for a meal. "Church," from the Greek word *ekklesia*, literally means "a calling out" or "assembly" and refers to actual gatherings of disciples, or to the disciples in a local area.[1] These "called out ones" shared a common life in Jesus Christ. A church had no identity outside the presence and power of the resurrected Jesus among those who believed.

Although there is no definition of church, the New Testament does set out nearly a hundred images reinforcing key aspects of the church's nature such as the Body of Christ, community of the Spirit, people of God, family of God, and bride of Christ. The use of diverse social and relational images points to the fact that the church is alive and cannot be contained. The images are more than mere descriptions of what the church *does*; they are definitions of the very identity of its being. It is not *like* a family but *is* the very "family of God."

Not just salty, but the very character of salt. Not like light but, as Jesus said, "You are the light of the world" (Matthew 5:14).

One of the most striking images used to describe the church in the New Testament is the Body of Christ. The body image illustrates the diversity, fellowship, and interdependence of believers under Christ as the head.[2] As we examine the life of the early church, we see the mutual nature of such a community, like a healthy family where people are committed to each other because of their common bond. Thus those churches were personal, intimate, committed, and small enough to facilitate healthy relationships. Jesus' life and mission continued through this Spirit-empowered community. The same can be true for us; the more we are united deeply in Jesus, the more beautiful and free the diversity of the body.

We are not like a body; we *are* the living, breathing Body of Christ.

As with the human body, though the Body of Christ is one it is made up of many working parts. As the apostle Paul writes, "[God] has given each one of us a special gift according to the generosity of Christ. . . . Under his direction, the whole body is fitted together perfectly. As each part does its own special work, it helps the other parts grow, so that the whole body is healthy and growing and full of love" (Ephesians 4:7, 16). The form we are to resemble is no less than the very form of Jesus, "measuring up to the full stature of Christ" (Ephesians 4:13). I can only tell you so much about Jesus, whereas in community, we can experience the living reality of Jesus. Spiritual maturing is growing into his likeness. We are, both individually and collectively, the dwelling place of the living Jesus.

An Ecological Perspective

We can view church from two primary perspectives: as a religious organization with institutional structures, or as an organic community with relational structures. The essential difference is that institutional structures are imposed upon from the outside, whereas living structures rise from within and support life. One is conserva-

Mechanistic Structures (Organized Religion)	Organic Structures (Relational Movement)
Rigid institution (pyramid)	Flexible movement (vines)
Church is building, institution, or event	Church is people ("Where two or more . . .")
Program, one day a week	Lifestyle, seven days a week
Build programs and/or buildings	Reproduce indigenous communities
Uniformity, conformity, predictability	Unity, diversity, spontaneity
Conserve and control	Empower and release
Centralized and hierarchical	Decentralized and horizontal
Low level of trust in people	High level of trust in people
Top-down, hierarchical	Bottom-up, grassroots
Static, product-focused	Dynamic, process-focused

tive, the other is ready to risk; the one guards boundaries, the other crosses them; the one conserves and controls, the other empowers and releases.

The basic tension between these two structures is one of perspective, between the parts and the whole. Fritjof Capra, the noted physicist and philosopher, explains that "the emphasis on the parts has been called mechanistic, reductionistic, or atomistic; the emphasis on the whole holistic, organismic, or ecological."[3] He later concludes: "Ultimately—as quantum physics showed so dramatically—there are no parts at all. What we call a part is merely a pattern in an inseparable web of relationships."[4] With all living systems, the whole is *different* from the sum of the parts.

In contrast to mechanistic or institutional structures where the parts only exist *for* each other, the parts of organic systems also exist *by means of* each other and in symbiosis with their environment.[5] In all living systems, relationships are primary. To break down those relationships by institutionally structuring them is to dissect a living organism (which kills it). Good organization often serves as a poor substitute for a living, breathing body of believers under the guidance of Jesus. The structures of a spiritual community should emerge from our life in Jesus and embody our pilgrim character. Such communities are flexible and fluid—able to move together as the Spirit leads.

It's one thing to talk organic, it's another to live it. Our friend Doug Johnson in Cape Town, South Africa, is one who lives what he talks. Doug directs a recording studio and is one of the pastors of a fellowship that is in the process of shedding institutional expectations to move more freely as the Spirit leads. Doug sent us an e-mail that gives a glimpse of what they are wrestling with as a community: "It is a slow journey unbundling the baggage of the past and letting the Holy Spirit begin to create what is 'right.' It is not too difficult to see what is wrong, but what to do with it is much more difficult. The best analogy I have is that the church is meant to be family. There is nothing organizational about the structure of the church—the only reference we have is family. The average church in the world today is not a family—it is an orphanage, run by people who can manage orphanages well. The biggest problem with orphanages is that they do not produce mature sons and daughters— only a family can do that. However, the danger that we face today is that many have seen that the orphanage is wrong and have walked away from it, only to become street kids. An orphanage is often better than living on the streets! The challenge we face today (and hence the need to begin to define what church is), is to begin to build authentic family."

As with any healthy family, the church is by nature always in the process of becoming—to be living in the present while embodying both the product of the past and the seed of the future. South African theologian David Bosch describes it well: "Proclaiming its own transience, the church pilgrimages toward God's future."[6] The moment a church ceases to be on the move in the world, engaging with culture, responding to God's Spirit, seeking to reconcile relationships with God and one another, it ceases to be a living organism and reverts to mere religion. Disciples and communities of the Way were never meant to settle or to make a permanent residence because they are continuously on journey toward the ends of the earth and the end of time. God has called us to be on the move, and the world will not tolerate anything less than authentic pilgrim disciples on the journey of awakening.

Centered and Moving in Christ, or Bound by Structures

If we listen carefully, the questions we hear people ask reveal their values and assumptions of church. "What church are you a member of?" "Where's your church located?" "Who's your pastor?" "What denomination are you?" Such questions and people's answers betray how far Christendom has strayed from our simple roots in Christ. The common understanding of church today, whether Protestant or Catholic, evangelical or charismatic, is primarily as an organization or institution.

The New Testament understanding of the Body of Christ stands in stark contrast to the two most common expressions of Western Christianity. First, the *church denomination* is completely foreign to the life of Jesus and the New Testament. Its existence relies on structures, hierarchies, and policies not based on the life of Jesus (though often proof-texted on select biblical passages). They may do well at capturing some biblical doctrines, but not all, and they are sometimes used as hoops to jump through. They are often characterized by rules and expectations (explicit or implied) that define who is in and who is out. The criteria may be based on a range of acceptable or unacceptable behaviors or standardized belief systems that govern from who God supposedly is or isn't to who to vote for.

Denominational programs have been used to bring institutional control and conformity to the second expression of Western Christianity, the *congregational church*. Such organizational expressions tend to be identified with their building, pastor, or worship style. For instance, a church is primarily known by its physical location and hours of operation; there are times when it is either open or closed. A congregation might be referred to as "Reverend Smith's church," as if one owned a group of people, or it may have a pastor who runs things like a CEO, wielding first and final authority. Worship might be liturgical, traditional, postmodern, contemporary, evangelistic, uplifting, Spirit-filled, driven by excellence, rave, or just plain "refreshingly different."

Though these religious structures often do good, the systems were not initiated by Jesus, endorsed by the New Testament apostles who were closest to Jesus, or practiced by our spiritual ancestors in the early Church. Beyond that, we've come to believe these structures are dangerous to the Body of Christ, for at least four reasons.

First, institutionalized religion establishes authorities who compete with Jesus. They displace the presiding presence of Jesus with executives, boards, and CEO pastors. In both of these religious expressions of Christianity—denominations and congregations—clergy take over the role of Jesus in leading the people. It's as if Jesus is reduced to being a historical figure, not a living reality! The Body of Christ is artificially fragmented into professional clergy, who are separate and above the passive laity; this creates a spiritual consumerism that burns out the staff and bloats those who just absorb the energies of whoever is doing the work. The structures take precedent over the leading of the Holy Spirit: "Is there an authority other than Jesus, his Word and Spirit?" or "Are the people of God free to be led by the Spirit of God?"

Second, religious structures blind us from seeing the beauty of unity in diversity throughout the Body of Christ. They imply sets of criteria for deciding who can be considered in and who is out of the church. These rules may bring some degree of uniformity within a denomination or congregation by defining their unique identity and mission. But they also foster disunity, competition, and fragmentation among groups of Jesus followers within the same area. Sadly, church as we know it today binds the people in ways Jesus never modeled and hinders people from moving freely together as a united Body of Christ in a city or region. It also explains why there are few good stories of Christian unity, despite much time and money invested. There are strong warnings throughout the New Testament against dividing what God has put together. For instance, to the church at

Corinth Paul speaks against their fighting and division: "You are act-ing like people who don't belong to the Lord. When one of you says, 'I am a follower of Paul,' and another says, 'I prefer Apollos,' aren't you acting like those who are not Christians? . . . My job was to plant the seed in your hearts, and Apollos watered it, but it was God, not we, who made it grow. The ones who do the planting or watering aren't important, but God is important because he is the one who makes the seed grow" (I Corinthians 3:3–9).

Third, institutionalization of religion contributes to fragmentation of family and marriage. Common church replaces an intergenerational understanding of the family of God with age or status-specialized programs that divide and control rather than unite and mobilize people. How many have been told, "Just give us your children for this hour on Sunday and we will teach them what they need to know about God"? Or "You singles, come away in your own special study group because it is better for you (since you can't relate to those in families)." Or "You elderly folks need to be contained in this class, where you will be entertained (since you are too old to be of much use otherwise)."

Whatever happened to the older men and women passing on their wisdom to the next generations? Is the current lack of spiritual fathers and mothers a symptom of a system that has deviated from its original design? Don't the older believers need the refreshing perspectives of the young? Could our institutional understanding of Christianity actually be contributing to the breakdown of the fam-ily in the West? What might happen if churches adopted a more holistic "tribal" approach to relationships that involved intergen-erational interaction, mentoring, and rites of passage to mark the milestones and seasons of life in community?

Fourth, religious institutions hinder authentic engagement of culture. The interrelationship of church as living organism to its environ-ment or ecosystem is fundamental to the health and reproduction of the gospel across cultures. However, the modern church is in a strange place of being in the culture yet outside the culture. The sta-tic structures often become self-absorbed and governed by political or economic drivers. They typically connect with culture to the degree that culture serves the purposes of the institution. Only as the church is free from institutional expectations will the diverse members of the Body freely move by the Spirit's leading to respond to the needs and opportunities in their cultural context.

When the Spirit of God came upon 120 women and men in the upper room in Jerusalem, God became incarnate again. Whether locally or regionally, we are called to be one body moving in Jesus.

> A church which pitches its tents without constantly looking out for new horizons, which does not continually strike camp, is being untrue to its calling. . . . [We must] play down our longing for certainty, accept what is risky, live by improvisation and experiment.
> —Hans Küng,
> German Catholic theologian

In the New Testament, the word *church* is never used to refer to a building, institution, or denomination. As in the first century, communities must be flat (not hierarchical), fluid, and fast on their feet. Contrary to a smooth-running organization, an organic church is alive, messy, and sometimes unpredictable—just like a healthy family. Life brings forth the structure, not the other way around. Consequently, the Body of Christ is in a dynamic and "chaordic" process of interacting with Jesus and one another in a constantly changing environment.[7]

Jesus did not define his followers by any religious designation or boundary, but only by relationship with him. In contrast, today's common understanding of church is defined by its boundaries or bounded sets. In a *bounded set*, belonging and functions are determined by static, predefined structural boundaries. If an object fits the checklist of criteria, then it belongs. However, in a *centered set*, belonging is determined by the dynamic relationship of the objects to the center. If the object is moving toward the center, it is considered to be in the set. An object that in some sense may be considered near the center but moving away from it is seen to be outside the set. Thus, the boundary is determined by the relation of the objects to the center, not by essential characteristics of the objects themselves, as with a magnetic field whereby some particles are attracted and others repelled by the same force.[8]

As disciples, our belonging is determined by our relationship to Jesus, the center. Being defined by our living center instead of some inanimate structure is consistent with the identity of God's people being a nomadic or pilgrim people who are always on the move. Such a definition reflects an organic worldview where life is always in motion, either toward the center or away from it. It follows that as we are moving closer toward Christ the center we are at the same time moving closer to each other. It is only by change of direction that anyone moves across the boundary, in toward Christ or out from the center.

All followers of Jesus are part of the Universal Church[9] that includes them regardless of geography, culture, or history. But the greatest emphasis in the New Testament is placed on a local group of disciples as the visible incarnation of the Body of Christ in a given time and place. In the early years, when the church was primarily around Jerusalem, the Jesus followers met in homes, synagogues, and even the temple in Jerusalem. As the church expanded beyond Jerusalem and Judea, two organic expressions of the Body of Christ emerged. First, there was the local gathering or church that met in a home, made up of an extended family of believers.[10] Second, there was the city or regional church, consisting of the disciples of a larger geographical area.[11]

The New Testament church in a city or region was a fellowship of smaller churches. This didn't mean that if twenty or thirty churches were in a city the church was fractured. The apostle Paul often referred to all disciples of Jesus in a city or region as one church, as in "the church in Corinth." It was one church, one Body, even though it met in many places. This isn't so very different from the reality of a Native American tribe having various clans in a number of locales but sharing the same core culture, language, and heritage.

Although Paul knew of various local churches in a city, he wrote one letter with the assumption that it would suffice for all in the city. Acknowledging their common life and inheritance in Christ, the first disciples understood themselves as family. And so meeting house to house was not a strategy to build community, but rather the natural outgrowth of life. As the basic unit of society, the family was the matrix from which the church was birthed and reproduced. These organic, relational patterns facilitated the extensive growth and reproduction of the early church for three centuries before being squeezed into submission by the Roman religious authorities.[12]

We are not to be bound by doctrines or personalities, but defined only by our common life in Jesus. The community is defined by the individual believer's relationship to the center, the living Jesus Christ. Not even theology, the community, or mission, but Christ himself is the focus: "For no one can lay any other foundation than the one we already have—Jesus Christ" (I Corinthians 3:11).

A new birth in Jesus brings about a change in the direction of one's life. Our life is based on our new and continuing relationship to the risen Christ. Likewise, regardless of what we may call ourselves, a group is only a church to the extent that we are moving in unity in response to Jesus. Jesus is the center, and the Holy Spirit is the one who binds us together. This is both individual and communal. Each person or family has the invitation and freedom to follow Jesus. This freedom spirals outward, from the individual to the family to the local community to the city or region to which each belongs.

Declaration of Unity

I belong to everything that belongs to Jesus, and everything that belongs to Jesus belongs to me. It's not "Us and them." It's just us! For there is only one body of Christ. And the problems of the Church, the whole Church, are our problems! For we are the Church! And we can do more together than we can do alone. "One shall chase a thousand, and two shall put ten thousand to flight."

—Robert Fitts Sr., spiritual teacher and author

Jesus as center is stronger than our greatest differences. He transcends national, political, and linguistic boundaries. Structures are irrelevant except to the degree that they hinder the free movement of the people with Christ. Church is no longer something to join, or even start, but the living extension of Jesus Christ in time and space. As my Native American friend Ray reminds me, you can't join that which you already are.

Only to the extent that the people of God free themselves from false authorities and live by the reality of Jesus as our only center and authority will we see transformation of our cities and countries. As we give up our loyalties to static structures and institutions, we create room for the Holy Spirit to draw people from diverse contexts toward the living Christ. Jesus followers can assemble and reassemble wherever they live, in homes locally or in larger venues regionally. These communities are movement-oriented, with an organic nature that constantly tracks toward Jesus and welcomes others on the Way.

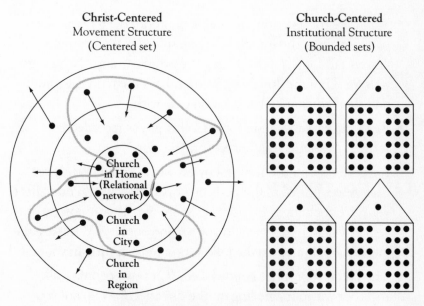

Christ-Centered
Movement Structure
(Centered set)

Church-Centered
Institutional Structure
(Bounded sets)

Church
in Home
(Relational
network)

Church
in
City

Church
in
Region

Church Paradigms in Contrast

Jesus prayed there would be unity among his followers in his prayer in John 17:20–21: "I am praying not only for these disciples but also for all who will ever believe in me because of their testimony. My prayer for all of them is that they will be one, just as you and I are one, Father—that just as you are in me and I am in you, so they will be in us, and the world will believe you sent me." The New Testament is full of exhortations to maintain unity and guard against division. Paul gives encouragement to the church of Ephesus: "Always keep yourselves united in the Holy Spirit, and bind yourselves together with peace. We are all one body, we have the same Spirit, and we have all been called to the same glorious future. There is only one Lord, one faith, one baptism, and there is only one God and Father, who is over us all and in us all and living through us all" (Ephesians 4:3–6).

Reflection and Discussion

Take a few moments to consider and discuss these questions with friends.

- What are the essentials for being church? Fold a blank sheet of paper down the middle. On one side, put the heading "Essentials for Church." Name the other column "Nonessentials for Church." Encourage a friend or two to do the same, and then compare what you come up with.

- Read the prayer of Jesus for his followers, as recorded in John 17. What is Jesus' prayer and passion?

- Imagine that all the Jesus followers where you live truly see themselves united as the Body of Christ. How would that affect you? What changes would you see among other followers of Jesus? What changes would you see in your city? What are the greatest hindrances to the followers of Jesus uniting in your city?

- The Hebrew prophet Amos asked, "Can two people walk together without agreeing on the direction?" Who are you walking with? Why?

8

PEOPLE OF THE WAY

> The way of Christian witness is neither the way
> of quietist withdrawal, nor the way of Herodian
> compromise, nor the way of angry militant zeal. It
> is the way of being in Christ, in the Spirit, at the
> place where the world is in pain, so that the healing
> love of God may be brought to bear at that point.
> —N. T. (Tom) Wright, Bishop of Durham, England[1]

The "Way" was one of the church's earliest self-designations.[2] They perceived themselves as an alternative culture *in* the world. These people of the Way considered themselves neither Jew nor Gentile but something new, transcending both identities. Above all, they were one in Jesus Christ, for as Paul says, in Christ "there is no longer Jew or Gentile, slave or free, male or female. For you are all Christians—you are one in Christ Jesus" (Galatians 3:28).[3]

Labels and names can originate with the founder of a group to set a sense of "tribal identity." For instance, Jesus generally calls us "disciples." This emphasizes our identity as people who learn from him and emulate him. Outsiders from Jesus who felt contemptuous or perhaps threatened sometimes threw out other labels. "Believers" was sometimes used as a term of derision. Meanwhile, in Acts 11:26 we learn that disciples were first called "Christians" at Antioch, one of the more multicultural cities in the ancient world, with city sectors for Jews, Africans, Romans, Greeks, and Asians, and likewise church leaders named from each of those backgrounds! So "Christians" holds the intriguing hint of ones who were like their master, because *Christ-ian* literally means "little Christ."

The church became not just a subculture within the dominant culture but a new counterculture in the Greco-Roman world. The Good News of Jesus' resurrection life spread across cultural borders to engage people on their own turf. This was not merely spiritual renewal; it was a social revolution that took root across geographical, cultural, social, and gender boundaries. Those following the Way of Jesus embodied a distinct lifestyle. We catch glimpses of this from the historical accounts of thoughtful observers and participants. For instance, the Greek apologist Athenagoras, writing around 177 A.D., revealed some characteristics of the early believers: "But among us you will find uneducated persons, and artisans, and old women, who, if they are unable in words to prove the benefit of our doctrine, yet by their deeds exhibit the benefit arising from their persuasion of the truth: they do not rehearse speeches but exhibit good works; when struck, they do not strike again; when robbed, they do not go to law; they give to those who ask of them, and love their neighbors as themselves."[4]

We gain additional perspective from another early observer, Dionysius of Alexandria, who wrote in his Easter Letter of 263 A.D. about how early followers acted during a period of social crisis:

> The most of our brethren were unsparing in their exceeding love and brotherly kindness. They held fast to each other and visited the sick fearlessly, and ministered to them continually, serving them in Christ. And they died with them most joyfully, taking the affliction of others, and drawing the sickness from their neighbors to themselves and willingly receiving their pains. And many who cared for the sick and gave strength to others died themselves, having transferred to themselves their deaths. . . .
>
> Truly the best of our brethren departed from life in this manner, including some presbyters and deacons and those of the people who had the highest reputation; so that this form of death, through the

great piety and strong faith it exhibited, seemed to lack nothing of martyrdom.

But with the heathen everything was quite otherwise. They deserted those who began to be sick, and fled from their dearest friends. And they cast them out into the streets when they were half dead, and left the dead like refuse, unburied. They shunned any participation or fellowship with death; which yet, with all their precautions, it was not easy for them to escape.[5]

We have much to learn from the spiritual DNA of our ancestors of the Way, especially these men and women of the churches just noted. My favorite story of a local church in the Bible itself is that of Thessalonica.[6] The mentor-apostle Paul and two of his protégés, Silas and Timothy, ministered only a few weeks in Thessalonica, the capital and commercial center of Macedonia. According to Acts 17:1–2, the team was in Thessalonica for only three Sabbaths before they were driven out of town. Yet they left a thriving community that made a significant impact in the region.

We know that God loves you, dear brothers and sisters, and that he chose you to be his own people. For when we brought you the Good News, it was not only with words but also with power, for the Holy Spirit gave you full assurance that what we said was true. And you know that the way we lived among you was further proof of the truth of our message. So you received the message with joy from the Holy Spirit in spite of the severe suffering it brought you. In this way, *you imitated both us and the Lord. As a result, you yourselves became an example to all the Christians* in Greece. And now the word of the Lord is ringing out from you to people everywhere, even beyond Greece, for wherever we go we find people telling us about your faith in God [I Thessalonians 1:4–8, emphasis added].

If the core of following the Way of Jesus can be transferred to people in three weeks or less, then it must be easily accessible—even if the implications and applications of living like Jesus take the rest of one's life! We see that this group of Thessalonians followed the example set by Paul's team and quickly became a model for believers throughout the whole country. Paul and his companions planted the seed of the gospel and left. Their leaving was a clear demonstration of their faith not so much in the people but in the inherent power of the seed. How can we explain the healthy growth and development of this church? In the first letter from Paul to this new cluster of Jesus followers, we discover at least five essential factors that facilitated the growth and influence of this young Thessalonian fellowship of disciples: seed, sowers, soil, Spirit, and sacrifice.[7]

The Seed

The "gospel" (1:5) represents the seed that bears fruit in followers and communities of the Way. Paul and his companions did not connect these new believers to a curriculum, denomination, or their own personalities, but rather to the person and ways of Jesus. They recognized that their sincere love and readiness to obey Jesus were key to the movement. The early churches based their identity not on some mystical communion with a prophet, teacher, or god, but on the life and mission of the resurrected Christ in their midst. Their identity and communion with one another was as "Christ followers." As messengers of the Good News, their task was simply to sow the gospel seed in the context of the culture and let the Holy Spirit do the work![8] Paul and his companions believed that if they were faithful to plant the seed, Jesus would be faithful to bring it toward fruitfulness. These early believers practiced "Less is more." They were careful not to set up false expectations or crippling dependencies on a teacher of the Word rather than on the Word himself.[9] Knowing they would not remain long in any one location, the apostolic band established communities that had the full potential to survive and indeed reproduce a movement of Jesus followers. Wherever they traveled they freely scattered the same gospel seed that had changed their lives.

As apostles, they were stewards of the gospel seed with the full expectation that the seed would take root, grow, and bear fruit in such a way that more seed would be scattered to new fields. In their follow-up letter, Paul, Silas, and Timothy exhort these new believers to "stand firm and keep a strong grip on everything we taught you both in person and by letter" (II Thessalonians 2:15; 3:6). The root meaning of the word *teaching* here is the same for the word *paradigm*, which implies a pattern that is meant to be handed over or passed on. The very nature of the gospel is that it is not dependent upon highly skilled professionals but is easily transferable by even the freshest of believers.

The Sowers

The use of *our*, *we*, and *us* throughout the letters points to the fact that Paul did not work alone. Those who planted the seed functioned in community to model the Way of Jesus and to prevent a focus on any one personality. Throughout the first century, we see the pattern of Jesus and his disciples continued in the work of apostolic bands or communities of believers living and spreading the gospel across cultural barriers. There are at least sixteen apostolic teams mentioned in Acts and the New Testament Epistles.[10] These teams were made of a mix of men and women. They demonstrated diverse gifts, but all were surrendered to Jesus and each other for the common purpose of initiating disciple-making communities. Wherever Paul traveled, his message was a blend of word (sharing) and life (showing).

I remember well the first time this passage hit me. About forty of us were at a spiritual retreat in the San Bernardino Mountains. After some prayer and singing, I was to teach on the basics of becoming a community. But just before I went before the group, I was reminded of the verse Paul and his companions wrote: "We loved you so much that we gave you not only God's Good News *but our own lives, too*" (I Thessalonians 2:8). A wave of emotion came over me and I did something I hadn't ever done before that time. As I walked forward, I just began to cry uncontrollably in front of everyone. It seemed like the longest time that I stood there alone. I tried to speak, but more tears just came. Then, off from the side, came the unexpected. Jim, one of the newest to the group, quietly walked toward me and put his big arm around me as I stood there sobbing. The more I tried to speak, the more I cried. Finally I shared the verse and confessed I had been guarding my heart without even knowing why. In that moment, Jesus began a work in my heart, granting me a new courage to be vulnerable in sharing my love and needs to my community of friends. From that point on I began to appreciate the importance of receiving as much as I had valued my ability to give.

> Christ has no body now on earth but yours, no hands but yours, no feet but yours; yours are the eyes through which Christ's compassion looks out on the world, yours are the feet with which He is to go about doing good and yours are the hands with which He is to bless us now.
>
> —St. Teresa of Avila
> (1515–1582)

The apostolic bands taught the Way of Jesus and lived it in such a way that it would be readily imitated and passed on. This points to the fundamental role of Paul's personal example in his missionary methodology. These teams modeled, taught, and reminded their hearers of the "ways in Christ"; they expected these new disciples to pass on what they had received. Paul encouraged his disciple Timothy to "give your complete attention to these matters. Throw yourself into your tasks so that everyone will see your progress. Keep a close watch on yourself and on your teaching. Stay true to what is right, and God will save you and those who hear you."[11]

Spontaneous reproduction requires an atmosphere of freedom and flexibility where apostolic teams and local communities work together without institutional policies, controls, or expectations. Throughout his ministry, we see Paul regularly developing new disciples, mentoring young apostles, nurturing relationships among churches, and functioning within teams. Paul continued in the pattern by which he was discipled. After his dramatic conversion on the Damascus road, Paul was instructed by many, beginning with Ananias in Damascus, then mentored for several years by Barnabas, and nurtured by the church in Antioch. He was shaped and sustained through his relationships with mentors, communities, teammates, and protégés alike.

Through years of experience in a variety of contexts, we have seen a direct correlation between reproduction and connectedness. Those teams and churches with strong relationships are more fruitful. Conversely, those with few or no relational connections struggle to grow and are slow to reproduce.

The Soil

There was a group of people in Thessalonica that represented a soil "chosen" of God (1:4). Regardless of where or how they were sharing the Good News, the apostles were always looking for people God had prepared beforehand for them to meet. They trusted these communities to carry on this pattern in their surrounding region.[12]

The Spirit continues to prepare soil today. We have friends in Germany who prayed to be directed to the people in their town who were ready to embrace Jesus. While praying, one young woman had a vision of a home that the Spirit prepared for them to connect with. She even felt she had the street address, so they checked the city map and drove to the stranger's house where the dream and address matched. They knocked on the door and were greeted warmly with, "We've been waiting for you to come." Sounds a lot like the New Testament![13]

We can be confident that wherever we go the Spirit has been there before us. Jennifer and I continue to see the Spirit lead us to persons of peace like Keith, whom we met on the bus; our new neighbors Jeff and Beth; and John, whom I met as I was the last one on the ferry after the Seattle earthquake. Just pray with your eyes open as you relate to the people around you, and see what happens.

Give me a divine appointment today with someone who is
hungry for God or in need,
and give me grace to minister the love of Jesus in the power
of the Holy Spirit.

—Robert Fitts Sr., spiritual teacher
and author

The Spirit

Paul and his companions confessed that they did not come on their own strength but "with power" from the Holy Spirit. The story of Thessalonica and the early church is not the story of religious devotees working hard but of Spirit-empowered disciples following God's lead. In the early church, the presence and power of the Holy Spirit dominates the unfolding story of the gospel spreading from one region to another. In Acts 9:31, Luke reports the power behind the movement: "The church then had peace throughout Judea, Galilee, and Samaria, and it grew in strength and numbers. The believers were walking in the fear of the Lord and in the comfort of the Holy Spirit." It is the Holy Spirit who ensures both qualitative growth ("strength") and quantitative growth ("numbers"). The early movement was primarily characterized by the readiness of common people to listen and follow the Holy Spirit, which often countered the best of human reason.[14]

In our own experience, as we began our first church in Riverside we *believed* in the Holy Spirit but had limited *experience* in the power of the Holy Spirit. It didn't take long to see a few new churches start that were simple, healthy, and growing. We even saw them reproduce and spread to other areas. But it was far from the movement we read about in Acts. The more we read the New Testament and the more we lived out the life of Christ the best we could, the more we realized that our best efforts weren't good enough. We actively pursued growing in the reality of the Spirit; we learned from many along the way, especially our friends from England and Latin America who had begun to experience miracles as described in the Book of Acts.

"Being church" is a spiritual endeavor. "'It is not by force nor by strength [or programs, marketing, professionals, or money], but by my Spirit,' says the Lord Almighty" (Zechariah 4:6). Anything not birthed by the Spirit of God is just an organization built, led, and empowered by humans. Jesus' promise in Matthew 16:18 still stands: "Upon this rock I will build my church, and all the powers of hell will not conquer it." Jesus is the one who plants, nurtures, and matures the church. Skilled and motivated people may be able to create religious organizations, but only the Spirit of God can birth genuine spiritual movements.

The Sacrifice

The Thessalonian believers received the gospel in the midst of what the letter calls "severe suffering" (1:6). We also know that Paul and his companions experienced "toil and hardship" (2:9) before they were forced to flee Thessalonica. Luke portrays a positive correlation between the sufferings of disciples and the growth of the church in Acts.[15] Suffering and persecution have a way of stripping away our façades and reducing us to the core essentials of what we believe. And like throwing seed to the wind, persecution also forced disciples to scatter to new regions with the gospel seed. As Paul and Sosthenes wrote the young church at Corinth, "Through suffering, these bodies of ours constantly share in the death of Jesus so that the life of Jesus may also be seen in our bodies" (II Corinthians 4:10).

We realize the ideas of sacrifice and suffering are not popular themes in Western Christianity, but they are the realities of the world. Times of hardship have a way of shaking us back to the essentials of life. When things are comfortable and on autopilot, we really don't need God or one another. When we encounter struggle, it moves us back to a deeper sense of dependency upon Jesus and one another. When Jennifer and I look back upon the last sixteen years, the greatest times of growth have been during or coming out of hard times. And the tougher, the better. As we follow Jesus, we will face suffering, injustice, and betrayal. Though we may have no control over whether we get hit, we do have a choice in how we respond. If we are strong and we do things for God in our own might or wisdom, then we get the glory. It is when we operate in our weakness, trusting God and his wisdom that we experience his grace and give him all the honor and glory.

> If we want to serve the true God, we must break out of the circle of self-absorption and pay heed to the bloodied faces of our fellow human beings. If we do not share life with the oppressed, we do not share life with God.
>
> —Leonardo Boff, Brazilian priest and theologian, *The Way of the Cross*

Acts 29 and Beyond

Thessalonica illustrates the beginning of churchwide fulfillment of Jesus' prophecy in Acts 1 that his disciples would be witnesses in "Jerusalem, throughout Judea, in Samaria, and to the ends of the earth" (Acts 1:8). This imperative was spoken to break an almost infinite number of barriers in order that people everywhere might hear and respond to the Good News. Even though Paul and his companions were in the city less than a month, the faith of the Thessalonian believers had become known: "And now the word of the Lord is ringing out from you to people everywhere, even beyond Greece, for wherever we go we find people telling us about your faith in God" (I Thessalonians 1:8). Just as God became flesh and dwelt among us, so his people are to break through any and all geographical, racial, linguistic, religious, cultural, and social barriers in order that members of "every tribe and language and people and nation" might be reconciled to God (Revelation 5:9).

Throughout history, we see significant movements often sprouting from humble beginnings. They originate mainly among the lowliest ranks of society, not the loftiest. In Acts 4, we read that the religious leaders were impressed with the passion of the disciples. They realized that the disciples "were ordinary men who had had no special training. They also recognized them as men who had been with Jesus" (Acts 4:13). The disciples' attitude was that of "Do what you may; we have a reality that is larger than anything you may do to us." These disciples did not have much, but what they did have was all they needed. They had the Good News of Jesus, a way of relating to one another, and the presence of the Holy Spirit. Their shared passion for Jesus and reliance on his Spirit fueled this first movement.

Acts 28 marks not the conclusion of the apostolic church but rather its beginning. Luke both described how the early church expanded and pointed to how these communities would continue in the future. We are now living in the days of Acts 29!

We believe it is now time to sow the gospel seed in the power of the Holy Spirit into Western soil—but in a way that will be readily carried on and reproduced by new spiritual seekers and religious refugees. The essentials just mentioned lie within reach of anybody. None are dependent upon education, credentials, money, or facilities. All the necessary resources are available today. The very nature of the church as a living system calls us to plant the seed (the essential DNA), nothing more and nothing less.

Then let the seed grow! It should have no structural expectations based on modern values (great buildings, a big budget, number of members), only organic expectations that it be healthy, growing, bearing fruit, and reproducing in the soil of the culture. The key to experience the life of Jesus in community is the same today as it was two thousand years ago: a radical love for Jesus, which translates into a radical lifestyle of walking in the fullness of his Word and Spirit.

Reflection and Discussion

The Way of Jesus represents intimate relationship with both Jesus and others in community. The first Christians were called "followers of the Way" because their new life was marked by a lifestyle accessible to anyone regardless of race, age, gender, or any other sociocultural distinctive. Take time to discuss the implications with a friend.

- In Matthew 16:18, Jesus said, "Upon this rock I will build my church, and all the powers of hell will not conquer it." What, then, is our role?
- Read the Gospel of Luke, 9:1–6 and 10:1–20, where Jesus sends his disciples out in teams of two. What did Jesus instruct his followers to do? What did he *not* mention?
- Which patterns of Jesus do you find most challenging to follow? How, then, will you live in the Way of Jesus today?

9

MATCHING WINES
WITH WINESKINS

When considering change, remember that you will
have a fight on your hands with those who want to
maintain the status quo, and your supporters will be
at best lukewarm, since you cannot show them a
proven model, only your vision for the future.
　　　—*Ray Lévesque (with apologies to Machiavelli)*,
Native American organizational consultant and spiritual leader

Ten years ago Jennifer and I went to the mountains with a group of
friends for renewal and refreshment. It was a time to pray and discern together how God was leading us in the early days of the first
church we started.

There were some who joined us for a season that expected me
or the team of leaders to direct more. They hoped we would become
the next hot church in town, hire staff, and support a large children's program. At the time, we were all meeting weekly in neighborhood churches throughout the city, but many struggled with the
fact that all the churches only gathered together once a month.
These changes were most difficult for those of us who had grown up
in church. Not everyone could adjust.

Despite many open questions, everyone who came to the
mountain retreat exhibited a strong sense of unity and willingness
to move forward. But I was becoming more and more uncomfort-
able, especially as we grew and reproduced new churches. Though
I am one who typically embraces change, I became more uncertain

about my own role as a leader. All those ideas of church planting movements and house church networks that we'd theorized and conferenced and lectured about were coming to pass . . . and I was right in the middle of it! Nothing had prepared me for this. I knew I had to radically shift my philosophy of what it meant to be a leader.

As Jennifer and I walked through the camp one evening, we reflected on the richness and simplicity of the retreat, and on our journey over the past year. It wasn't that easy to learn how to let Jesus build his church! Just when we thought we were getting a handle on it, God led us to remove something else. Over that first year, we had replaced the large weekly celebrations with simple gatherings in homes, apartments, and businesses. We'd given up our dedicated building, all programs, preaching, professional staff, and budgets. As we were walking under the moonlit sky, I turned to Jennifer and said, "I feel like Jesus keeps stripping stuff away from us as a church. I'm not sure how to lead this . . . if he keeps taking stuff away one of these days there's going to be nothing left!"

"Nothing but Jesus," Jennifer quickly responded. Then after a pause, she added, "Along with me, our family, and some good friends."

Did we really need anything more?

As has happened many times in our married life, Jennifer is used by the Spirit to implant an "ah-ha!" moment. At the time and many times since, I've thought, "Is that so bad—just Jesus and us and others? Or are we too dependent on the comfort that comes with the organization? How much flexibility can we handle? Do we have the courage to hold onto Jesus and him alone? What would that mean? Could this be the real test of genuine spirituality?"

Such an approach demands that we give more attention to Jesus and his Spirit's leading than to what a few leaders could think up. We were learning there is an inverse relationship between Spirit (divine) and structure (human). The more structures we build, the less we "need" the Spirit; but the more we welcome the Spirit, the fewer formal structures we need. Maybe we seek to solidify structures in order to hide our impoverished and uncertain spiritual state. I didn't want to give in to temptations to go institutional. I did, though, want to embrace whatever was biblically true about following Jesus. I still wanted what I'd prayed for that night I turned my life over to Jesus: to be, do, and say whatever my Lord Jesus directed, and go where he wanted.

About this time, I met George Patterson, who became a key mentor to me at this critical season. Those privileged to know George know him to be full of enthusiasm and wisdom. Having pioneered an indigenous movement of churches in Honduras for twenty years, George wrestled through many of the questions we were facing. He was relentless in challenging me to question anything that distracts from simple obedience to Jesus. One afternoon he told me, "Jonathan, you need to lower the bar of your standards for leadership . . . until they are nothing but biblical. Build upon the life and teachings of Jesus."

We came to recognize the value of George's counsel. We needed to discard nearly everything we had been taught about leadership. The prevailing paradigm in the West is a leader who controls people from the top of the organization, whereas the Jesus paradigm is that of a servant-leader, who models the radical lifestyle of a living movement. In fact, the root of the English word *leader* (*leith*) means "to go forth," "to cross the threshold," or "to die," describing the self-sacrifice of a pioneer. We began to realize the radical difference between movement leadership and institutional leadership. While typical church leadership is driven to conserve and control from a managerial viewpoint, movement leadership is marked by equipping, empowering, and releasing people to freely give what they have freely received.

We wanted to experience the same vitality as did the first Jesus followers. So we continued the process of simplifying our understanding and practice of church to the essence of Jesus. As we released our dependency on extra stuff and structures we were then able to embrace more of Jesus' teachings and life. This was the case for the first disciples, and it's just as true for us today. It wasn't easy for the first disciples to release their expectations that Jesus would establish a new religion or kingdom on earth. For instance, even up to his ascension, Jesus' disciples thought he would establish a political reign where each would have a place in his cabinet. Throughout his ministry, we occasionally see several of them vying for position. Even the mother of two disciples (James and John) asked Jesus to give her sons a high position in his kingdom. She didn't get it about Jesus either! And, after the arrival of the Spirit at Pentecost, we see some disciples struggled with whether they should require new disciples to submit to certain Jewish laws.

Not much has changed since the time of Christ. We have the same weaknesses as our ancestors; we're still not content with Jesus alone. But the truth is that the more we embrace Jesus, the less we need religion. The more religion, the less need for Jesus. The more we add to Jesus, the less we experience him because it all gets in the way of the Way.

When Jennifer and I began our quest, we were searching for a simpler way of doing church. Many who joined us were glad to leave the heaviness of institutional religion, but were slow to embrace a new way of life. We soon realized that going to church is a lot easier than being the Body of Christ. As Charles Brock, my friend and longtime missionary to the Philippines, explained, the typical American pastor just wants church members who attend, donate money, and agree with decisions. But Jesus talks about actively denying ourselves, obeying him, and loving one another. Many fall prey to passive spiritual consumerism. They want the benefits of community without taking any responsibility for being an active member of the Body.

What Went Wrong?

I first met Erik on the ferry just a few months after my family and I moved to the Northwest. We've been getting together every couple weeks since. We talk about everything: family, work, poetry, the latest films, our enjoyment of the outdoors. With his nominal Jewish upbringing and background in medicine and my Christian upbringing and background in ministry, there are always spiritual threads woven throughout our conversations.

Just a few weeks ago, Erik and I were conversing over a cup of tea when he asked, "How long were you in the ministry?"

"About twelve years as a profession."

"Was there one event that impacted you, or was it a series of events that moved you to where you are now?"

I thought for a moment and then answered, "I was like the proverbial frog in the kettle . . . they say you can drop a frog in a pot of hot water and it will jump out immediately. But place a frog in a pot of water straight from the pond, turn up the heat slowly, and the frog doesn't even notice the rising temperature until it's too late."

"Sounds like the ministry was the opposite of spiritual awakening," Erik replied.

"I never thought of it that way, but you're right. Though I grew professionally and even theologically, my spiritual sensitivities were being deadened. For the most part, the church today has lost touch with its roots in Jesus. We've lost what it means to be the living, breathing Body of Christ. We read throughout the New Testament how we are to gather in community. It's supposed to be natural and participatory: 'When you meet, one will sing, another will teach, another will tell some special revelation God has given, one will speak in an unknown language, while another will interpret what is said'" (I Corinthians 14:26).

Erik continued, "That doesn't sound like any church I've heard of. . . . It seems like what you believe would threaten many people in church . . . at least the Christians I've known."

I answered, "Yes, Jesus is a lot more radical than the church today."

Our discussion then meandered through church history as we discussed how unpopular radical movements are with the ruling powers. Since the first century there have always been those who use the name of Jesus for political or economic gain. One way to look at church history is to follow the political moves against the people of God. There have always been remnants such as the Moravians, radical reformers, and other movements persecuted by the religious establishment, both Protestant and Catholic (heretics are, after all, in the eye of the controller).

"Those in power are always threatened by those who do not conform," Erik responded.

"Yes. I'd say we both would have been killed by the same religious authorities."

"What do you mean?"

I explained that some prominent leaders of the Protestant Reformation persecuted Jews because of their blood and simple Jesus followers for their beliefs (they didn't align with the political structures of Protestants). Many radical Jesus followers such as the Anabaptists and Swiss Brethren were given a "third" baptism, which meant being tied to a large rock and then thrown into the Rhine River. The grassroots revolutionary movement with a distinct lifestyle based on the resurrected Christ has been all but squelched by religious authorities throughout history.

Both those raised in church and those without a church background can see the chasms between Jesus and churches as they are today. For example, my friend Scott, who had no upbringing in church, told me why he doesn't go to church: "What's the point? Why should I go to church to sit in an auditorium of strangers to listen to a guy I don't know, tell me how to live a life that I don't even know if he's living or not? He doesn't live in the world I live in."

> One of our great allies at present is the church itself. Do not misunderstand me. I do not mean the Church as we see her spread out through space and rooted in eternity, terrible as an army with banners. That, I confess, is a spectacle that makes our boldest tempters uneasy. But fortunately it is quite invisible to these humans [From a conversation of Screwtape, a senior devil, instructing a junior devil on how to tempt humans].
>
> –C. S. Lewis (1898-1963),
> Irish-born author,
> *The Screwtape Letters*

How did this kind of gathering of the first followers of Jesus turn into an event where one or two professionals perform on stage with the support of a few song leaders, while the audience sits passive?

The turning point was when Emperor Constantine issued the Edict of Milan in 313 A.D., officially ending the persecutions of Christians and making the church the official religion of the Roman Empire. This was the start of Christianity as a "Western religion." Greek philosophy and methodologies soon displaced the Eastern worldview and values that characterized the early Jesus followers and their Hebraic roots. Under political rule, church began to be transformed into the institutional form we know today. This also ushered in the us-and-them, clergy-and-laity division. The problem was that 98 percent of the church was "them," and so the professionals took over. The rest learned to sit and be quiet and join in singing when told to. The organic, intimate Body of Christ was systematically displaced by political powers in the name of religious tolerance.

Today, in our struggle to be the Body of Christ in a dramatically changing global culture, we realize that our problems are deeper than they seem. The real issues are not methodological or structural; they are theological and deeply spiritual. The church was never meant to have a permanent (or stationary) residence because it was to be always en route toward the ends of the earth and the end of time. We see the cultural shifts exposing the modern encrustation and enculturation of the church. Our identity has been hijacked!

Once a way of living, modern Christianity (so called) has become almost entirely confined to dedicated buildings, worship services, and structured programs. The problem with the church is not that it's out of touch with the culture, but that it's out of touch with Jesus. Our powerless ecclesiology (understanding of church) reflects our powerless Christology (understanding of Jesus). We know *about* Jesus without *experiencing* Jesus.

Jennifer and I have been increasingly thankful for the handful of people who walked with us during those early days of our journey as we asked deep questions of Jesus, the church, and ourselves. We questioned the religious paradigm that had defined church for the last fifteen hundred years. This Christendom paradigm was initiated by a political order from the Holy Roman Empire, affirmed by the Protestant Reformation, and later fueled by the culture of

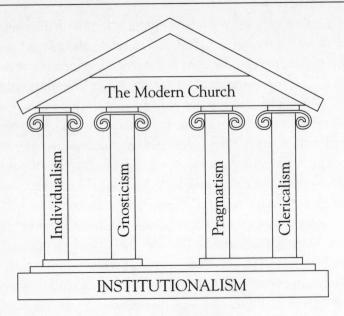

Modern Church

modernity. The marks of the modern church are perversions of the simple patterns of Jesus and the early church: the Cornerstone of the resurrected Christ was usurped by the authority of the religious institution. Community was displaced by radical individualism. A direct experience of *living* the faith was replaced with *knowing* the faith by rationalism and Gnosticism. Divine revelation was replaced by pragmatism (if it works, it must be of God). The priesthood of all believers—the authority and opportunity for each disciple to go directly to God—was removed by the professional clerics (an elitist priesthood or form of shamanism). All of this led to a syncretistic mix of modernism and Christianity. After centuries of persecution, religion was initiated to control what Rome failed to destroy.

Even the most celebrated churches of the day—the so-called contemporary, seeker, postmodern, or emerging churches—are not as radical as they'd like to think, but rather the next evolutionary link of the new-and-improved modern church.[1] Many remain systemically modern (perhaps even hypermodern) with their reliance on external religious forms that often inoculate the masses with a religious experience of sorts but do not lead to lasting spiritual fulfillment or transformation. They may well be contemporary, but they can hardly be described as culturally indigenous or authentic to the life of Jesus.

Sadly, despite many charismatic renewals over the past fifty years, institutionalism remains. Even the most gifted leaders who teach freedom in Jesus and long for a greater outpouring of the Holy Spirit perpetuate structures that prevent free-flowing movement of the Body of Christ. With a few exceptions, church in the West is still described in institutional terms: a worship service whereby passive laity sit in a sanctuary listening to a didactic monologue from a professional. Most of what we see today are primarily cosmetic changes expressed in the superficialities of style: music style, clothing style, program style, architectural style. Styles may change, but the systemic structure remains entirely modern.

The compromised state of the church is nothing new; we are just now beginning to notice it. Nearly a hundred years ago Sadhu Sundar Singh, a wandering holy man of northern India, offered these observations of American Christianity:

> In America one sees a good deal of Christianity, but it does not address the spiritual needs of the people. Just as salty seawater cannot quench thirst, much of American religion cannot satisfy a spiritually thirsty person because it is saturated with materialism. Although America is a "Christian" nation and there are many sincere Christians in America, the majority of the people there have no faith. There, where it is so easy to have religion, where religion is offered on every side and no one is persecuted for their beliefs, life should be peaceful. Instead, there is a mad rush and hustle and bustle after money and comfort and pleasure. In India, many Christians suffer bitter persecution but continue to find happiness in their new faith. Because it is so easy to have faith in America, people do not appreciate what a comfort there is in faith.[2]

For centuries, the church fit with the culture, so we did not see anything wrong. The church settled itself comfortably inside the surrounding culture with little critical discernment. But now, with the end of Christendom, we see hints that the church was captive to its culture all along, and still is. So when our family and our network of friends began moving into simpler, smaller groups, we were trying to figure out how to follow Jesus. We weren't focusing on turning away from church, but rather moving toward Jesus. As my friend Doug, a recovering pastor turned mortgage broker, confessed, "I've become disillusioned with Christianity. . . . I have given up on Christianity as an illusion; I now realize I must go directly to the source, which is Christ."

The problem with the Western church is that it has defined the gospel one way (scripturally and spiritually according to Jesus) but then has established structures and practices that run contrary (institutional, individualistic, pragmatic, and political). We have a normative view of belief, but not of practice. No longer faithful to its simple nature, the church sacrificed its spiritual integrity for cultural relevance and institutional conformity. Generations of uncritical enculturation have left us with a diluted, nominal, and impotent church. From a psychological and historical perspective, the renowned psychiatrist M. Scott Peck observes:

The absence of meaningful Christianity from institutionalized religion is hardly a recent problem. The history of the Church for the past 1600 years has innumerable instances of institutional blasphemy. It is the Church that marched off in crusades to murder Muslims in the name of Jesus. It is the Church of the Inquisition that killed and tortured in the name of Jesus. It is the Church of Rome that stood by during the Holocaust, doing nothing in the name of Jesus. Why? How could the Christian Church be so consistently blasphemous? At what point did Jesus get lost in the shuffle? When did the Church lose sight of what community is all about?[3]

The problems with the church transcend Western contexts. Because the Western church has been the dominating missionary influence until recently, the destructive effects of modern Christianity can be seen worldwide. For example, my friend Kasereka observed the effects of missionaries who brought more than the gospel to the Wanande people of Eastern Zaire: "I discovered that what we had been calling 'orthodox Christianity' was 'Western syncretistic Christianity.'" He concludes, "our Christianity was doubly syncretistic. Doubly syncretistic, as the Nande Church struggles to be 'orthodox,' while really trying to be a Western church."[4] Blinded by their good intentions, many Western missionaries never realized they were creating converts to a religious system, not disciples to the risen Christ. As my friend and mentor Wilbert Shenk claims, "This should not surprise us, since the model and practice of church taken to Asia, Africa, and Latin America was that of Christendom, and nominality has cropped up wherever Western missions have gone."[5]

Any ideologies or organizational structures imposed upon a people stunt the natural growth and reproductive capacity of the gospel in that area. While in Mongolia, I heard of a church that was started by American missionaries among a community of nomads. Like 60 percent of the population, these nomads live in *gers*, a typical stick-framed circular hut covered with canvas and camel hair. Even though these were small structures (about five to eight meters in diameter), the missionaries brought in a keyboard and sound system. Since they didn't have electricity, they had to place a gas generator to power up the electronic church service. It was a good thing they had the sound system because the generator drowned out the voices of the people. They also took the liberty of rearranging the furniture from the customary circular arrangement to neat rows so they all could see the back of each other's head. How would this ever spread to other *ger* communities?

The cries of our world and the crises within culture call the church to a radical self-examination. The word *radical* comes from the Latin *radix*, which means "relating to or proceeding from a root." To recover the radical nature of the church implies going to the origin or fundamental source, which is often not easily discerned. We have no need to be attached to church structures, because *we* are the church. The only thing that holds us together should be the living Christ and our love for one another; anything else is some kind of artificial life support. To be radical means letting go of any excess baggage and holding on to Jesus.

New Wineskins for a New Age

When the old wineskin is dying, the new wineskin is
created by those who are not afraid to be vulnerable.
—*Graham Cooke, English spiritual teacher and author*

Jesus and his disciples attended a wedding in the little village of Cana in Galilee. They were celebrating this festive occasion when all of a sudden the wine ran out. This was devastating to the host and embarrassing to the family. After some prodding from his mother, Jesus turned six pots of water into fine wine. When the master of ceremonies tasted the water that was now wine, not knowing where it had come from, he called the bridegroom over. "Usually a host serves the best wine first," he said. "Then, when everyone is full and doesn't care, he brings out the less expensive wines. But you have kept the best until now!" (John 2:9–10).

They just needed to taste it, to see that it was indeed different. Even as the wedding party at Cana discovered that the new wine was better than the former wine, so our new life in Jesus is far better than our natural life.[6] The idea of new wine was used by Jesus as a symbol of his life and reflects the ever *newness* of God—a new creation, a new song, a new Spirit, and a new covenant.[7]

Later, Jesus gave a challenging parable regarding the relationship of wine and wineskins: "No one puts new wine into old wineskins. The new wine would burst the old skins, spilling the wine and ruining the skins. New wine must be put into new wineskins.

But no one who drinks the old wine seems to want the fresh and the new. 'The old is better,' they say" (Luke 5:37–39).

In Jesus' day, there were no glass bottles as we have today. New wine was poured into wineskins. Wineskins were actually the skins of sheep and goats that were sewn together except at the neck, which served as the opening of the container. The skins were filled with grape juice, and the neck then sewn closed. The juice would then ferment, producing alcohol and carbon dioxide, which would cause the new skins to expand. It expands in all directions. Old skins would not work, since they had already been stretched and were no longer elastic. If grape juice were to be put in old skins, the expanding carbon dioxide would rupture the wineskins. The wine would run out and be lost and the wineskins would be ruined.

Our little band of Jesus followers wrestled with both the Scriptures and the Spirit as we explored four options for moving forward:

- *Put old wine in old wineskins.* This is a legitimate option because the wine matches the wineskins. Old wine does belong in old wineskins. Is the modern church (that is, the old) really good enough? Well, not for the new wine, but for Christianized or church-cultured people it may be good enough because the current structure works for them. There are those who are content to maintain the old wineskins of church by sticking with those who believe the old is better, but this is not what we were called to do. This parable does not give us license to judge those who prefer the old, nor to reject any of our roots. It's not our place to change old wineskins. Old wineskins aren't bad; they're just old. We can bless fellow disciples of Jesus, though they gather in different ways.
- *Pour new wine in old wineskins.* Many still try to change the modern church by pouring new wine into old wineskins, hoping the new wine will revive the old wineskins. But this is often shortsighted and more focused on the skin than the wine. This new life in Jesus is fresh and potent. If we try to pour the new wine into the rigid structures of old, they will burst and both the wine and the structures will be lost. Is it possible to renovate old wineskins? With

a lot of greasing they may regain some flexibility, but never as much as new ones. The process may also take a long time.

The life and energy of the new wine cannot be contained in the old structures. Just as first century religion could not embrace the new wine of Christ, so the religions of today, whether Eastern or Western, traditional or contemporary, program-driven or purpose-driven, are entwined with an inorganic structure of a particular culture. Our present-day wineskins are not capable of serving the new wine for today's rising number of religious refugees and spiritual sojourners. Without a radical paradigm shift, the modern church will continue to "convert" spiritual seekers to a syncretized form of cultural Christianity.

• *Pour old wine in new wineskins.* A few years later, we discovered another option: pour old wine into new wineskins. We've done this accidentally (more times than we'd like to admit) by bringing people into new wineskin gatherings who haven't shed the old ways. They may have left the system, but the system hasn't left them. It shows. They do what is natural to them: seek to impose structures, consumerism, judgmentalism, or programs. The net effect is that the old wine (sometimes it's actually turned to vinegar) spoils the new. This may be what Paul had in mind when he wrote, "My ambition has always been to preach the Good News where the name of Christ has never been heard, rather than where a church has already been started by someone else" (Romans 15:20–21).

• *Pour new wine in new wineskins.* We believe Jesus is always pouring out a new wine, and the wineskins must match the wine. Jesus invites us to join him to incarnate new wineskins for the new wine that God is bringing forth at this time. Since wine is living and expanding, it needs a living wineskin. We are the new wineskins for the new wine of Jesus. There is no structure beyond the body of believers centered in Christ. The new wine of Jesus is manifest in our lives, in who we are and how we live.

The Way of Jesus *is* the wineskin. In him we experience new wine and new wineskins—our life and our lifestyle. Jesus is our life, and the way *to* life and the way *of* life. He never wrote a book, built a building, or initiated an institution, but he did gather a new community of believers and lived with them. He left nothing else. He left nothing less.

God is bringing forth new wineskins for a fresh outpouring of wine, and it does not look like anything we've ever seen. So we must focus on Jesus and the wine he is pouring out, and not on the wineskin. Remember, the purpose of the wineskin is to furnish the appropriate environment for the juice of the choice grapes to ferment and season at just the right time. We should be open and flexible, like new wineskins, in order to have Jesus fill our hearts and communities. This new wineskin must be very simple and able to expand and grow with the new wine.

Renewal is not enough. We all need to go through a conversion something like what the apostle Peter experienced in Acts 10 and 11. Peter's conversion from an ethnocentric Jew to an advocate for Gentile missions was one of the most significant paradigm shifts in the history of the church.[8] Likewise today, the church must repent of any cultural tradition that hinders the movement of the gospel across cultures. The current spiritual-cultural crisis calls for nothing less than complete repentance, what the Greeks called *metanoia*, a transformation of the mind, a change of heart, and a new way of living. Just as Gentiles received salvation free of Jewish tradition, so all people have the right to follow Jesus without having to become Western or institutionalized.

Jesus is not bound by any culture or structure. His life and ways transcend all cultures. His body (the wineskin) is not to be culture-bound. Jesus calls his followers to undergo a systemic shift that goes to the root of our identity—one that questions all the assumptions of the Christendom model. What we really need are people living the life of Jesus in community, drinking the new wine of the Spirit and living as fresh wineskins in the world.

Only Jesus will bring forth the new wine! The new wine in Cana was not produced by human effort; it was the supernatural work of God. This will be as much his work as the new wine produced in

Cana was his work. This is the meaning of grace. We cannot produce the life of Jesus, even if we try for a lifetime.[9]

If the early church's new outpouring of the Spirit required a new way of living, how much more does the current outpouring require new wineskins in our day!

✣ Reflection and Discussion ✣

You may want to review what Jesus said in the Gospel of Luke 5:37–39 about the relationship of wine and wineskins before you consider and discuss these questions:

- Describe your current relationship with Jesus. How does religion or spiritual community affect your relationship with him? Does your current wineskin set you free or confine you?

- Which characteristics of a wineskin are most compatible with the gospel of Jesus and our emerging global culture?

- Meditate on what God said in Isaiah 43:19: "For I am about to do a brand-new thing. See, I have already begun! Do you not see it?" Ask Jesus to open your eyes and ears to catch what new thing he is doing in and around your life.

10

LET GO AND HOLD ON

Test everything. Hold on to the good.

—*I Thessalonians 5:21 NIV*

Along our journey, we have tried to listen to our culture in light of the Word and Spirit. As a community, we learned to critically discern the religious traditions that evolved during modernity. We began to evaluate how we were shaped by cultural influences (educational, religious, family, political, economic) and found we were a lot more entangled in modernity than we thought we were—and the rest of the world knew it. Even now they see the church's widening distance from Jesus. We started to sift out whatever portions of our worldview and methodologies were incompatible with the Way of Jesus.

The more we interacted with people from diverse cultures the more we came to see that the gospel is not Eastern or Western, but the "power of God at work, saving everyone who believes."[1] But if the gospel is captive to a culture, it becomes less than the good news and thereby cannot make its natural progression across cultures. For the church to recover her spiritual integrity in any culture requires nothing less than death to her old ways and resurrection to a radically new life.

"What will an awakened church look like?" My mentor and friend Wilbert Shenk responded to that question by citing what the Dutch theologian Johannes Hoekendijk once said in a classroom discussion. After listening to his students wrestle with problems associated with cultural diversity and authenticity, Hoekendijk intervened to give four marks of the authentic church:

First, it has developed its own way of sharing its faith in Jesus with other people.

Second, it is composing and singing its own songs.

Third, it conducts its ecclesial life in a culturally appropriate, rather than exotic, manner.

Fourth, it manages to spawn a heresy or two.

In attempting to embody the gospel in a new context, we must risk the possibility of getting it wrong. Shenk elaborates on Hoekendijk's observations: "A moribund church is notably free of heresy because it has effectively insulated itself from the hurly-burly that attends every effort to engage a culture for the sake of the Gospel. This is the risk and the promise of mission. Without it, the church will not throw off its nominality and be renewed according to its constitutional purpose."[2]

> Future and past cannot live off the present forms of religious experience, for these are too shallow; the future can live only from the most primordial communion with the sacred.
>
> –Thomas Berry, author and environmentalist

There is hope for those who are willing to die to self and structures, in order to let Jesus bring new incarnations of his life that are capable of spontaneous growth and reproduction. To the degree we die to self and become alive to Jesus will he transform us to be the Spirit-led community that is the hope and healing that religious refugees and spiritual sojourners are searching for.

We have seen the gospel embodied in a variety of ways. The more we experience the power of God at work in Western and non-Western contexts, the more we appreciate the power and simplicity of the gospel to take root in any culture or among any people. A number of beliefs and assumptions have emerged from our journey:

- There is a growing awareness and valuation of spirituality throughout the West, much as Jesus described the fields of first-century Palestine as being ripe for harvest.
- Spirituality has been held captive by cultural ideologies, traditions, and structures in Eastern and Western religions alike.
- The gospel of Jesus answers the spiritual and relational longings of all cultures (specifically the needs for identity, love, community, truth, and power).
- Jesus relates to every culture. Both his gospel and his Body (the church) can be translated to and experienced in any culture.
- There's a way of spiritual life and community that has been lived since creation and has touched all major cultures of the world.
- When the gospel of Jesus is received free of religious baggage, it can take root and grow rapidly in and across cultural boundaries.
- There is no such thing as a cultureless gospel. The gospel must be embodied by a people in culture.
- For the gospel to spread across cultures, it must be free from the control and baggage of any one culture, including Western Christendom and religious structures.
- Only as the church dies to itself and lays down the image it thought it was to be or has become will it have the opportunity to be organically reborn as the Body of Christ in new and different cultural realities.

Let Go: Deconstruct Our Cultural-Bound Paradigm

The problem of God is more important than the problem of the Church; but the latter often stands in the way of the former.

—*Hans Küng, German Catholic theologian*

In the Kingdom of God, death precedes life. As disciples of Jesus, we cannot expect to faithfully incarnate Jesus until we die to ourselves and the structures we've created that attempt to box God in and control his people. Unless we lay aside our rights, comforts, traditions, politics, and other self-interests, we will inevitably transplant our own culturally conditioned traditions instead of the powerfully simple Way of Jesus. As Jesus said, "The truth is, a kernel of wheat must be planted in the soil. Unless it dies it will be alone—a single seed. But its death will produce many new kernels—a plentiful harvest of new lives" (John 12:24). The journey toward fruitfulness begins with death.[3]

Jesus set the pattern for us to follow. Just as God became flesh and dwelt among us, so now we as the Body of Christ are to carry on the mission of Jesus among the peoples of the earth. Before people will consider the truths of Jesus, they must observe and feel (both spiritually and physically) these truths. The gospel is communicated and experienced in word *and* deed. The most powerful testimony of the reality of Jesus is not a church service, but a healthy community. Our attitude should be the same as that of Christ Jesus: "Though he was God, he did not demand and cling to his rights as God. *He made himself nothing; he took the humble position of a slave* and appeared in human form. And in human form *he obediently humbled himself* even further by dying a criminal's death on a cross" (Philippians 2:5–8; emphasis added).

Just as Jesus gave up his godly rights and privilege, we must give up our rights and comforts for the sake of Jesus and the world around us. Only as we are different *from* the culture can we make a difference *in* the culture. This calls for all-out abandonment of our comforts, and even our "rights." Everything that has become a necessity for church must be challenged: financial dependencies, dedicated buildings, imported programs, hierarchical professionals, suprachurch agencies, and other such institutional expectations that prevents a community from functioning as a living organism. We must clear away anything that hinders the body from functioning and reproducing—anything that is heavy, complicated, and culture-bound.[4] Make no concessions. Any vision or dependency other than Jesus is idolatry and dilutes our experience with Jesus.

There are several questions that have helped us let go of our culturally bound paradigm of the gospel, church, and self:

- In your experience, how have you been shaped by cultural influences (educational, religious, family, political, economic)?
- What are the common cultural or traditional standards used for determining the success of churches today?
- How much of what we do as church is translatable to other cultures?
- What could we give up and still be church?

We desired simply to experience the life of Jesus in community. In our journey, we tried to clear away anything that distracted from Jesus and hindered the Body of Christ from functioning and reproducing.[5] It meant letting go of anything and everything that compromised the nature of the gospel or the freedom to move as a group and individuals according to how the Spirit led. This was deconstruction with a purpose: to make room for God to birth a new thing. What looked like a pile of rubble was actually just the beginning of something ultimately constructive. But we had to move on, from letting go to discerning what to hold on to.

Hold On: Embody the Way in New Cultures

> He who has Jesus and everything else has no more
> than he who has Jesus and nothing else.
> —C. S. Lewis (1898–1963), Irish-born author

An elder from the Echota Cherokee tribe struggled with his identity as a Jesus follower while being true to his culture. He longed for his people to experience the Way of Jesus in their native culture. The elder found great wisdom in a story of Mahatma Gandhi. In the early days, when he had just come from South Africa to begin his work of gaining freedom for India, Gandhi was asked, "What would you suggest to us as Christians that we do to make Christianity more *naturalized* in India, not a foreign thing, identified with a foreign people and a foreign government, but a part of the life of the people and making its contribution to the remaking of India?" Gandhi replied without a moment's hesitation: "I would suggest four things: first, that all of you Christians, missionaries and all, must begin to live more like Jesus Christ. Second, I would suggest that you practice your religion without adulterating it or toning it down—practice it as it is. Third, I would suggest that you emphasize love and make it your working force, for love is central in Christianity. Fourth, I suggest that you study the non-Christian faiths more sympathetically to find a more sympathetic approach to the people."[6]

In Jesus we discover not only what to believe but also how to live—to know him and follow his Way. Although there's no definitive list, patterns for living out the Way of Jesus are woven throughout the New Testament record. We see these patterns of living rooted in the life and work of Jesus Christ, visible in the apostolic church, and evident across cultures and throughout history:

- *Jesus*: Are these patterns seen in the life and teachings of Jesus Christ?
- *Apostolic church*: Are the patterns evident in the expansion of the first-century church?
- *Culture*: Can the patterns be lived out in a variety of cultural-historical contexts?

The very nature of the gospel calls for "one way": the Way of Jesus. At the same time, its location and reach into many places and cultures require variety and flexibility; it is one way with many expressions. Whatever forms the gospel takes, they must be both authentic to the life of Jesus and indigenous to the culture. Here are some questions that have helped us discover the essential life and patterns of Jesus.

- What can other cultures teach us about being authentic followers of Jesus in our culture?

- What might an indigenous movement look like where we live?

- What are the greatest threats and challenges for translating the Way in our culture?

- How can we guard against drifting away from Jesus' simple plan for us?

As we center on Jesus and move in the fullness of his Spirit, we can expect our lifestyle and gatherings to reflect the life of Jesus. Here are some principles we've been learning about living the Way of Jesus:

- Love is our primary pattern, as Paul wrote to the Corinthian believers: "Let love be your highest goal, but also desire the special abilities the Spirit gives" (I Corinthians 14:1).

- Watch out for centering on anything other than Jesus (community, doctrine, mission, even the Bible). In navigating a long voyage, a shift of one degree can make a world of difference.

- Everything we do should be simple enough to be lived out in any culture, with no (co)dependencies such as special equipment, professionals, buildings, or anything money can buy. Less is more.

- We must constantly lower our standard for leadership to be nothing more than what Jesus modeled (repeat the process of model, assist, watch, and leave).

- God's design and plan is that *every* believer be a functioning part of the Body of Christ. There is no place for either spectators or superstars.

- We begin living the Way of Jesus with our closest relations and then spiral out to other spheres of relationships. Expect the gospel seed to spread and reproduce.

- We will make mistakes. Expect some heresy; just don't institutionalize it.

- Since there's no difference between the sacred and the secular, we live from our center in Christ integrating every sphere of life: family, work, community, and all creation.
- We believe the Holy Spirit is at work in every culture. We pray for our communities, expecting God to reveal how he wants us to join him. Pray prophetically; act apostolically.

How will the community of faith live true to God's original design in this rapidly changing world? Although we cannot predict the future, we can safely predict that this movement will emerge from the fringes of Christendom, and even from the ruin of modernity. Those who move forward according to this Way can expect persecution and opposition. As Jesus said: "For you will be expelled from the synagogues, and the time is coming when those who kill you will think they are doing God a service. . . . I have told you all this so that you may have peace in me. Here on earth you will have many trials and sorrows. But take heart, because I have overcome the world" (John 16:2, 33).

Traveling Light

> He who would travel happily must travel light.
> —*Antoine de Saint-Exupéry (1900–1944),*
> *French pilot and author*

How we pack our bags defines our journey.

In this quest to understand what it means to truly follow Jesus, we've found the process of letting go and holding on to be a continuous one. We always need to be checking for how our load might be getting weighty, much like what I learned when I began backpacking as a youth.

I remember a practical joke my friends and I used to play on some of our rookie hiker friends during weeklong trips in the wilderness. At rest stops, we would add rocks to their packs while they weren't looking. Since we added just a rock or two at a time, they thought the pack felt heavier because they were tired from hiking, until they unpacked their gear at camp and discovered what we'd done.

There is a long tradition in traveling light with just one bag or satchel.[7] In this way, our energies can be put into the journey and the new vistas. Simplicity defines pilgrimage and defines the Way of Jesus. Whether by conscious choice or through some other turn of events, most of us are carrying excess weight that slows us down, drains our energy, and robs us of the joy of our journey. When our load is heavy, we focus our eyes on the ground beneath our feet rather than enjoying the sights and sounds on the Way. But no matter where we are, we can always ask, "What can I do to lighten my burden on this journey?"

> The spontaneous expansion of the church reduced to its elements is a very simple thing.
> —Roland Allen (1868-1947), Anglican missionary to China and Africa

Our life in Jesus and the corresponding lifestyle can be likened to a baton that is passed from runner to runner. A baton is a simple tube that is light, mobile, and open-ended. It is so light and so simple that even the newest runner can live it out. It is mobile, designed to be passed on. It is open-ended; it can be lived out in any cultural context. It is a way of life that by its very nature is designed to be passed on to others. It expresses what it means to be in relationship with Jesus and our world. It *is not* a methodology, model, program, or exhaustive theology. It is simply the Way of Jesus.

Within a few years of our first church start, our very young movement began to witness fourth-generation reproduction of simple churches across diverse cultures and locations, free of money and professionals. It was dynamic and fluid. We made many mistakes along the way. As with all living organisms, some were healthier than others. But we were seeing the genesis of an organic movement with our friends, both locally and globally:

- *In an urban multihousing setting.* Bob shared with me that he began gathering with a few families around Jesus in his apartment complex. As they continued to grow, they held a baptism in their apartment pool one sunny afternoon while kids continued to swim and splash around them. This community grew and reproduced to neighboring apartment complexes.

- *In a poor village in Belize.* Teresa walked three miles and took two buses to come to an evening seminar on life in Jesus. We later found out that she went home to Pomona Village, where there was no church, and shared with her husband what she had learned. They started to meet together, and soon friends and neighbors came to Christ; a church was started that continues to meet from house to house.

- *In a rural farming community.* Paul and Kieva went on vacation and camped out in Northern California. They met some organic farmers and invited them over for a meal. After a few weeks, a church was started that continues to meet from farm to farm.

- *In the marketplace.* We've seen businesses transformed into agents of societal change as they learn to expand their values and vision beyond their financial bottom line. From a large San Francisco brokerage house to a Seattle coffee house, from a Beijing trading company to a Dallas import-export business, and from a recording studio in South Africa to a medical doctor in Switzerland who is establishing healing prayer rooms for his patients, people are embodying the life of Jesus in and through their business and community.

> When the solution is simple, God is answering.
>
> –Albert Einstein (1879–1955), theoretical physicist

To live in the Way of Jesus: nothing could be simpler. Nothing could be more difficult. Nothing could be more *real*. Nothing could appeal more to the social and spiritual longings inherent in our world. The less weight we have along the Way, the faster we can move and enjoy the journey.

✥ **Reflection and Discussion** ✥

Our friend Joel offers an exercise to help catch what Jesus is saying to us today. As you read the letters to seven churches in Asia found in the second and third chapters of the book of Revelation, notice three exhortations: to repent, to believe, and to hope. As you read and pray, consider writing yourself a letter with the following in mind:

- *Repent*—What (or who) will I turn away from? What will I let go of?
- *Believe*—What (or who) will I turn toward? What will I hold on to?
- *Hope*—How or where is the Spirit leading now?

Part Three

AWAKENINGS

"Awake, O sleeper,
rise up from the dead,
and Christ will give you light."
So be careful how you live, not as fools but as those
who are wise.
Make the most of every opportunity for doing good
in these evil days.
Don't act thoughtlessly, but try to understand what
the Lord wants you to do.

—Ephesians 5:14–18

11

LISTENING TO OUR LONGINGS: ANCIENT AND PRESENT

Blessed are those who hunger and thirst.
—Jesus of Nazareth, Matthew 5:6

Tell me, men of learning what is Longing made from?
What cloth was put in it that it does not wear out
    with me?
Gold wears out, silver wears out, velvet wears out,
    silk wears out,
every ample garment wears out—yet Longing does
    not wear out.
Great Longing, cruel Longing is breaking my heart
    every day;
when I sleep most sound at night Longing comes
    and wakes me.
—From an old Cymric (Welsh) poem[1]

I often feel something deep within me is slowly being uncovered as our family is being reborn. The Cymru Celts would say we were being consumed by *hiraeth*, a Welsh word that loosely translates as "intense longing" or "remembrance of a time long past." It's the rubber-band feeling that pulls us back to connect with home, land, and love. As we left the securities of home and career in our move from California to Washington, we felt we were being called back home, except we didn't know where home was. The profound stirring within our spirits moved us to begin walking the path we continue to walk to this day: to listen to our heart longings and to listen to the Spirit within each family member.

The Celts—my ancestral people, and Jennifer's—have by nature always been a migrating, searching people. Sometimes their wanderings were born out of a spirit of exploration, as with the voyage of St. Brendan the Navigator, while at other times famine or invasion sent them away on their journeys. Author Frank MacEowen describes the Celts as like the mist, "slowly moving across the landscape, perpetually in-between and always seeking for that place we can call home."[2]

As I have left who I was and journeyed toward the future, I see that I am still in between, but I'm more at peace with the process. The further removed I become from my previous life, the more the Life of Jesus is emerging from within me. Detached from religion, my lifestyle is embodying a new freedom in the Spirit.

Across Western cultures, I see similar signs of spiritual awakening. The global cultural and spiritual shifts are exposing longings of the heart that have been long ignored or suppressed in the modern era.

I caught a good picture of this spiritual emergence late one evening while I was riding the ferry home from Seattle. After I locked my car and walked up the stairs to catch a better view of the city lights, I saw that the boat was nearly empty except for one man in bicycle gear sitting by a window. As I came closer I saw it was Colin, a guy I had met just a few weeks earlier at an Insight Meditation workshop on Bainbridge Island. We share several mutual friends but had never connected much personally.

We were drawn into deep conversation just as the boat was leaving the dock. After sharing a bit of our personal stories, Colin asked, "So how did you end up moving to the Seattle area?"

He was intrigued to hear about my previous life of pastor, turned seminary professor, turned entrepreneur, turned business consultant. I told him how I had given up on religion and my related vocation and how I was rediscovering a simpler spirituality for me and my family.

"I knew there was something about you!" He then began describing his own background: growing up in Seattle, his technical training, various jobs he had held, and the ambivalence of starting his own software company. He paused, smiled at me, and said, "I'm spiritual, but not very religious. I'm Buddhist and I believe in God and Jesus." He continued, "Buddha gives me a way of life."

"Tell me more," I asked.

"Buddhism provides me spiritual discipline and practice—a way to center myself in the midst of my life and work. My community is primarily in my company. I also volunteer as a basketball coach for youth at risk, and I occasionally attend the Sangha gatherings on the Island for some spiritual connection. . . . I know there's more. I'm still searching."

I shared more of my story and how we were experiencing Jesus in life and community.

Colin replied, "I can't remember the last time I was tempted to go to church. It's just not an option for me. The Christian church simply doesn't answer my spiritual needs, model the way Jesus lived, or provide a way of holistic living."

Colin represents many of our friends who are part of a spiritual renaissance in the West. They have more questions than answers when it comes to their own spirituality. Most are eclectic seekers who believe in some sense of the Sacred (or the Universe, Spirit, God, or some other supreme being), enjoy the contemplative practices of Eastern lifestyles, hold little tolerance for institutionalized religion, and are growing in their environmental consciousness.

My family and I are like Colin in that when we moved to the Northwest we turned our questions away from "What is church?" to "What is life?" As we started meeting people and listening to their longings, we realized that they were asking many of the same questions we were. It was then that we realized the church was giving us answers to many questions we weren't even asking. The church was not listening to our longings or allowing us to express our desires or our questions about our hopes and fears. Most people, engaged in the busyness and stress of daily life, do not wake up in the morning to questions such as "What is church?" No, their questions are more like: "Is life worth living?" "How will I support my family?" "Who cares for me?"

Three Ancient-Present Longings

> There is a desire within each of us, in the deep
> center of ourselves that we call our heart. We were
> born with it, it is never completely satisfied, and it
> never dies. We are often unaware of it, but it is
> always awake. . . . Our true identity, our reason for
> being, is to be found in this desire.
>
> —*Gerald May, psychiatrist and author,*
> The Awakened Heart

We have desires we cannot explain and questions we cannot answer.

I've always in some way known there was more than meets the eye, even through those many years when I conformed to the American way of materialism, humanism, and individualism. I trusted my eyes, my mind, and my will. "If it's going to be, it's up to me." I assumed that if I worked hard, with good ideas and good people, I could make a difference. All that has changed.

Now I'm not so linear or driven; I'm more content with openness and process. I'm moved more by my questions and desires than my answers and possessions. I've become a pilgrim again. My young children and my Celtic heritage have been encouraging me to embrace life as a journey. Lauren, David, Rachael, and Nathan remind me daily of the joy of discovery and relationships.

As I've explored my Celtic roots, I am learning to listen to longings that have been suppressed. These longings reflect my identity and place of belonging. They raise questions that are not easily answered: Who am I? Where did I come from? Who do I belong to? How should my family and I live? What is the source and meaning of life? How can we live in peace? What happens after death?

This is a journey of faith, one that requires deep listening to the desires and themes of our own life story. At the core, it is a journey of the heart. "That is why we live by believing and not by seeing," writes the apostle Paul (II Corinthians 5:7).

From the rich tapestry of stories from cultures across the globe and across time, I see three common patterns of spiritual restlessness and fulfillment. Our longings are *social*, for connection to one another; *ecological*, for connection to the earth and creation; and *spiritual*, for connection with the Creator, the transcendent. These common longings are expressed in richly diverse ways, but they seem to grow out of our very humanity. Everyone is born with a body capable of experiencing both pain and joy. We desire solitude and community. We want to love and be loved. We strive and rest. We know we are part of the earth and yet distinct from it. The very nature and direction of our longings are at the same time paradoxically universal across cultures and unique in their expression.

Social: Connecting with One Another

> I am because we are.
>
> —Proverb, *Xhosa people of Southern Africa*

We are all longing for belonging.

One evening, I met my good friend Erik for an ale and conversation at our island pub. As we have done in our regular get-togethers over the past couple of years, we talked about our lives. Erik was exploring new ways to father his two teenage boys in the aftermath of his recent divorce. He shared a few poems of William Stafford and then asked me what I had been learning the past week. I told him that I had been trying to slow down and listen more: listen to Jesus, my wife, my children, my friends, and my community.

Erik remarked, "You have a community that is real . . . you have others to journey with who share similar values and vision for life."

"Well we're working together to figure out how to be a community of friends. Like others, we hold in tension both the longing for community and the fear of community—fear of intimacy, rejection, being needy."

Erik continued, "I've hungered for healthy community for years—with colleagues at the university, in men's groups, and at various religious gatherings, but I was always left wanting. Whether it was a Unitarian church or a Buddhist meditation group, they all left me hungry. I'd like to be part of such a community, but I'm scared and excited about the possibility."

I believe Erik demonstrates what we are now witnessing on a larger scale: a movement in the West to recover a deeply communal sense of being. It encompasses a paradoxical longing for and fear of community. Though Western society has advanced the sense of rugged individualism and its inherent, corresponding loneliness, our desire to be together has not lessened. Humanity is essentially relational, even tribal. We are meant to live together, to care for one another in the spheres of life. As M. Scott Peck states in opening his book *The Different Drum*, "In community is the salvation of the world."[3] Driven by a desire to heal a fragmented world, we long for an integrated, connected life at the local level—for love, belonging, and security. Yet individualism continues to hold as a defining ideal in North America. In some ways, it can be said that Western culture is characteristically "postcommunity," evidenced by alienation, fragmentation, and the breakdown of family systems. Such trends, however, do not mean that people desire or need isolation and anonymity. The facts point to the contrary.

> The unrelated human being lacks wholeness, for he can achieve wholeness only through the soul, and the soul cannot exist without its other side, which is always found in a "you."
>
> —Carl Jung (1875-1961), Swiss psychiatrist and author[4]

Many studies over the past few decades have noted the erosion of the social fabric in the United States. In his acclaimed book *Bowling Alone: The Collapse and Revival of American Community*,

Robert Putnam documents the crisis of declining social capital over the last twenty-five years. Attending club meetings is down 58 percent; having friends over to each other's home is down 45 percent; families eating dinner together are down 33 percent. These shifts reflect our increasing disconnection from one another and the breakdown of basic social structures. The rise of personal freedom has come at a great cost. We are now feeling the effects of loss of family and communal interdependence, and of increasing individualism and independence.

Somewhere deep down, we know that if we are to survive we must come together and rediscover ways to connect with each other, and with the earth that supports our collective life. We are social beings who need one another not just for physical survival but also for spiritual sustenance as we journey together. So our individuality only makes sense in the context of community, where we are free to become ourselves. But the fact is that we have few good Western cultural models of individuals in healthy relationship and community who are searching together for meaning and fulfillment in life.

Ecological: Connecting to Creation

> We belong to the ground. It is our power. And we
> must stay close to it or maybe we will get lost.
> —*Narritjin Maynuru Yirrkala, Australian Aborigine*[5]

> The Lord God formed a man's body from the dust
> of the ground and breathed into it the breath of
> life. And the man became a living person.
> —*Genesis 2:7*

We are all pagans.

This may sound foreign, even heretical, for many readers. However, *pagans* in the original sense of the word simply means "people of the earth," because our bodies were fashioned from the dirt, live off the earth, and will return to it when we die. Whether conscious of it or not, we are drawn to nature. In the words of the medieval Rhineland mystic Hildegard of Bingen, "Holy persons draw to themselves all that is earthly."

Though often ignored by modern culture in innumerable ways, this longing has been in us as individuals and as peoples from the beginning. We are distinct from the earth, but not separate. All so-called primitive tribal cultures and most world spiritualities are grounded in this reality. Their connection to the earth is both natural and mystical—the basis of their culture, life, and spirituality, their sanctuary. Some may call it creation spirituality, deep ecology, natural mysticism, or ecospirituality, but we are all integrally related to the natural world.

I write this today from a high point overlooking the Strait of Juan de Fuca. It's nearly 11:00 P.M. With the city lights of Victoria, British Columbia, in the east, the luminescence of a full moon shimmers across the waters like a river of light until it crashes on the rocks below me. I'm drawn into the beauty and brilliance of the light bouncing off the water, casting silhouettes of jagged rock cliffs, towering firs, and twisted madrona.

I know I am not alone. Creation reflects the powerful glory and the constant presence of the Creator. Yet I experience this as the paradox of God's transcendence seeming to clash with his immi-nence. God is beyond us, but also here with us in all of creation—in every sunset, alpine wildflower, herd of elk, and mountain stream. I am reminded of the Psalmist who wrote:

> The voice of the Lord echoes above the sea.
> The God of glory thunders.
> The Lord thunders over the mighty sea.
> The voice of the Lord is powerful;
> The voice of the Lord is full of majesty.

—Psalm 29:3–4

Answering our longings for connection with the earth begins with understanding the relationship between the earth and its Creator:

"The earth is the Lord's, and everything in it. The world and all its people belong to him. For he laid the earth's foundation on the seas and built it on the ocean depths" (Psalm 24:1–2).[6] The human relationship with the earth is one of those themes woven throughout the entirety of Scripture, from the account of creation and the Tree of Life in the Garden of Eden in the first pages of Genesis to the new creation and the Tree of Life in the New Jerusalem in the last pages of Revelation.

Despite our rising awareness of the interconnectedness of all living things, ironically we also feel alienated and estranged from the created order and from the source of creation. This valid longing is the source of the unquenchable search for fulfillment through Mother Earth, Gaia, gods, or God. Especially in Europe and North America, we see a revival of premodern earth-centered spiritualities. At the 1996 North American Conference on Christianity and Ecology, theologian and cultural historian Thomas Berry asserted: "You cannot tell the human story except by telling the universe story. This means that modern cosmology must be a part of Christian education and made integral with theology."[7]

> All praise be yours, my Lord, through Sister Earth, our mother, who feeds us in her sovereignty and produces various fruits and colored flowers and herbs.
>
> —St. Francis of Assisi
> (c. 1181–1226)

All the revolutions of the industrial, information, and technological ages distanced us from creation. Still, we retain a deep value and enchantment with the earth and ecology. The apostle Paul wrote to a group of Jesus followers in first-century Rome: "For we know that all creation has been groaning as in the pains of childbirth right up to the present time. And even we Christians, although we have the Holy Spirit within us as a foretaste of future glory, also groan to be released from pain and suffering. We, too, wait anxiously for that day when God will give us our full rights as his children, including the new bodies he has promised us" (Romans 8:22–23).

We might say today that the earth is again groaning, but this time from the environmental abuse that results from our separateness from creation. Nearly three thousand years ago, the Hebrew prophet Jeremiah wrote: "They have made it an empty wasteland; I hear its mournful cry. The whole land is desolate, and no one even cares" (Jeremiah 12:11). The earth also groans in response to the spiritual and social alienation of all creation. The earth feels the effects of our alienation with the Creator and one another that manifests in prejudice, genocide, and other social atrocities. The Hebrew Scriptures make clear the interdependence of our relationship with the Creator and the health of our land.[8] In response to the effects of our spiritual and social separation, even the earth is calling for reconciliation.

Indeed, creation is one undivided whole in Christ. As Creator and Sustainer of the universe, Christ brings reconciliation of *all* things. The Way has much to say about ecology[9]: "Christ is the one through whom God created everything in heaven and earth. He made the things we can see and the things we can't see—kings, kingdoms, rulers, and authorities. Everything has been created through him and for him. He existed before everything else began, and he holds all creation together. For God in all his fullness was pleased to live in Christ, and by him God reconciled everything to himself. He made peace with everything in heaven and on earth by means of his blood on the cross" (Colossians 1:16–17, 19–20).

One of the primary marks of Celtic spirituality is the belief in the essential goodness and sacredness of creation. The Celtic cross itself reflects the centrality and celebration of creation. The great round circle is held in tension by the two arms of the cross, holding together heaven and earth, creation and redemption. As Celtic author J. Phillip Newell has observed, "Everything in creation has issued forth from the invisible and contains something of the unseen life of God."[10] Jesus himself is the heartbeat at the center of all creation, sustaining all that is. Intricate, twining Celtic knot work is essentially a cosmological statement about the interrelatedness of all things within the divine Creation. Newell describes well

Celtic Cross

the Celtic view: "The Spirit of God is 'impregnated' throughout the whole of creation. Where there is life and goodness, there is God. God exists wherever there is love and creativity. . . . The whole of life is sacred, every day, every hour, every moment."[11] Indeed, all of creation is a sacrament ushering us to God.

Spiritual: Connecting with Creator

> Our hearts are restless until they rest in God.
> —*St. Augustine, Bishop of Hippo (396–430* A.D.*)*

We are all mystics.

The nature of our reality as human beings is metaphysical, literally "beyond the physical" realm of being. We all seem to know, without even being taught, that there is more to life than what we see. Across generations, cultures, and history, we are all searching for peace in our souls. The words of the French mathematician Blaise Pascal are as true today as they were four centuries ago: there's a God-shaped vacuum in every person that only God can fill. During times of mass social change, our spiritual hunger intensifies. This certainly describes our time; even scientists are studying the "neurobiology of faith" and identifying a "God spot" in the brain.[12]

With the demise of modernity, the spiritual void in the heart of Western culture is fully exposed. We are, in fact, spiritual beings with physical bodies.

Many are moving from one religious or spiritual fix to another, but all of us are searching to connect with the transcendent. We Americans know how to do religion but are awkward at being spiritual. We've been handicapped for a long time. In her book *The New American Spirituality*, Elizabeth Lesser writes: "We could say that the history of human suffering is our inability to come to terms with spiritual hunger. Like one big cosmic joke, humans were born yearning for a home of tranquil abiding, yet without the map to get there."[13] Like a child taking her first steps, we are full of enthusiasm, fear, and awkwardness, all at the same time. We know we are spiritual, but we don't know *how* to be spiritual, even those of us who know how to do church (or thought we did). Yet still we search for a connection with what is outside us—for ultimate reality, Spirit, the Universe, the divine, or God. Whatever is beyond our perceptions, we want it. Whatever our culture denies, whatever our culture tries to affirm, ultimately, the human heart is still restless until it finds rest in God. We want to touch God. We want to be touched.

> God has made everything beautiful for its own time. He has planted eternity in the human heart, but even so, people cannot see the whole scope of God's work from beginning to end.
>
> —King Solomon, ninth century B.C., Ecclesiastes 3:11-12

The longing for interconnectedness has increased with the growing realization that fragmentation and separateness characterizes our Western culture. The triple spiral of the Celtic triskele serves to illustrate the interconnectedness of our longings. For many of us, the longing for life within us seems a distant dream from the life we are living. We are disconnected from ourselves and one another. We yearn for simplicity and wholeness. But in our busy lives, we learn to suppress our heart's desires. In doing so, we settle for survival rather than fully living the desire of our hearts. We grow numb to our desire.

Celtic Triskele

Many who reject organized religion find themselves running from one spiritual practice to the next in an effort to find spiritual meaning. Others seem to have traded their old dependency on religion for a new dependency on the latest "spiritual" personality or program. Could it be that what appears to be a spiritual sojourn has actually reverted into a new religion of running away from God—instead of toward him? Or might it be why the longings intensify, because our numbness pushes in and condenses our hearts into stone?

Many are experiencing new forms of "separation anxiety": waking up to the effects of our separateness from ourselves, our families, God, and the earth. Often the more we listen to our longings the more the pain of loss intensifies. We can easily grow weary of this new hunger and thirst. But it's part of the process of coming alive again.

These are the birth pangs of awakening.

Reflection and Discussion

Where our heart wanders during those still moments will often show us the direction of our true longings. And those longings often echo our original design and destiny. Find a quiet place to listen. Perhaps with a journal or a good friend, explore these questions:

- What do you thirst for? What do you long for the most? Where do you desire more connection: with Spirit, with others, or with the earth?
- How have you sought to fulfill your longings? Are you satisfied?
- With a close friend, exchange perspectives on the longings or unfulfilled needs you see in each other's life.

12

EMBRACING OUR
PRIMAL DESIRE

The soul must long for God in order to be set
aflame by God's love; but if the soul cannot yet
feel this longing, then it must long for the longing.
To long for the longing is also from God.
—*Meister Eckhart, fourteenth-century*
Catholic mystic, Spricht

Our longings are deep within the heart of humankind. We will stop
at virtually nothing until we are satisfied.

We first met Marcel and Maria at the end of their quest. Maria
led the search over the preceding four years, buying and reading all
she could on spiritual practice and alternative healing. She enrolled
in numerous classes and acquired the products. She tried it all. But
every time she would begin a path, she was stopped short by the bad
vibes within her spirit, or by some external circumstance. Neverthe-
less, she persevered in her search. Finally, a friend invited Marcel and
Maria to a weeklong seminar on Christ-centered healing in southern
Switzerland.[1] Marcel was a bit skeptical at first but agreed to attend a
workshop. His heart opened after he experienced healing from the
chronic back pain of a twenty-year-old hockey injury. Together, Marcel and Maria experienced the love and power of Jesus in a deeply
personal way. They left the seminar with physical healing as well as
an inner joy and peace that continue to radiate through them.

One evening while Marcel was preparing a fondue dinner at their
home outside Zürich, Maria showed me all the books, recordings,

and courses she had sampled over the years. Marcel confessed, "If we'd found Jesus four years ago we would have saved a lot of money." When they added up the cost of their spiritual quest it came to more than $100,000. Maria expressed guilt for having "wasted so much money."

Moved by their story, I shared with Maria what God said through the Hebrew prophet Jeremiah six hundred years before Jesus: "'If you look for me in earnest, you will find me when you seek me. I will be found by you.'[2] Thank God, he met you in your searching!"

Our longings reflect our very nature as human beings, revealing the interconnectedness of our identity. All our longings converge in the deepest desire of our lives: loving union with God. That is because God created us for union with himself; it is the original purpose of our lives. The loving part of it implies mutual choosing, not one-way absorption of the other. This suggests a reason we feel a certain loneliness, emptiness, and separateness; they're all shadows of something or someone lost. Our heart reflects our original design: the nature of God that was breathed into humanity at the beginning.

> Thirsty hearts are those whose longing has been wakened by the touch of God within them.
>
> —A. W. Tozer, twentieth-century theologian with no formal training

We are spiritual, designed to enjoy communion with the Creator. The great point of resemblance between the Creator and us is found in our spiritual nature. Our likeness to God is not, as some of the early Latin Fathers fancied, a bodily likeness. *Imago dei*—bearing the image of God—transcends physical reality. As Jesus said, "For God is Spirit, so those who worship him must worship in spirit and in truth" (John 4:24). The life inbreathed from God is *the* distinguishing mark of our humanity.[3] This points to our immortal nature and destiny, because God is the Eternal Spirit. To be created in the image of God means that we humans have the ability and the privilege to know, love, and commune with God directly.

We were created to enjoy a special relationship with God. We cannot know our unique design or fulfill our destiny outside of relationship with the one who designed us. The fourteenth-century Christian mystic Meister Eckhart said that we are all born with the "God seed," an inherent tendency toward spiritual growth: "The seed of God is in us. Given an intelligent and hard-working farmer and a diligent field hand, it will thrive and grow up to God, whose seed it is and accordingly its fruits will be God-nature. Pear seeds grow into pear trees, nut seeds into nut trees, and God seed into God."[4]

At the root of our humanity is our desire to connect with our Creator. Our hearts echo God's desire to enjoy communion, to be as it was in those first days of creation when God walked with Adam and Eve in the garden in the cool of the day (Genesis 3:8). The hunger of our hearts for spiritual intimacy was placed there by God to draw us back to him. The Hebrew Talmud summarizes it well: "God wants the heart." But God can only have intimacy with those who want relationship with him. The capacity to love implies the capacity to choose. Genuine love cannot be forced. So he blessed us with an essentially relational and spiritual nature that has the ability to accept or reject communion with him.

> I don't see myself as so much dust that has appeared in the world but as a being that was expected, prefigured, called forth. In short, as a being that could, it seems, come only from a creator; and this idea of a creating hand that created me refers me back to God.
>
> –Jean Paul Sartre (1905-1980), French existentialist philosopher, *Interview with Simone de Beauvoir*

We are relational, designed to live in community with one another. God created us *out of* community and *for* community. We see this in Genesis 1:26–27, where God said, "Let *us* make people in *our* image, to be like *ourselves*. . . ." Our spirituality is not just a part of who we are. We have been created out of the triune Godhead, the source of spiritual community. We are made to live in conscious and practical interrelationship with God and the rest of creation.

Later in the creation account, we see that man and woman are both created in God's image for community with each other. Adam alone could not reflect the fullness of God, and Adam needed companionship. So after God caused Adam to fall into a deep sleep, he took a part of the man's side (not his head or feet) to fashion woman and complete his creation of humanity. When God brought her to Adam, "At last!" Adam exclaimed. "She is part of my own flesh and bone! She will be called 'woman,' because she was taken out of a man" (Genesis 2:21–24).

Gender is one way we bear the image of God. "God created people in his own image; God patterned them after himself; male and female he created them" (Genesis 1:27). Being created in God's "image" means being created male *and* female, to enjoy communion with both the Creator and one another. Though we are one humanity, we are male and female. We are one and different. It is in the tension of our sameness and difference that we reflect the fullness of the Creator. Likewise, it is in the context of community that we truly discover ourselves and our individuality, and also our inherent interdependence with all creation.

> God is infinite while we are finite. We can never fully comprehend the infinite, but we do have within us a spiritual sense that allows us to recognize and enjoy God's presence.
>
> —Sadhu Sundar Singh (1889-1929), wandering holy man of northern India

In the Way of Jesus, love and community give living testimony of the reality of God. When people accept us, they accept God. As Jesus told his first followers: "So now I am giving you a new commandment: Love each other. Just as I have loved you, you should love each other. Your love for one another will prove to the world that you are my disciples" (John 13:34–35). To paraphrase Mother Teresa, Jesus often comes to us in the distressing disguise of other people in need. Will we embrace the poor or the outcast and so embrace Jesus?[5]

We are creative, designed to enjoy and care for creation. To be created in God's image is to have a place and purpose in creation. Whether the place assigned to humanity in creation is to be considered a feature of likeness to the divine or the consequence of that likeness is a question that has been much discussed. The meaning and purpose of our role on this earth are based on embracing our *imago dei*; "Let us make people in our image," God said, "*to be like ourselves. They will be masters over all life*—the fish in the sea, the birds in the sky, and all the livestock, wild animals, and small animals" (Genesis 1:26, emphasis added).

God created, then he rested. The cycle of creation and rest continues. For the first six days, God labored and brought forth creation. Then we read: "On the seventh day, having finished his task, God rested from all his work. And God blessed the seventh day and declared it holy, because it was the day when he rested from his work of creation" (Genesis 2:2–3). God began the pattern in the first week of creation that we are to continue. Later in the book of Exodus, we read that God instructs his people to continue the cyclical pattern of work and rest: "It is a permanent sign of my covenant with them. For in six days the Lord made heaven and earth, but he rested on the seventh day and was refreshed" (31:17). The Hebrew word for "refreshed" is *naphash*, which literally means "to breathe or exhale," akin to the word used for God breathing life into Adam. This is the same word used when God began the pattern of work and rest. All creation moves with the rhythm of inhale and exhale, work and rest, presence and absence.

We are both invited and called to share in the care of God's creation as eco-stewards.[6] The earth is our household! God has entrusted us with a creation-based economy. Our role on earth is not to be a "user" or consumer, but a steward of life. God has purposed to fill the earth with his image—through us. We are called to care for the earth—to be agents of reconciliation between God and all creation.

Desires and Delight

> Most men lead lives of quiet desperation and go to
> the grave with the song still in them.
> —*Henry David Thoreau (1817–1862),*
> *American writer and philosopher,* Walden Pond

The lack of connection and meaning has led many of us to settle for lives of quiet desperation, as Thoreau said, exhausted by the emptiness and frustration of unsatisfied dreams. The proverb from the tenth century B.C. laments that "hope deferred makes the heart sick, but when dreams come true, there is life and joy" (Proverbs 13:12). Desire cannot be alleviated through talking, any more than scratching gets rid of an itch. The more you scratch, the more you itch, and the more you scratch.

Recognizing the emptiness of life, many people have embarked on an unending quest for connection with the infinite. They search wild and wide, rather than committed and deep. I believe most of our societal excesses and addictions can be traced to our heart's unfulfilled longings. As our heartsickness deepens, we look outside for something to fill the void. We try to drug it away legally or illegally, drink it away, work it away, play it away, shop it away, sex it away, or eat it away. The addiction is not the problem, but rather a fruit of the root issue, which usually relates to painful relationships or the lack of love. These habits or addictions may bring relief or remission for a time, but the longings always return. (Actually, the longings have never left!)

Life is relationship. Ultimately, our primal desire is rooted in a longing to know that we belong, that we are loved, and that we have a place on this earth. Our hearts long for reconciliation in these three domains. The renowned psychologist Martin Buber, best known for his book *I and Thou*, also believed the sacred is found in our connections with other, with nature, and with God the Eternal Thou. He postulated that "all actual life is encounter."[7]

Into every life, God has placed these desires for reunion, or deeper union, with God. For to be fully human and fully alive is to be in right relationship with the one who created us. It is beyond both the rational and emotional. It is more like a gravitational pull back to where we belong, to a place of wholeness and reconciliation. This is not simply an inner longing for subjective experiences with the transcendent; there is also a search for an ultimate reality or overarching story that might restore our relationship with all creation. These longings offer a clue to who we really are and why we are here—evidence of our intimate identity and ultimate purpose.

> *Trust in the Lord and do good.*
> *Then you will live safely in the land and prosper.*
> *Take delight in the Lord,*
> *and he will give you your heart's desires.*
> *Commit everything you do to the Lord.*
> *Trust him, and he will help you.*
>
> —Psalm 37:3–5

❖ Reflection and Discussion ❖

Reflect on the promise expressed in Jeremiah 29:13, and then compare it with the words of Jesus in the Gospel of Luke 11:9–13.

- What do these verses reveal about the nature of God?
- How have you sought after God? How have you seen God seek after you?
- What one thing would you like to ask of God? You might want to pray for the faith to ask.

13

AWAKENING TO OUR IDENTITY

Are not our desires inseparably intertwined
with the continuation of life? Even the idea
of eliminating desire is fruitless. The desire to
eliminate all desire is still itself a desire. How can
we find release and peace by replacing one desire
with another? Surely we shall find peace not by
eliminating desire, but by finding its fulfillment and
satisfaction in the One who created it.

—*Sadhu Sundar Singh (1889–1929),*
wandering holy man of northern India

I have a psychologist friend who has counseled many Vietnam veterans still struggling with the horrors of battle and alienation with their homeland. I remember hearing a story of a man awakened by excruciating pain in his lower legs, only to realize that his legs were no longer there. It's what doctors call "phantom pain."

I believe we suffer a similar phantom pain in our spirit. We feel the pain of something lost in our soul, and we want to be made whole and restored. But we ask, What does it mean to be whole? Restored to *what*? Or restored to *whom*?

Embracing the Phantom

The decisive question for man is: Is he related to
the infinite or not? That is the telling question of

> his life. Only if we know that the thing that truly
> matters is the infinite can we avoid fixing our
> interests upon futilities and upon all kinds of goals
> which are not of real importance.
> —Carl Jung (1875–1961), Swiss psychiatrist

"I didn't realize I was spiritual until about three years ago."

I was surprised to hear such a confession from Erik. It wasn't all that unusual except when you consider the source. Erik is a Stanford-trained psychiatrist and tenured professor who now serves as an executive of a large health care system. With such a background, why did it take Erik nearly fifty years to "discover" he was spiritual?

As he and I reflected together on our lives, we realized that we have been culturally conditioned to suppress our inner longings. We are given culturally appropriate things to desire that can be brought up in our everyday discussion. Who has not shared a longing for more money, less work and stress, an exotic vacation, or a change of circumstance? The list could go on. But I have observed that even if these appropriate desires are met, there is still a longing for more. Sometimes the desires that occupy our mind are just distractions from the deeper, nagging desire of our soul. When the rational exterior is broken down, it reveals a hungry soul—the soul of culture and the souls of people longing for connection and fulfillment that cannot be satisfied by anything of the physical realm.

Later in the same conversation, Erik expressed another level of frustration: "I know I'm spiritual, but I don't know *why*."

We are spiritually restless and we don't know why. Like Erik, many people are coming to realize we are not merely human beings who have an occasional spiritual experience but in fact spiritual beings having a human experience. Though many don't know why or what to do about it, these new realizations provoke new questions that have no easy answers . . . or no answers at all.

In the preceding chapter, we began to look at our longings, which are really about the meaning of our existence and what brings us fulfillment in life. But as we explore the source of these longings, we enter into a new realm of questions: Who am I? Who are we? Who am I beyond my career, my mind, beyond my personality?

Personal answers to universal questions: that is what we all seek.

Awakening to the Source of Our Story

He who has a why to live can bear almost any how.
—*Victor Frankl (1895–1969),*
Holocaust survivor, author, psychiatrist

But where do these spiritual longings come from? Why do we long for a holistic solution that will affect and integrate every area of our lives—spiritual, physical, emotional, social, financial, and family? I believe the incessant spiritual wandering of our day is because we have lost the story of who we are and why we are here. We need restoration (a "re-story-ation") of the narrative that tells us the source of our identity, for until we know *why* we are spiritual we will never know *how* to be spiritual. As we realize the source of our identity, we begin to catch some bearing to ask questions regarding how we will live out our spirituality.

The word *spirituality* comes from the Latin root *spiritus*, which means "breath" and refers to the breath of life, or the animating principle. This same idea is expressed in Genesis 2:7, which reads, "And the Lord God formed a man's body from the dust of the ground and breathed into it the breath of life. And the man became a living person." So our deep desire for spiritual connection is a mark of our true nature, God's very life breathed in us. As we realize who is responsible for our spirituality, we can then look to why it exists in the context of the ultimate purpose of creation. As we reflect on understanding our own spiritual nature, we come to better understand the nature of God, for we were created in his image.

Original Blessing:
The Desire and Design of God

God is the good and all things which proceed from
him are good.

—*Hildegard of Bingen (1098–1179)*,
German abbess and author

We find the origin of our spiritual longing in the creation story. We
are *imago dei*, the image of God. Humanity is related to God as
its Creator and to the larger created order because God is originator of all. Genesis eloquently makes clear that the image of God
is expressed in relationship between God and humanity, male and
female, and Creator with all creation: "God breathed his essence
into the dirt" to create Adam (Gen-
esis 2:7). My Native American
friends remind me "Adam" literally
means "red dirt" in Hebrew. Our
origin as God's personal creation,
bearing his image, is the source
of the longing of our hearts and of
our inseparable relation with our
Creator.

For in him [God] we live and
move and have our being. . . .
We are his offspring.

  –Apostle Paul, speaking to
  first-century Athenians,
  Acts 17:28

Through the creation story, we see God's original blessing, simply that he designed and created us in his own image and likeness.
The use of both *image* and *likeness* in Hebrew strengthens and
emphasizes the idea of our likeness to God (cf. Genesis 1:26; 5:1).
The Hebrew word for image, *tselem*, comes from the root meaning
of shade or phantom; we each bear a phantom reflection of our Creator. Likeness, from the Hebrew *demuwth*, tells us that the divine
image we bear corresponds to the original pattern. We see this
passed down through humanity: Adam "became the father of a son
in his own likeness, according to his image, and named him Seth"
(Genesis 5:3). Humanity continues to reflect God's own attributes.

It is this creation in the likeness of God that makes us more than a composite of base compounds and water. We have been birthed from red earth by the very breath of God. After the creation of Adam and Eve, "God looked over all he had made, and he saw that it was excellent in every way" (Genesis 1:31). Excellent! All creation reflects the glory and greatness of a personal and transcendent God. God is the life within all life. We are integrally connected to both Creator and creation, and though we are created from the soil of the earth we are distinct from the rest of creation for we have the stamp of God within us. We are the very image and likeness of God.

Celtic theologians such as Pelagius (c. 354–418) and others espoused that God's goodness is the original defining characteristic of humanity. Pelagius maintained that the image of God can be seen in every newborn child and that, although obscured by sin, it exists at the heart of every person, waiting to be released through the grace of God.[1] These Celtic theologians did not deny the presence of evil and of its powerful influence in humanity, but they maintained that the image of God is still at the heart of humanity.

In our very design, then, we see the source of our primal longings for life, for connection with God, with each other, and with creation. Created out of God's love, our original design is to enjoy the fullness of this love in communion with the Creator, with one another, and with all creation. Glory is a bright reflection from a source of light, and we partake in the glory of God as we become fully alive to who we are.

So Why the Distortions?

With this original blessing, how is it then that creation is so filled with pain and destruction, sorrow and imperfection? How is this a part of our identity?

Late one night, my friend Tony gave me a lift to the ferry terminal. We'd just participated in a gathering of civic and business leaders discussing the challenges of and opportunities for sustainable business that is both socially and environmentally responsible. In talking about environmental threats, we got on the subject of creation and the Fall. Tony affirmed the idea of God's original blessing but asked me, "Then where did all the [expletive deleted] come from?"

Many of my friends, like Tony, believe in "spirit," know they are connected to the universe, and have a reverence for the earth. But they have no real explanation for evil. They don't like the idea of the Fall and all the associated shame, guilt, and judgment that goes with it. They want wholeness and reconciliation, but they can't explain why we don't have it. They've heard evil is an illusion, a social construction with no real basis, an error of modern man, or the result of ignorance. Though some, like Tony, are hesitant to admit it, they are beginning to question the culturally received assumptions about natural human goodness and our ability to solve our problems, as well as the belief that we are evolving to become more civil human beings. In her book *Turning to One Another*, writer and philosopher Margaret (Meg) Wheatley represents this widely held position: "Most cultural traditions have a story to explain why human life is so hard, why there is so much suffering on earth. The story is always the same—at some point early in our human origin, we forgot that we were all connected. We broke apart, we separated from each other. We even fragmented inside ourselves, disconnecting heart from head from spirit. These stories always teach that healing will only be found when we remember our initial unity and reconnect the fragments."[2]

Like Meg, we feel the results of alienation and evil, but can't explain where they come from. So what happened?

Original Separation: Deception, Rebellion, and Fragmentation

The sin behind all sin is separation.
—*Meister Eckhart (c. 1260–1327),*
philosopher, mystic, and theologian

We can't fall from where we have never been.

The book of Genesis records the story of the conspiracy and compromises that led to our current state of brokenness. In the form of a serpent, Satan (from a Hebrew word that means "opposer") the deceiver tempts Eve to eat of the Tree of the Knowledge of Good and Evil. He plants questions in Eve's mind about the truthfulness of what God told her and Adam about the Tree and its significance: "God's holding out on you. . . . There's more. . . . You can be like God!"

The truth was that they already were like God, but Eve and Adam believed the lie and chose to move away from their fellowship with God and toward another path. Hence sin entered the world, a path of our own choosing. From then on, it would spread to all creation, inborn to our very nature. Before their actions, all of creation was in harmony. Life was perfectly good. Afterward, things looked different than they had before. They were aware of their nakedness for the first time, and they tried to cover up their vulnerability, guilt, and shame. The form this takes varies with the culture. Generally speaking, Western cultures emphasize guilt that is based on issues of doing and guilt-based theology. In contrast, Eastern cultures tend to be more shame-based and focus on broken relationships. The Eastern perspective reflects the understanding that the consequence of sin is separation.

One of Satan's grand schemes from the beginning has been to prevent humanity's communion with God. My friend Salvatore calls this the original "Luciferic deception," which marks the genesis of religion. Lucifer is another name by which Satan is known; it comes from the Latin for "light bearer." As the story of Adam and Eve illustrates, not all light is good. Some light can blind and actually prevent us from enlightenment. Lucifer, disguised as an angel of light, blinded Adam and Eve with his dazzling promises.[3] Having led, and failed, the first rebellion in the heavenlies, resulting in eternal separation from God for the heavenly rebels, Lucifer then turned to deceive and destroy God's crowning joy and creation.

In this ancient narrative we see that in partaking of the fruit of the Tree of the Knowledge of Good and Evil, Adam and Eve compromised their face-to-face relationship with God, which resulted in at least two forms of spiritual bondage. The first is the spirit of religion, which displaces a direct relationship with God by a system of rules, rituals, and mediators between us and God. This breeds various expressions of complacency, fear, pride, counterfeit dogma, guilt, and shame. The second is the spirit of unbelief, which at the core trusts self over God. This breeds spiritual cynicism, arrogance, or apathy.

The spirits of unbelief and religion are both the cause *and* the effect of our spiritual alienation (Ephesians 2:1–3). The first breeds a spiritual independence, looking for salvation in self-effort. The latter fosters spiritual codependence by imparting a system of belief or regimen of practice for attaining favor with God.

> It is the image of God reflected in you that so enrages hell; it is this at which the demons hurl their mightiest weapons.
> —William Gurnall (1617-1679), English theologian and author

The spirit of religion builds its work on two basic foundations: fear and pride. It seeks to have us serve God in order to gain his approval, rather than live from the truth that we have received our approval through the grace of God. We like religion because it tells us what to do externally, and when we do it our conscience feels better, but it takes the place of the inner peace that results from right relationship with God. When we're gripped by the spirit of religion, we substitute human activity for the power of the Holy Spirit in our lives.

Just as the primary characteristic of the Pharisees was their tendency to focus on what was wrong with others while being blind to their own faults, the spirit of religion tries to make us more prone to seeing what is wrong with others than to seeing the need for our own correction. Those with a religious spirit often claim to be open to more understanding, but most of the time that only goes one way—to get everyone else to be open to what they teach, while they remain steadfastly closed to others. This is the essential character of false mediators.[4]

Lucifer was the original spiritual mediator, pretending to be a keeper of esoteric knowledge essential to our spiritual well-being. Whether we call anyone who comes between us and God mediator, priest, shaman, pastor, guru, or reverend, the net effect is the same. We were designed for direct access, but Lucifer slithers his way in between God and us as his creation, enticing us to take a path that subjects us to spiritual bondage.

The Problem of Sin

In its common forms, Western Christianity understands sin as alienating behavior, the "bad things we do." But increasingly we see another form emerging: the sin of alienating ignorance or wrong beliefs. As a friend of ours said: "We are not separate from God; it's just that we've forgotten. The ego is the soul in the state of forgetfulness of its union with God. The occasional mystic experience, or revelation, is a glimpse of that union, of the oneness of everything."

It's like those times when I travel away from my family. It's not enough for me to reflect on memories or look at pictures, or even talk with them on the phone. It helps, but the satisfaction is only temporary. More often than not, it actually worsens my homesickness. There's nothing like being with them—in person. So it is with Jesus. Thinking about him and visualizing him does not replace an intimate relationship with Jesus. Relationship is more than rationalization or visualization. Ignorance or faulty beliefs are not an acceptable rationale for evil.

Both common views of *sins*—bad behavior and wrong belief— ignore the root nature of *sin*. Jesus demonstrated in his life and teaching that sin is actually the underlying human tendency to deliberately separate ourselves from God. In the Epistle to the Romans, we read, "For all have sinned (specific choice and action); all fall short of God's glorious standard" (3:23). Everyone is separated from God, both by nature (sin) and by choice (sins). That is, specific sins are possible because we are free to choose to commit sins. We have a tendency to commit sins because of the underlying tendency to separate ourselves from God. It's really a core attitude of saying, "God, you go your way and I'll go mine."

Our problem with God is indeed beyond remembering.

Matters of Choice and Consequence

Have you ever wondered why God would create us in his image, knowing our inevitable capacity to turn away? Did he create us with inherent imperfections? Did God create sin? Is this some sort of cosmic manipulation? Over the centuries, such questions have spawned countless hours of discussion and debate at pubs and seminaries, campuses and campfires. We are driven to decide because the issues involved lie at the core of our identity.

God created us free. Free from oppression. Free of toil and hardship. Free to walk with him in the Garden. Free to walk away from him. Free to listen to the voices of rebellion. Free to choose to remain in spiritual darkness or walk in the light.

God desires and invites all of us to love him without restricting our personal freedom.[5] To force us to love God would contradict his very nature. Freedom means the freedom to choose, and choice implies the existence of things among which to choose. So central is freedom to God's nature and to the basic nature of man that C. S. Lewis writes, "Try to exclude the possibility of sufferings which the order of nature and the existence of free wills involve, and you find that you have excluded life itself."[6] God will grant those who do not love him their free choice to forgo intimate communion and instead live in eternal separation from him.

Though created in and for the light, we are born into darkness and alienation. This is the blessing and the curse of free will. It also illustrates the interconnectedness of all life. All offspring inherit qualities of their parents. Each generation and each individual will be characterized by both the uniqueness and commonness in relationship to one's family. It is so in the entire created world: plants, animals, and humans. I, for example, am a mix of southern and northern European. My maternal grandfather emigrated from Greece, and my paternal great-grandparents emigrated from Scotland. I didn't have any choice in this. For better or worse, I live everyday with the reality of those decisions. Now I have the freedom to return to my ancestral homeland in the rugged Highlands of Scotland or the olive groves of Greece, or anywhere I choose. Likewise, all my decisions will affect my children and my children's children.

The spiritual hunger we have been describing is, I believe, a manifestation of how deeply we feel our separation from God. This fragmentation is in fact a separation from our very identity, which makes it possible for us to do all the destructive things we do. We have used our freedom to create slavery, division, alienation, sickness, greed, and ultimately death. As Sadhu Sundar Singh explains: "We have been endowed with spiritual senses so that we can feel and enjoy God's presence. But the influence of sin deadens these senses till we are no longer able to see beyond ourselves, nor beyond the material world. As long as we follow this path of darkness, we cannot believe God, so we starve ourselves until in the end we have committed spiritual suicide. Our end is total enslavement to the material world."[7]

> Sin is what you do when your heart is not satisfied with God.
> –John Piper, American theologian, *Future Grace*

The evidence of this original alienation is seen in our destruction throughout all creation. The Hebrew word for *polluted* is *chaneph*, which means "straying from God's path." The land, through pollution, is led astray from God's original blessing to be fruitful. It begins to "cry out" to its Creator for a divine solution.[8] In his book *Creation Spirituality*, Matthew Fox writes, "Humans are quite capable of sinning against creation, of missing the mark of our purpose in being on this planet and in this universe. In this sense, sin is a turning away from creation and its author, the divine one who dwells in all things. Sometimes we sin by omission—by not realizing or admitting sins against the biosphere (rightly called ecocide) or against earth species (biocide) or against soil (genocide). Yet these are truly *mortal* sins, for they will prove to be deadly for generations to come."[9]

We are just like those whom Sophocles (496–406 B.C.) described in saying "men of ill judgment oft ignore the good that lies within their hands, till they have lost it." Personal loneliness, social atrocities, political corruption, and environmental destruction all reflect the damage we humans cause as we exercise our free will to reject the original blessing of communion with God and creation.

We can rightly understand our spiritual alienation in light of our original design. Contrary to most church traditions, regardless of denomination, our identity is not in the Fall and our sinfulness. With such a worldview, God tends to be distant, a king and judge, and the only salvation is escape from this fallen world. Such a perspective downplays God's original work with humanity. It poses the notion that God placed us into the world despised, unwanted, and powerless, when in reality we were created out of love, with the capacity to love and to exercise our free will. Created in original blessing, we have rebelled against God by heredity and by choice, thereby falling short of experiencing the glory of our original design.

But all is not lost. The fingerprint of God's original blessing can still be seen in all creation. We still possess some unique "godlike" characteristics, even if they are distorted. The Celtic theologian Pelagius taught that sin and human foibles had not eliminated the image of God in humans but had overwhelmed it or covered it up. At this point, despite sin, wonderful vestiges of God's inherent greatness and our likeness to the divine can still be discerned in humanity. It is still the light of God within every person that brings forth the hunger for wholeness and restoration. We originally bore, and again may bear, the divine likeness in this respect.

However, to reach spiritual restoration requires us to reconnect the paradoxical tension between original blessing and original alienation. Many of the people I encounter on their journey of spirituality and self-discovery accept the original blessing but ignore the original alienation. Such a focus on the self ignores our sin. It makes the self a god and turns selfish fulfillment of our full potential into life's ultimate destination. Meanwhile, many Christians accept original sin but ignore the original blessing. Goodness without sin and sin without goodness both prevent us from receiving God's grace. To come to an authentic understanding of ourselves and fulfill our longings, we must hold in full tension both original blessing and original alienation. Only in the tension of these two realities will we be in the place to recognize the path to redemptive transformation.

By returning to our origins, we can find meaning and discover a pattern of living that fulfills our destiny.

✥ Reflection and Discussion ✥

Find a quiet place to listen and reflect. You might want to grab a journal or enlist a good friend and explore these questions:

- When did you first become aware of your spiritual yearnings?
- How does your view of your origin (evolution or creation or other) influence your spirituality?
- How does being created in the image of God shape your view of God? of yourself and others? of your spirituality and religion?
- What do you most identify with: original blessing or original alienation? How does this affect your desire and ability to be spiritual, to pursue God?

14

AWAKENING TO
OUR DESTINY

My purpose is to give life in all its fullness.
—*Jesus of Nazareth, John 10:10*

Deep within us, our hearts yearn to be restored, and re-story-ed, to experience again the fullness and joy of our original blessing—to enjoy our sacred standing as image bearers of God and cocreators with him. God placed these deep desires within our hearts as a living invitation to return to him. They evidence our humanity. They define us, shape us, and invite us to move back to center. However, we must choose.

In his love, God created us with both the freedom to love and the freedom *not* to love. Also, in his love, he offered a way back to experiencing true relationship. The first chapter of the letter to the Ephesians gives a look into God's timeline and motives: "Long before he laid down earth's foundations, he had us in mind, had settled on us as the focus of his love, to be made whole and holy by his love. Long, long ago he decided to adopt us into his family through Jesus Christ. (What pleasure he took in planning this!) He wanted us to enter into the celebration of his lavish gift-giving by the hand of his beloved Son. . . . It's in Christ that we find out who we are and what we are living for. Long before we first heard of Christ and got our hopes up, he had his eye on us, had designs on us for glorious living" (Ephesians 1:4–6, 11, *The Message*).

We've come to see that God's plan to restore humanity to the place of original blessing is not remedial, but rather primal. We each have been chosen, before and beyond the foundations of the world! In the original blessing, God created us for communion with himself but also gave us the capacity to rebel, to declare our independence from him. And so we have. And all creation bears the consequences. But through Jesus, God provides a way to be restored to our original design.

Celtic streams of spirituality paint a picture of grace as enabling our original nature to come forth from darkness into the fullness and the freedom of the Light. Redemption is restoring the work of God's original creation. This grace is not regarded as *planting* something new in essentially bad soil, but rather *releasing* the goodness that is in us, albeit in bondage to evil. Literally, redemption means purchasing back something that was lost, through the payment of a ransom. This is not some rational formula, nor merely a ticket to heaven; nor is it some impersonal union with the universe. We actually become a new creation in Christ. By his redemption, God sets us free from our bondage to sin and spiritual death, to be who we were originally designed to be.

Original Atonement: Redemption

By definition, religions provide rituals and procedures for attaining favor with God, enlightenment, salvation, and all other manner of "spiritual" gifts. But the good news of Jesus is we no longer need religion. We can be reconciled to God directly through Jesus as mediator. The word *atonement* can be broken into three parts, expressing this truth in simple but profound terms: "at-one-ment." Through God's atoning grace and forgiveness in Jesus, we are reinstated to a relationship of being at one with God, in spite of our sins (acts) and our sin (nature). The reconciliation of God and humans is brought about by the redemptive life, death, and resurrection of Jesus, not by human effort.[1] The cross nullifies all religion and all our efforts—whether righteous or unrighteous. Atonement is the act by which God restores a relationship of harmony and unity between himself and human beings.

Sadhu Sundar Singh illustrates well the sacrificial work of Christ with a story:

> Once a young man fell over a cliff. By the time he was rescued he had lost so much blood that he was almost dead. His father rushed him to a doctor, but the doctor said, "He will certainly die, unless someone can be found who is willing to provide enough blood for a massive transfusion." Now the father's heart overflowed with such love for his son that he offered his own blood, though he knew it would cost him his own life. So by the sacrificial love of his father, the young man was given new life. We, too, have fallen headlong from the mountain of righteousness and lie broken and wounded by sin, with our life fast ebbing away. But if we turn to the Master, he freely gives us his spiritual blood so that we might be saved from death and regain life. Indeed, he came to us for this very purpose.[2]

Since the Fall, God has been seeking to redeem us and reconcile us to himself. These themes can be seen like a scarlet thread from the beginning to the end of the Bible. Reconciliation is a passion for God.[3] This passion is embodied in his son, Jesus, who is called the last Adam—the Lifegiver. Just as God breathed into the womb of the earth to bring life to the first Adam, Jesus was conceived by God in the womb of a young Jewish girl. Whereas the first Adam left the Garden of Genesis in separation from God, the Garden of Gethsemane was where Jesus embraced his redemptive work that made our restoration possible. Whereas spiritual death was introduced through the first Adam, the second Adam brings spiritual life.

> The longest journey is the journey inwards of him who has chosen his destiny, who has started upon his quest for the source of his being.
>
> —Dag Hammarskjöld (1905-1961), Nobel laureate, former secretary-general of the United Nations

By his holiness and grace, God extends a complete pardon for our sins—past, present, and future. Now we live with the reality that we are dead to sin and separation, but alive to God in Christ Jesus. We are "brand new," and we are in the process of being restored to our original design.[4]

Reconciliation is the central message of the New Testament. It's all about healing relationships with God, one another, and the world. To a gathering of Jesus followers in first-century Corinth, the apostle Paul explains: "A new life has begun! All this newness of life is from God, who brought us back to himself through what Christ did. And God has given us the task of reconciling people to him. For God was in Christ, reconciling the world to himself, no longer counting people's sins against them. This is the wonderful message he has given us to tell others. We are Christ's ambassadors, and God is using us to speak to you" (II Corinthians 5:17–20).

Redemption activates the restorying of our identity in loving union with God. But then what?

Invited to Be Fully Alive

Our hearts long to be reconciled with God, to be one with him. This is the *why* of our spirituality. Though we may remain in darkness, we are being called back to the Light. The yearning is never going away. Born in spiritual rebellion, we have an open invitation to be reborn, to return to the original blessing given to our most ancient ancestors. All humanity is graced by design and desire to be holy and whole—to be one with God.[5]

Now, the choice before each person in every age is whether to remain living in alienation or receive the invitation to return and enjoy the original blessing again. The Latin root of *invite* is derived from *vita* (life). The very word *invitation* itself indicates a summons to life and fulfillment of our heart's desires. What could be more (super)natural? The promise is clear: "But to all who believed him and accepted him, he gave the right to become children of God. They are reborn! This is not a physical birth resulting from human passion or plan—this rebirth comes from God" (John 1:12–13). Jesus is God's invitation to be restored to a state of original blessing.

To *receive* love often calls for greater responsibility than trying to *earn* love. If we can expect to earn love, then love is not a gift; it is payment for what we earned. Just as people give love freely to their children, whether they deserve it or not, so God freely loves us. Maybe this is what Augustine meant when he said, "Love God and do as you please." As our friend Hseih Sun said, "God is often more offended by our rejecting his grace than he is by our sin." If Christ is in me and I am in Christ, there is no reason to strive. Who am I to think that my striving could "do" a work for God, or earn his favor?

A great illustration of God's love and restoration comes from the parable of the prodigal son, one of the best-known stories told by Jesus. The story begins with two sons; the younger requests his inheritance while his dad is still alive (which was the equivalent of wishing your father dead). He leaves home and squanders his fortune on wild living while the older brother remains home, working faithfully for his father. The wayward son ends up broke, homeless, and with nothing to eat but the mush he was feeding the pigs. He begins to feel the shame and separation. No doubt there is a good deal of self-pity mixed with his remorse. However, his change of heart leads him to return to his father's house, hoping for a servant's job. When he does, his father, who has been waiting for this moment for a long time, throws aside all dignity, runs down the road to meet him, and throws a party to celebrate his return.

> People say that what we're all seeking is a meaning for life. I don't think that's what we're really seeking. I think that what we're really seeking is an experience of being alive, so that our life experiences on the purely physical plane will have resonances within our innermost being and reality, so that we actually feel the rapture of being alive.
>
> —Joseph Campbell (1904-1987), mythologist and author, *The Power of Myth*

Notice that the returning prodigal never earned his father's love by anything he did—by coming back or by repenting. Love had never been absent from his father's heart, only he could not express it with his son far away in a foreign country. So it is with us. We do not earn God's forgiveness and love through repentance. Repentance is the way we open our hearts to *receive*: "In repenting of sin we are not turning away in order to be someone else, but re-turning to our true selves, made in the loveliness and goodness of the image of God."[6]

The apostle Paul was speaking with religious and philosophical leaders when he explained God's original plan for restoration of all peoples: "His purpose in all of this was that the nations should seek after God and perhaps feel their way toward him and find him—though he is not far from any one of us. For in him we live and move and exist. As one of your own poets says, 'We are his offspring.' And since this is true, we shouldn't think of God as an idol designed by craftsmen from gold or silver or stone" (Acts 17:27–30).

Here is the good news for all people in every culture and every generation: the identity we originally bore we may experience again. We see here several truths that are significant, whether or not we are conscious of their reality:

- We are all the offspring of God.
- God desires all peoples to seek after him and find him.
- God is not far off, but rather all around us.
- God is not created in our image as an idol formed by the art and imagination of mortals. Instead, we are created in his image.
- God invites us to be restored to him as expressed in his original blessing.

Jesus removes all barriers so we can experience again the blessing. Within the garden of intimacy with God, Adam and Eve chose to turn away. Now, outside the garden, we are given the choice again.

But this time it's a choice to turn back to God—back to the place of his original design and desire.

Good News

> The glory of God is man fully alive!
> —*Saint Irenaeus of Lyons* (*c. 130–202* A.D.)

To our every spiritual and relational yearning, Jesus is indeed the gospel—the essence of good news. To the alienated, the gospel brings reconciliation. To those who are powerless to change, the gospel is transformational. To those who are without hope, Jesus brings the promise of life and living abundantly. To the lonely, the gospel provides the security of loving community. To those searching for meaning, the gospel gives a new identity and purpose for living. To those who are wondering why they are spiritual, the gospel reveals God's original design, and his divine plan. To those left cynical, or disenchanted with religious institutions, the answer is, as the bumper sticker says: "After religion, try Jesus." The gospel is not what we did or can do, but what Jesus did for us. The promises of Jesus are fulfilled in the presence of Jesus.

Jesus' resurrection brought victory over darkness and death, releasing again the image of God in us. Later, in his letter to the Jesus followers in Rome, Paul writes, "So you should not be like cowering, fearful slaves. You should behave instead like God's very own children, adopted into his family—calling him 'Father, dear Father.' For his Holy Spirit speaks to us deep in our hearts and tells us that we are God's children."[7] We can experience both the intimacy and magnitude (imminence and transcendence) of God through his life *in* us.

In short, the gospel brings faith, hope, and love. These are not emotional conveniences to make our lives happy, but transformational and eternal realities that are grounded in the person of Jesus Christ. Through faith in Jesus we experience the transforming power of Jesus in our lives. Faith answers both primary longings: to believe (spiritual) and to belong (social). The gospel guarantees a present and future hope in the face of an uncertain, even dark, horizon. It also states a solid hope for an ultimate ecological restoration in the "New Heavens and New Earth," as prophesied by the prophet Isaiah (65:17; 66:22) and the apostle John (in Revelation 21:1–5).

This points to the reality of God's design before time, embedded in creation, actively working today, and the present hope that God's original design will be completed in the future: "All creation is waiting eagerly for that future day when God will reveal who his children really are. Against its will, everything on earth was subjected to God's curse. All creation anticipates the day when it will join God's children in glorious freedom from death and decay" (Romans 8:19–22).

Finally, the gospel is the beginning of experiencing genuine love, a radically different kind of love (*agape*) from the oftentimes self-serving "love" of the world. Love answers the cry for belonging: "There are three things that will endure—faith, hope, and love— and the greatest of these is love" (I Corinthians 13:13).

⬥ Reflection and Discussion ⬥

Find a place where you can quiet your mind, breathe deeply, and allow yourself to feel God's presence. Read the following prayer. If it resonates with you, consider using this prayer to express your heart to Jesus.

Jesus,
    Thank you for loving me. I recognize I have been living in spiritual darkness and separation from you. I have tried religion and my own ways and have found it tiring and impossible.
    I believe you came to bring new life. You died on a cross and you rose again to life.

I now turn to you. I give myself to you—my body, mind, and spirit. Forgive me for my every thought and action that has furthered my separation from you and others around me.

I give you the place in my heart that you really deserve. I invite you, Jesus, to come and live your life in me and through me!

Thank you for hearing my prayer and for sending me your Holy Spirit.

Amen!

15

BACKSLIDING TO ENLIGHTENMENT

To reach something good it is very useful to have
gone astray, and thus acquire experience.
—*St. Teresa of Avila (1515–1582)*

It's a beautiful winter day in Seattle. The cold, clear skies in January make for a breathtaking ferry ride from Bainbridge Island to the city, with Mount Baker to the north, the Olympic Mountains to the west, and Mount Rainier to the south. I'm en route to facilitate a community task force of local business owners, youth activists, social services, and the police department with a common vision for serving the homeless youth of Capitol Hill. I take the bus to the edge of downtown, to the last bus stop in the ride-free zone. I choose to walk the remaining blocks to conserve my cash. It's now been over ten months with no steady income since we shut down our company. I am starting to feel the effects. I begin to see the homeless.

No vanilla mocha today. $1.25 buys me a drip coffee; that's the price of bus fare. I take a seat at a cold granite table in the back, with a view of a guy removing beans from the roaster. The air is warm with the rich smell of fresh-roasted Nicaraguan beans.

I have an hour before my meeting, but instead of reviewing my notes my mind wanders as I thaw my hands around my coffee cup. I imagine myself as a fresh-picked coffee bean from California shipped to the Northwest to be roasted. I was a lot greener than I thought! The last three years have yielded a long, dark roast. I realize that I've never felt so fulfilled and at the same time so fruitless—so free and yet so powerless. Maybe this is similar to what the apostle Paul was feeling when he wrote on two separate occasions he was being poured out like a "drink offering."[1]

Shaken Back to Life

Sometimes we have to travel to the edge of ourselves to find our center.
—*Buck Ghosthorse, Lakota Sioux elder*

My first few years in the Pacific Northwest were the most grueling of my life. They were also the most rejuvenating. I knew the transition from professional ministry in Southern California to launching a new technology company in Seattle would be huge. I just didn't realize how revolutionary it would be. Each year seemed to bring the pain and joy of an entire decade. We moved to simplify our lives, and in many ways it has been simpler. I had no idea how much spiritual, emotional, and intellectual baggage weighed me down and affected my life, my marriage, and our children.

Life can only be understood backwards; but it must be lived forwards.
−Søren Kierkegaard (1813-1855), Danish philosopher, *Writings*

When Jennifer and I left the ministry, some friends and family thought we were backsliding (that's a derogatory Christian subculture term used to label people who seem to be dropping out or moving backward in their faith). In many ways, they were right. Our goal, though, was not to move away from Christianity, but to move more freely with Jesus. It reminds me of when we were married fifteen years ago. My intent was not to leave my father and mother but to cleave to my wife—I needed to leave before I could cleave. The value of backsliding is determined by what you're sliding back to. Our journey led us to let go of everything that weighed us down so we could move more freely with the Spirit.

We know now that if we want to walk in freedom we must be set free of both the religious structures outside of us *and* the religious spirit within us. Dietrich Bonhoeffer explained this well in his book *Christ the Center:* "It is the structures of religion that must go, not the proper consideration of Christ."[2] And as we have seen, religious structures can take many shapes: external and internal, Eastern and Western, formal and informal, contemporary and traditional.

Paul's warning to the young believers at Corinth two thousand years ago is as fitting today as it was then. He writes, "I fear that somehow you will be led away from your pure and simple devotion to Christ, just as Eve was deceived by the serpent" (II Corinthians 11:3). Here, the language of purity doesn't mean perfection but rather "unmixed," as is twenty-four-karat gold. We've come to realize that such simplicity is beyond our own good intentions and spiritual practices. It's something only the Creator can do to restore us to his original design. Just as precious metal is refined through fire, so we are purified through the Refiner's fire. And the process doesn't always feel so good.

God loves us too much to let us continue in our current state of being, so he strips us down to the bare essentials. Jesus tells us we will all be stripped down for one reason or another: "My Father is the gardener. He cuts off every branch that doesn't produce fruit, and he prunes the branches that do bear fruit so they will produce even more" (John 15:1–2). If we have no deep feelings of inadequacy and weakness, how would we need or depend on God? We wouldn't. We'd be doing stuff *for* him, not with him. If we had no deep longings for spiritual connection with God, why would we move toward him in the first place?

There have been seasons over the last few years where I felt as though all life support had been stripped away—no position, no income, nothing external that gave me meaning. But it was in the stripping that I began to realize who I was. I had to be stripped of what the New Testament calls "every weight that slows us down, especially the sin that so easily hinders our progress" (Hebrews 12:1). In a world infatuated with style, all of us are constantly tempted to clothe ourselves with stuff that will keep people from knowing how empty we really are. Like athletes at the ancient Greek games, we must strip down to our nakedness. Only as we release our hands from all we've clutched dear are we ready to receive the fullness of our inheritance as children of God. I just wasn't expecting the process to hurt so much. It seemed as though God was taking me up on my desires and the many times I prayed, "More of you and less of me."

From our experience, we can tell you: be prepared. When we commit to following Jesus, it's just a matter of time until God calls us into a season of suffering and humility and puts on us such demands of obedience that we will depart from the ways of other good Christians. He seems to let other good people do things that he will not let us do.

When we follow the Way of Jesus, we give God permission to complete the work he has begun. As we encounter the loving discipline of God, we can choose to submit or to remove ourselves. Even if we try to remove ourselves, we may find that we can't because God is holding us to our heart's desire. He won't let us out of the battle because he holds us to the decision we made during peacetime. God's faithfulness is stronger than our faithlessness.

After we gave up everything we knew, we prayed: "Is there anything else that you want?" There have been many times when we let go of everything, only to experience the agony of more stripping. But we have learned, and are still learning, patience. Initially Jennifer and I looked at the stripping as circumstances gone awry, or questioned ourselves: "What did we do wrong?" or "What more are we to do?"

But we are learning that it is in the loving discipline of God that we see his hand pruning all excesses to create more fruit in and through our lives.

One season of pruning took place when we were lacking stable income. We were living month to month, when the authorities notified us that a financial investment we made the year before was exposed as a fraud (the CEO is now in a federal penitentiary). We cried out to God as we realized the staggering implications this could potentially have for our future. We could lose our home. We went months not knowing how we would pay the bills or buy food. Yet again, God showed his grace during that dark period by providing for us in miraculous ways: small consulting gigs, an unexpected IRS refund, bags of groceries appearing on our porch, anonymous cashier's checks in our mailbox.

> All praise to the God and Father of our Lord Jesus Christ. He is the source of every mercy and the God who comforts us. He comforts us in all our troubles so that we can comfort others. When others are troubled, we will be able to give them the same comfort God has given us. You can be sure that the more we suffer for Christ, the more God will shower us with his comfort through Christ.
>
> —II Corinthians 1:3-5

We also grew closer as a family. We were especially strengthened by the response of our daughter Lauren, who was nine at the time, "It's going to be OK—God will take care of us." Her faith encouraged Jennifer and me toward greater trust in God for our finances. It has released us from the mind-set that we honor God and do good with "our" money, moving us to the conviction that we belong to God and everything we have belongs to him. We are his stewards.

In the wake of financial uncertainty, the season turned more discouraging when some friends walked away from us. This came about suddenly and without any explanation. It was during an especially vulnerable time for us as a family. It felt as if we were climbing a rock face and the ones who were belaying us just got up and left us clinging on the side of the mountain with no protection. It was a painfully slow and lonely descent to safety. But in the passing of time, we realized that God had a greater plan. He used this circumstance to remove relationships from our lives and bring us into a deeper dependence upon him. Then he surprised us by blessing us with many new friends who were also walking in the Way of Jesus.

Even if we feel alone in this reduction process, we're not. Jesus is with us and he brings us companions in our journey at just the right time.

During a three-year period, everything we valued was tested: our finances, marriage, friendships, family relations, and community. We've come to believe that it's only when we have lost everything that we are truly free to discover our core selves and our spiritual identity. The author of Hebrews describes this phase as a shaking:

> His voice that time [when God spoke from heaven in giving Moses the Ten Commandments] shook the earth to its foundation; this time—he's told us this quite plainly—he'll also rock the heavens: "One last shaking, from top to bottom, stem to stern." The phrase "one last shaking" means a thorough house cleaning. Getting rid of all the historical and religious junk so that the unshakable essentials stand clear and uncluttered. Do you see what we've got? An unshakable kingdom! And do you see how thankful we must be? Not only thankful, but brimming with worship, deeply reverent before God. For God is not an indifferent bystander. He's actively cleaning house, torching all that needs to burn, and he won't quit until it's all cleansed. God himself is Fire! [Hebrews 12:26–29, *The Message*].

No discipline is enjoyable while it is happening–it is painful! But afterward there will be a quiet harvest of right living for those who are trained in this way. So take a new grip with your tired hands and stand firm on your shaky legs.

–New Testament Letter to the Hebrews (12:11-13)

Our journey has stripped us of what we thought we needed in order to live a life of one deeply satisfied in Jesus. But it was the fallacy that Jesus wanted our commitment to him that has crumbled. He simply wants us. We've learned to live again, though not the way we once lived. It's as if Jesus is saying, "You've invited me into your heart; now I'm inviting you into mine. Just remain in my loving presence . . . rest in me and see what I will do." Only when we die to the things of this world will we be able to see through the things of this world.

Though God is doing the real work, we also have a role. We must submit and hold still and stop squirming so he can complete his work. It's really a matter of vulnerable love, ruthless trust, and raw endurance. In the midst of such an agonizing process, the depth of pain is matched by his gracious love and healing power. As our friend Dave said, "God brings us to the end of our human resources, and then he releases his." God insists that our spiritual life originate not from our own strength but from our union with him, so the times of isolation and stripping become instruments for God to work in us our new identity and deeper faith in him.

Embracing the Wellspring of Life

If you have not chosen the Kingdom of God, it
will make in the end no difference what you
have chosen instead. We shall have missed the
end for which we are formed and rejected the only
thing that satisfies. Does it matter to a man dying
in the desert by which choice of route he missed
the only well?

—C. S. Lewis (1898–1963),
Irish-born author, The Weight of Glory

One afternoon, Erik, my psychiatrist friend, asked me, "Who is Jesus to you? Is he a spiritual teacher who lived in the past? Is he 'out there' in the cosmos? Or is he somehow personal for you?"

I paused before answering, "Yes."

When Erik asked me to explain more about my answer, I told him that I didn't mean it in the theological sense, but in the experiential sense. Since I've become a refugee from religion, I've been struggling to understand *and* experience Jesus without any props or artificial life support. I've come to see how our beliefs are shaped by social or religious expectations. That is not necessarily bad, but it can be difficult to discern between what I've been told to believe and what I know in the core of my being I do believe. It is easy to accept a surface level of understanding, and never go to the depths. But shallow beliefs often lead to behavioral conformity without holistic transformation.

When Erik asked, "Who is Jesus to you?" I told him he echoed the words of Jesus when he asked his closest followers, "Who do people say I am?" His disciples replied, "Some say John the Baptist; others say Elijah; and still others, one of the prophets." But it really doesn't matter what other people say or think, so Jesus went deeper: "But what about you?" he asked. "Who do you say I am?" Peter then answered, "You are the Christ."[3]

Jesus looks beyond our proclamation to our heart attitude. When the religious leaders of the day confronted Jesus and his disciples for not conforming to religious customs, Jesus replied by quoting from the Hebrew prophet: "You hypocrites! Isaiah was prophesying about you when he said, 'These people honor me with their lips, but their hearts are far away. Their worship is a farce, for they replace God's commands with their own man-made teachings.' For you ignore God's specific laws and substitute your own traditions" (Mark 7:6–8).

In my earlier life as a church leader, I was becoming like those who have correct theological understanding and righteous ethics but are not experiencing communion with God. It reminds me of what our good friend James of Santa Cruz, California, said when he was getting annoyed with some Christians for trying to make a case for the existence of God: "Maybe the reason so much emphasis is on 'proving God' through rational means is that many 'Christians' are missing the experience of God *in* their lives." This is why we can be theologically correct but at the same time spiritually bankrupt.

The Bible does not exist to prove the existence of God. In fact, nowhere in the Bible does it tell us to prove God's existence to others. Rather it assumes God's existence and tells the story of the human relationship with God. We experience the reality of Jesus as we submit to him without reservation. Theological correctness does not bring spiritual fulfillment; nor does it bring right living. Spiritual fulfillment comes only from the Spirit working in us, not from how hard we work at getting it.

We've come to see that incomplete understanding can be just as crippling as complete deception. We can know *about* the indwelling Jesus, and still not experience him. This is why so many faithful churchgoers remain unchanged, and why the many spiritually curious who visit church for the first time don't return. Our society has been inoculated with Jesus; we've had just enough exposure to keep us immune from the truth that will set us free. We hear such statements as "I've tried Christianity" or "I'm a Christian," but it's clear the people speaking have never had a vital encounter with the risen Jesus. They speak of their issues with the church and Christianity; they may even pose a heavy theological question, but rarely will they mention the name of Jesus. Our friend Marsha suggests simply asking, "'Tell me about this Jesus. . . .' If they start talking dogma, church, or Christianese, gently interrupt with, 'No . . . tell me about the Jesus you know and experience personally. . . .'"

Though we had many genuine encounters with Jesus in traditional churches, there is more to Jesus than what we were led (even programmed) to believe. Jesus is alive and at work today, as he was when he walked this earth. "Jesus Christ is the same yesterday, today, and forever" (Hebrews 13:8–9). We are now relating to a far more loving and powerful Jesus than we had previously known.

Can we use another lens to look at Jesus? If we look at him through our own tradition, our own needs, our own wounds, we might get a glimpse. However, we will miss his freedom and his fullness because we are looking through the narrow, constricted viewpoint of our selves. The only way to truly see Jesus is for him to reveal himself to us. We can only go so far, but he meets us in our hunger.

Jesus said, "I am leaving you with a gift—peace of mind and heart. And the peace I give isn't like the peace the world gives. So don't be troubled or afraid" (John 14:27). The world is full of ways to gratify our heart longings, but the satisfaction is at best temporary.

Jesus brings eternal fulfillment for both social and spiritual longings. To the Samaritan woman he met at the well, Jesus said, "If you only knew the gift God has for you and who I am, you would ask me, and I would give you living water. . . . People soon become thirsty again after drinking this water. But the water I give them takes away thirst altogether. It becomes a perpetual spring within them, giving them eternal life" (John 4:10–14).

A few days later, Jesus was speaking to a large crowd of people gathered to celebrate the last day of the feast of tabernacles: "If you are thirsty, come to me! If you believe in me, come and drink! For the Scriptures declare that rivers of living water will flow out from within." When he said "living water," he was speaking of the Spirit, who would be given to everyone believing in him (John 7:37–39).

This message is nothing less than radical. The hearers would have been familiar with images of God as the provider of streams of life—but not from within. This stream of life from within had not been experienced because the Holy Spirit had not yet been given. In some versions of the text, we read that the streams would flow out of the belly or heart. These streams of ever-flowing fountains will be constant and life-giving. As we are centered in Christ, his life will flow through us and bring life to others. The Kingdom of God is within us: "All who proclaim that Jesus is the Son of God have God living in them, and they live in God" (I John 4:15).

So, as the offspring of God, there is an untapped well within each of us. *Wherever you are, the stream is.* Paul said, "For to me, to live is Christ." He did not say, "To me, to live is to strive to be like Christ or to believe correct doctrine about Christ." He said, "To me, to live *is Christ.*" Paul's understanding of life in Christ would be like Jesus living and walking the earth again, but in another body—in Paul's body. To the Colossian believers, Paul wrote, "When Christ, who is your real life, is revealed to the whole world, you will share in all his glory" (Colossians 3:4). Here, the word *glory* speaks of the radiant beauty of God shining through us. We all come short of that glory, but the indwelling Christ restores the lost glory to our original design.

Paul considered that Jesus was not just a part of his life; Jesus was the only life he had, and the only life he wanted. The only life that is pleasing to God is the life of Jesus lived out in us and through us by faith. We can be confident that we will experience the reality of Jesus at work within us as we seek after him. " 'For I know the plans I have for you,' says the Lord. 'They are plans for good and not for disaster, to give you a future and a hope. In those days when you pray, I will listen. If you look for me in earnest, you will find me when you seek me. I will be found by you,' says the Lord" (Jeremiah 29:11–14).

⟡ Reflection and Discussion ⟡

Take a few moments of quiet to remember a time when you went through a shaking, a crisis, or a dark night of the soul. It could have been relational, spiritual, physical, emotional, or financial. You might wish to journal your thoughts and share them with a trusted friend.

- What was stripped away? What deeper realities held true?
- How did God reveal (or not reveal) himself through this experience?
- Who walked with you through this time? Who didn't?
- Meditate on Romans 8:28. What spiritual lessons did you learn?

16

CHRIST-CENTERED
(RE)INCARNATION

I tell you the truth, unless a kernel of wheat falls to
the ground and dies, it remains only a single seed.
But if it dies, it produces many seeds.
—*Jesus of Nazareth, John 12:24*

Just as in the seasons of nature, where plants must die back in winter
before they can bloom in the spring, the pilgrim's way often requires
walking through dark valleys before enjoying the mountain views. In
the course of our journey we've grown to appreciate the ebb and flow
of life. It's the most challenging times that move us to strengthen our
faith in the one who orders all the seasons and surprises of life.

In John 12, Jesus reminds us that there is no harvest without
death. A seed of wheat can be preserved for many years as long as it
is not exposed to moisture and heat. However, when the seed is
planted in the ground and watered, the nutrients in the seed rot to
become the initial "soil" for the life-germ to grow into a new plant
that will reproduce more seeds.

In the same way, our spiritual life in Jesus begins with death. We
cannot embody the life of Jesus in our lives until we die to ourselves:
our rights, our ambitions, our control—even our hopes. But we are
not regenerated through some sort of karmic rebirth. We do not
have to wait until we die to experience our next life. We can be
born again now.

We realize "born again" has become a dubious term in some cir-
cles. But we use the term to describe the process of receiving new

life in Jesus. Paul explains to the new believers in Galatia, "Christ's life showed me how, and enabled me to do it. I identified myself completely with him. Indeed, I have been crucified with Christ. My ego is no longer central. It is no longer important that I appear righteous before you or have your good opinion, and I am no longer driven to impress God. Christ lives in me. The life you see me living is not 'mine,' but it is lived by faith in the Son of God, who loved me and gave himself for me" (Galatians 2:20, *The Message*). By being born again, we begin to (re)incarnate the life of Jesus; we demonstrate his transforming presence through our lives and into our world.[1] This parallels how Jesus embodied the invisible nature of God when he took on human flesh and blood. And as "the Word became human and lived here on earth among us," so we incarnate the very life of Jesus in our bodies (John 1:14).

> The willingness to be born—and this means the willingness to let go of all "certainties" and illusions—requires courage and faith. Courage to let go of certainties, courage to be different and stand in isolation.
>
> —Erich Fromm (1900-1980), German psychotherapist and author

In the third chapter of John's Gospel, Jesus explains that to experience new and eternal life, we must be born of water *and* reborn of the Spirit. This cannot be understood in a literal human way, as Nicodemus tried. Rebirth is a spiritual mystery, a miracle. As Jesus promised, this life is like no other: "Flesh gives birth to flesh, but the Spirit gives birth to spirit" (John 3:6). As we begin to love and trust Jesus, we begin to be transformed and experience the reality he promised: "If you believe in me, come and drink! For the Scriptures declare that rivers of living water will flow out from within" (John 7:38). This the New Testament declares, and this a disciple trusts.

In anticipating his own rejection and suffering, Jesus confessed: "Now my soul is deeply troubled. Should I pray, 'Father, save me from what lies ahead'? But that is the very reason why I came! Father, bring glory to your name" (John 12:27–28). Even Jesus, the Prince of Peace, Wonderful Counselor, Son of God, and Son of Man, was troubled!

No one can evade the darkness. Our lives have been rich with experiences, but none as transformational as during periods of darkness when we couldn't see any light ahead. As the Psalmist wrote: "Weeping may go on all night, but joy comes with the morning" (Psalm 30:5). We now expect to see light in the darkness, hope in despair, life in death, and rebirth in burial. "The Harrowing," one of our favorite poems by Parker J. Palmer, captures these harsh and hopeful realities:

> The plow has savaged this sweet field
> Misshapen clods of earth kicked up
> Rocks and twisted roots exposed to view
> Last year's growth demolished by the blade.
> I have plowed my life this way
> Turned over a whole history
> Looking for the roots of what went wrong
> Until my face is ravaged, furrowed, scarred.
> Enough. The job is done.
> Whatever's been uprooted, let it be
> Seedbed for the growing that's to come.
> I plowed to unearth last year's reasons—
> The farmer plows to plant a greening season.

But why burial? We resist the thought of it, but it is necessary, as Jennifer found out one spring morning when she started to plant our garden. She spread the seed packets out on the porch as she planned the layout of the garden. She interrupted her project to make lunch inside. When Jennifer came back, she was surprised to find the crows opening the packets and eating the seeds! They were being eaten, because they had not been buried. Just as seeds must be buried to let their tender shoots sprout, so we must submit to a burial process to be reborn.

There were times during our harrowing and burial season that we tried to push away the dirt, saying, "No! No!" But we eventually learned to submit to the burial process. It took nearly two years to fully appreciate the deep work that God was doing within us while we were covered in the chilling soil of circumstances. We just couldn't see, discern, or understand it at the time. But we've come to realize that no matter how dark our season of soul, God is still at work within us. While our lives are buried in Christ, miraculous things are going on. A miracle is being activated. The God of light penetrates the darkness and does a work within our darkness that we cannot see, a transformation, a metamorphosis.

> Sitting down to brood over our sorrows, the darkness deepens about us and creeps into our heart, and our strength changes to weakness. But, if we turn away from the gloom, and take up the tasks and duties to which God calls us, the light will come again and we shall grow stronger.
>
> –J. R. Miller, *Streams in the Desert*

As much as a part of us screams "No more! I want to get out!" when we're confronted with pain or darkness, we know that we cannot accept God's love and yet reject his discipline. After all Jesus has brought us through, after tasting his saving presence, after receiving his blessings of life and family, are we now going to abandon him because this change process doesn't feel good? Or is costing too much? Or is lonely at times? Certainly not! Life is not easy, but turning our back on Jesus would be literal hell on earth, the place of separation from God.

God's power thrives in the midst of our weakness. Only to the degree that our own power is dismantled will we experience the power of the Holy Spirit. As John the Baptist confessed, "I must decrease that he may increase." It's a matter of making room for someone else to be in charge. Likewise, Jesus told Paul, "My gracious favor is all you need. My power works best in your weakness" (II Corinthians 12:9).

The Chrysalis

All those who believe this are reborn!—not a
physical rebirth resulting from human passion or
plan but from the will of God.
                —*John, the disciple of Jesus, John 1:13*

The Monarch butterfly chrysalis is one of nature's most beautiful
metaphors for our transformation in Christ. A Monarch caterpillar
has no idea what's going on before it begins to form the jade green
shell that will house its rebirth. During the process of metamorphosis, the caterpillar loses nearly half of its weight and is completely transformed—the muscles, digestive system, heart, even the
nervous system are totally rebuilt. It's like sending a Volkswagen
Beetle into the shop for a week and then seeing it come out as a
Leer jet.

After struggling free of the chrysalis, the Monarch immediately
begins to inflate its wings with a reservoir of blood contained in its
swollen abdomen. As the wings inflate, the body of the butterfly
reduces to normal proportions. Once the wings have fully inflated,
the insect expels any excess fluid and rests, waiting for its wings to
dry and harden before taking its first flight.

In much the same way, following Jesus awakens in us a new
understanding of who we are and where we are going. The dark and
lonely season we believed we were experiencing has turned out, in
actuality, to be the chrysalis. Before we entered it, we were very busy
California caterpillars, crunching and munching and doing good in
one form or another. When we moved to the Northwest, we
entered a chrysalis period in which we began to transform in the
quiet darkness. We emerge only as we surrender our lives to Jesus
and the work of his Spirit within us.

In Christ, we undergo a metamorphosis, literally a changing of
form. By entering the caves of our heart, we encountered God and
our own selves. God used the dark period to strip us of our fears, so

we could rise from the darkness and live again, as he did. Have you ever felt you were in a thick forest with neither map nor trail? It is often in the darkness that the call comes.

In the Gospel accounts of Lazarus, Jesus arrives at the grave of his close friend who has been dead and buried four days. With both compassion and authority, Jesus calls in a loud voice, "Lazarus, come out!" Bound in his grave clothes, Lazarus staggers out of the tomb. Jesus tells his family to unwrap him and let him go. As religious refugees, Jennifer and I felt as though we were bound. We needed to be set free of our old ways. Jesus wants to liberate us from the container of our previous experiences and immerse us into a deeper experience of his love and power.

But it is important to let Jesus do the liberating. Suppose a child watches a Monarch butterfly struggle to force its body through the little hole of the chrysalis. What if it appears that the butterfly has gotten as far as it can and can go no further? Wanting to help, the child takes a pair of scissors and snips off the remaining bit of the cocoon. The butterfly then emerges easily. But it can never take flight. Instead, it spends the rest of its short life crawling around with a swollen body and shriveled wings. Though well-intentioned, the child doesn't understand that the restricting cocoon and the struggle required for the butterfly to get through the tiny opening is nature's way of forcing fluid from the bloated body of the butterfly into its wings.

In the middle of the journey of our life, I came to myself within a dark wood where the straight way was lost.

—Dante Alighieri (1265-1321), Florentine poet, *The Divine Comedy*

Sometimes a cocoon of struggles is exactly what we need. If we were allowed to go through our life without any obstacles, it would cripple us spiritually. We would not be as strong as what we could be. We could never fly. The way to fly in the long run requires pushing through in the short run. There are no shortcuts to maturity.

There are many times when we can go neither forward nor back. At such times, moving forward is outwardly impossible other than through the way of faith, through casting into God's hands all our hopes and dreams, and even our very will to live. Meister Eckhart calls this the *wayless way*, where the children of God lose themselves and, at the same time, find themselves.

Jennifer and I now see the value of the last few years. Even as we have lost many of our external securities and identifications, we have come to realize in a deeper way the richness of life in Jesus and the value of our marriage, children, and the friends we journey with. We know, however, that this is just the beginning. Through this process of loving discipline, God is purging and purifying us. This is for our benefit, to restore us to fulfill what he has created us for. There is no room for self-reliance or self-effort in *any* area. We are powerless. We need God. We are desperately dependent on the Holy Spirit not only for our calling but our very life. As Malcolm Muggeridge writes in *The End of Christendom*:

> It is precisely when every earthly hope has been explored and found wanting, when every possibility of help from earthly sources has been sought and is not forthcoming, when every recourse this world offers, moral as well as material, has been drawn on and expended with no effect, when in the shivering cold every log has been thrown on the fire, and in the gathering darkness every glimmer of light has finally flickered out—it is then that Christ's hand reaches out, sure and firm, that Christ's words bring their inexpressible comfort, that his light shines brightest, abolishing the darkness for ever.[2]

Reflection and Discussion

God loves us too much to leave us the way we are. Sometimes he uses difficult times to strip us back to what is real. Take a few minutes to reflect on your spiritual journey.

- Reflect on Paul's struggle with Jesus in II Corinthians 12:8–10. How can you relate to what Paul is saying?

- Read again the poem "The Harrowing." How can an uproot-ing (or a chrysalis experience) in your life be used by the Holy Spirit to prepare you for new opportunities?
- Give thanks for the transforming work of Jesus in your life. See how your attitude changes about current or past difficult situations when you respond with gratefulness.

Part Four

ENLIGHTENMENT

I pray that your hearts will be flooded with light
so that you can understand the wonderful future
he has promised to those he called. I want you to
realize what a rich and glorious inheritance he has
given to his people. I pray that you will begin to
understand the incredible greatness of his power for
us who believe him. This is the same mighty power
that raised Christ from the dead and seated him
in the place of honor at God's right hand in the
heavenly realms. Now he is far above any ruler or
authority or power or leader or anything else in this
world or in the world to come. And God has put all
things under the authority of Christ, and he gave
him this authority for the benefit of the church.
And the church is his body; it is filled by Christ,
who fills everything everywhere with his presence.

—*Ephesians 1:18–23*

17

FINDING OUR WAY
BEYOND RELIGION

For I will pour water on the thirsty land,
and streams on the dry ground;
I will pour out my Spirit on your offspring,
and my blessing on your descendants.
They will spring up like grass in a meadow,
like poplar trees by flowing streams.
—*Isaiah, Hebrew prophet, Isaiah 44:3–4*

I'm not who I used to be. I didn't realize just how much I had changed until I ran into someone from my past on a business trip to California.

It was a sunny afternoon in Pasadena when I walked into a coffee house and ran into my friend Alan. We hadn't seen each other since I had left the Los Angeles area some years ago. We exchanged greetings, and I joined him at his table while keeping a lookout for the person I was scheduled to meet.

After we'd shared news of our families, Alan asked, "Are you still in the ministry?"

"No."

"Are you teaching seminary?"

"No. Not anymore."

"So are you still starting churches?"

"Not really. It depends on what you mean by *church*."

"So what church do you go to?"

"I don't . . . but I am part of the Body of Christ."

With a puzzled smile, he then asked, "So what are you really doing?"

Hesitating, I answered, "I'm simply following Jesus with my wife and children. . . . And we meet regularly with friends."

Alan winced with confusion but remained silent. I felt far away from that place where we first met seven years earlier, while I was still in religion (and deeper than I would have admitted at the time). I now refer to that time as my "previous life," because there seems so little resemblance between how my family and I live now and those twelve years when I was a "religious professional" serving as a local pastor, church planter, seminary professor, and mission consultant. It feels like a lifetime ago.

Finally, he spoke. "Tell me more."

I struggled with how I could condense the past four years into the few moments remaining before my colleague arrived. I finally answered, "In short, I've been (re)incarnated; I have died to my old life. I don't believe in any religion anymore—including Christianity. I no longer need religion with its special buildings, dogmas, programs, clergy, or any other human invention, that displaces genuine spirituality. . . . I have been reborn. And I'm being reborn into a fresh experience of life and spirituality. I've come out of religion and back to God."

His raised eyebrows seemed to question me: "Have you gone heretical or New Age on me?"

"The truth is, I became tired of *doing* religion while *talking* about spirituality. Like the apostle Paul simply said, 'The Kingdom of God is not a matter of talk but of power.' I had enough of my words extending beyond my experience. There had to be more."

I shared with Alan a little of our journey and how Jennifer and I had come to abandon conventional religion. How we reacted against the human-made systems for understanding God that lack genuine community and transforming power. How we had been questioning the institutional paradigm that has defined church for the last fifteen hundred years. And how we were searching within a community for a spirituality that transcended our church experience. We longed for a simpler way of living.

That day in Pasadena, my conversation with Alan was cut short when my friend arrived for our meeting. As I walked away, I turned to Alan and said, "I'm not who I used to be. It's been a five-year metamorphosis. I'm just beginning to discover who I am. I didn't realize I had so much religious baggage. I'm lighter now. Something is coming alive in me again. The Spirit is making a Way through it all. He is making streams in the wastelands. I feel we've only just begun the journey."

One Spirituality, Many Religions

> This is what the Lord says:
> For my people have done two evil things:
> They have forsaken me—
> the fountain of living water.
> And they have dug for themselves
> cracked cisterns that can hold no water at all!
>
> —*Jeremiah* (*c. 600 B.C.*),
> *Hebrew prophet, Jeremiah 2:13*

Once upon a time, the Water of Life, wishing to make itself accessible to all creation, bubbled up in an artesian well and flowed freely without limit. Word spread fast. Soon people were traveling from all over to be nourished and healed by the pure stream. But humankind was not content to leave things in this Edenic state. Gradually some began to fence the well, charge admission, claim ownership of the property around it, and make elaborate laws as to who could come to the well. Soon the well was the property of the powerful and the elite. The water was offended. So it stopped flowing and began to bubble up in another place.

The people who owned the property around the first well were so engrossed in maintaining control that they did not notice that the water had vanished. They continued selling a poor substitute, and few people noticed that the true power was gone. But some dissatisfied people searched with great courage and found the new artesian well. Soon that well was also under the control of the property owners, and the same fate overtook it. The spring took itself to yet another place—and this has been going on throughout recorded history.[1]

As the parable implies, religions have become purveyors and gatekeepers of the divine. Even well-meaning leaders have built sacred edifices and established special rules and rituals to control access to the sacred. Each religion claims itself to be the sole custodian of the water and the pathway to partake of it. Religious institutions mediate the flow, mixture, and distribution of the water.

> If Christ is in me, the hope of Glory, then what in the hell do I need religion for?
>
> –A friend

Religionists dispense just enough to wet the palette, so those who are hooked will keep coming back. Always drinking, but never satisfied.

There is one humanity, one earth, one Creator; but there are many religions. Or as a Sufi master once said, "A river passes through many countries, and each claims it for its own. But there is only one river." The Water of Life runs through all cultures, both Western and Eastern, but the effect of capping the water is the same. Religion tries to convince us that we are broken and only a particular church or creed, liturgy or ritual, priest or shaman can fix us.

The first deception in the Garden was only the beginning of what would become an almost infinite number of ways to promise satisfaction or alleviation of our longings. Many who were once content with mediated spirituality are now leaving their religion to discover their own spirituality. They don't want second-hand religion, but first-hand experience. They search for new wells outside the walls of traditional religion—to the East, to indigenous spiritualities, and even within themselves.

But religion never leads to soul rest.

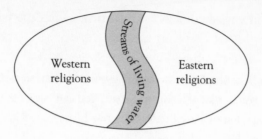

River of Life

Religion is humanity's attempt to reach God. God created humans, and, sadly, we responded by creating religion. Religions are humanly contrived systems for attaining favor with God (or some supreme being or spiritual state) for the purpose of achieving nirvana, salvation, enlightenment, or escaping penalties such as karma. Religion is about *doing* the things we must do to gain God's approval, to make up for past sin. The Way of Jesus is about being *done*—that's what Jesus meant when he said on the cross, "It is finished." At the crucifixion, the barrier inside the Jewish temple was torn from top to bottom, destroying the long-standing separation between the ordinary places for the common people and the Holy of Holies where only specially chosen priests could enter God's presence just once per year. Now it's all changed; "Because of Christ and our faith in him, we can now come fearlessly into God's presence, assured of his glad welcome" (Ephesians 3:12–13). Through his death and resurrection, Jesus has cut through both personal and structural strongholds that hinder our relationship with him.

The Fruits of a Religious Spirit

Nothing is more dangerous to the advancement
of God's kingdom than religion. But this is what
Christianity has become. Do you not know that it
is possible to kill Christ with such Christianity?
—*Christoph Friedrich Blumhardt (1842–1919),*

teacher, The Bruderhof

Jesus gave some wise counsel and warning regarding false spiritual teachers:

> Beware of false prophets who come disguised as harmless sheep, but are really wolves that will tear you apart. You can detect them by the way they act, just as you can identify a tree by its fruit. You don't pick grapes from thorn bushes, or figs from thistles. A healthy tree produces good fruit, and an unhealthy tree produces bad fruit. A good tree can't produce bad fruit, and a bad tree can't produce good fruit. So every tree that does not produce good fruit is chopped down and thrown into the fire. Yes, the way to identify a tree or a person is by the kind of fruit that is produced [Matthew 7:16–20].

There is fruit that may look enticing at first, like the fruit in the Garden of Eden; it looks plump and satisfying but in the end leaves a bitter taste. One of these bitter fruits to watch out for is the fruit of the religious spirit. Like most of Lucifer's deceptions, the religious spirit has two roots: fear and pride. The religious spirit would have us serve God in order to gain his approval, and distract us from our position of having received grace through the sacrifice of Jesus. A counterfeit belief rises up against the truth. Lucifer's most deceptive and deadliest disguise is to come as a servant of righteousness, using truths for the purpose of destruction. The many versions of religion appeal to people's various predispositions and vulnerabilities. Lucifer is quite skillful at quoting Scripture or using the wisdom of the Tree of Knowledge for his purposes. He can accurately point out what is wrong with someone else, but he always does it in such a way that tears down, not offering solutions that build up hope and freedom.

A religious spirit seeks to substitute activity for the power of the Holy Spirit in the believer's life. Soul rest becomes an illusion as religion entices people to try, and then try harder, and try their hardest. Time and again it leaves them tired, frustrated, depressed, and wondering if they're doing enough. Paul warns Timothy to watch out for these ones: "They will act as if they are religious, but they will reject the power that could make them godly. You must stay away from people like that" (II Timothy 3:5).

In religion, both the needs of the community and those of the individual are sacrificed for the "corporate" church. Christian community is reduced to a service, building, or denomination; the mission of the church degrades to institutional growth and expansion. The institution exists for itself—to promote, protect, and perpetuate the institution's dominion, where members are expected to get with the program. Religion has become increasingly intertwined with money to support the buildings and professionals. Without money, the typical church, like most institutions, would eventually crumble.

In the New Testament, Jesus himself confronted religion gone bad. His harshest words were reserved for those who preached a graceless, performance-oriented, try-hard religion. The religious leaders of Jesus' day were offering forgiveness, restoration, and freedom. The catch was that you had to jump through all their hoops. No matter how many you jumped through, they were always able to produce one more. In the Gospel of Matthew, Jesus says, "They crush you with impossible religious demands and never lift a finger to help ease the burden" (23:4). Jesus broke through the walls of religion. No more hoops, no more bondage, and no more religion!

> So Christ has really set us free. Now make sure that you stay free, and don't get tied up again in slavery.
>
> –Paul's Letter to the Galatians (5:1)

Although the fruit of religion may answer some of our spiritual longings, in the end it tends to suppress our spiritual nature and leaves us always yearning for more.[2] As our friend Judy confessed, "Church looks like it should be set up to bring fulfillment—but it doesn't." We come thirsty and can get spoons, buckets, even sprays of water in a church service to get an experience of the divine, but it's a mediated, regulated outpouring of that water. Rarely are we connected directly to the source.

Once we've tasted of the Living Water, we want more. It's hard to settle for regulated disbursement once or twice a week. We want to tap directly into the artesian springs of the Holy Sprit. These springs are beyond both East and West; they flow directly from the source of the Living Water: "Come. Let the thirsty ones come—anyone who wants to. Let them come and drink the water of life without charge" (Revelation 22:17).

✦ Reflection and Discussion ✦

Take a few minutes to explore these questions. You might wish to exchange your thoughts and feelings with a friend.

- What is the difference between religion and spirituality?
- How do we find our way through the noise of so many religions?
- How can we sustain authentic spiritual life and community without slipping into religious trappings or institutional bondage?

18

STREAMS OF
LIVING WATER

On that day living water will flow out from
Jerusalem, half to the eastern sea and half to the
western sea, in summer and in winter.

—*Zechariah (eighth century* B.C.*),*
Hebrew prophet, Zechariah 14:8

One day Jesus and his disciples were on their way to Galilee, when
they passed through Samaria. Tired from the long walk, Jesus sat
beside the well outside the village of Sychar while his disciples went
into town to get some food. Soon a woman came to draw water in
the heat of the afternoon.

Jesus asked her, "Please give me a drink."

With that simple request, Jesus confirmed his political incor-
rectness and chose love over tolerance. As was the pattern of his
life, Jesus transcended the human-made (read: "man"-made) preju-
dices of cultural, religious, political, and sexual differences. The
Samaritans were a racial mix of the former northern tribes of Israel
with the Assyrians and other non-Hebrew peoples. Though Samaritans shared some things in common with the Jews, such as some of
the Scriptures (although the Samaritans had their own unique ver-
sion) and acceptance of spiritual forbears such as Jacob, the Jews
would have nothing to do with them.

Jesus' simple request for water was not so simple. Jesus begins
the conversation by breaking through the major cultural and religious mores, by talking with someone no "good" Jewish man was

supposed to speak to: First, she was a woman. Second, she was a "half-breed" Samaritan. Third, she was considered defiled because she was living in adultery. Also, the fact that it was the middle of the hot afternoon hints at how marginalized this woman likely was in her own community, as the city's women would usually congregate at a well in the cool of the morning. Why else would she be there alone in the midday heat? Jesus' request may have been startling to her, because in those times to give and receive water was a form of covenant representing a degree of friendship.

Jesus began his conversation by affirming what Samaritans and Jews share in common: Jacob's well, a place of worship, prophets sent by God, and the promise of the Messiah. Jesus was not derogatory, but he cut through the long-standing religious differences by declaring "the time is coming and is already here when true worshipers will worship the Father in spirit and in truth. The Father is looking for anyone who will worship him that way. For God is Spirit, so those who worship him must worship in spirit and in truth" (John 4:23–24). True worship will no longer be dependent on or mediated by the religious trappings of special rituals, places, people, dogma, or priests of a particular culture.

If that was not enough, Jesus told her that he is the alternative to religion. He is the Living Water who would satisfy her deepest spiritual thirsts. He invited her into a direct relationship with God himself.

The woman was transfixed by her encounter with Jesus, and she ran to tell anyone who'd listen. So much was she a dramatically changed woman that the people of Sychar were drawn into the message of Jesus. "Then they said to the woman, 'Now we believe because we have heard him ourselves, not just because of what you told us. He is indeed the Savior of the world'" (John 4:42).

What first attracted the people of Sychar to Jesus was the transformation of the woman, but what caused them to believe was their own encounter with Jesus and the promise that the life they received would continue to flow through them.

Let the Rivers Flow

Jennifer and I have experienced this same kind of transformational work in our lives. We liken it to a type of spiritual detoxification whereby we give ourselves the opportunity to let go of anything that is unnecessary or unhealthy. As we trust the Spirit and embark on the process, our unhealed places are forced to the surface. That which we thought (or even hoped) was hidden, rises up to be released and healed. Sometimes messy and painful, but always ultimately healing.

One afternoon over coffee, my good friend Salvatore told me a story from Greek mythology. One scene of the "Twelve Labors of Hercules" reminded Salvatore of the stripping and newfound freedom Jennifer and I had experienced over the past few years.

Hercules traveled all over Greece for twelve years to perform incredible tasks given him by King Eurystheus of Tiryns. Eurystheus was pleased with himself for dreaming up a labor he was sure would humiliate his heroic cousin: Hercules was to clean out the stables of King Augeas. The king possessed vast herds of cattle, which had deposited their manure in such quantity over the years that a thick aroma hung over the entire Peloponnesus. Eurystheus made Hercules' task even harder: he had to clean the stables in a single day. As strong as he was, it would be impossible to clean thirty years' worth of dung within a day.

> The secret of happiness is freedom, and the secret of freedom, courage.
>
> –Thucydides, Greek philosopher (460-400 B.C.)

Hercules noticed two rivers, the Alpheus and the Peneus, flowing near the stables and pasture. As he stood on the bank of one, the answer to his problem flashed through his mind.

Hercules went to King Augeas and, without telling him anything about Eurystheus, said that he would clean out the stables in one day if Augeas would give him a tenth of his fine cattle.

Augeas couldn't believe his ears. "I do not think you can fulfill your boast, but try you may. If you, within a single day, shall do what you have promised, one-tenth of my great flock of cattle shall be yours. But if you fail, your life and fortune will be in my hands."

Hercules brought Augeas's son along to watch. First the hero tore a big opening in the wall of the cattle yard of the stables. Then he made another opening in the wall on the opposite side of the yard. Next, he dug wide trenches for the two rivers. When he released the Alpheus and the Peneus, the rushing torrents swept through the stables, flushing the long-accumulated filth out the hole in the wall on the other side of the yard.

Hercules returned to Augeas with the king's son as witness to report that the stables were cleaned within one day's time.

"You have succeeded by a trick," King Augeas cried out in rage. "The rivers did the work, not you. It was a ruse to take from me my cattle. You will have no reward."

Because Hercules had demanded payment of Augeas, Eurystheus refused to count this as a labor.

As illustrated in this Greek myth, water is a powerful agent with cleansing properties. Likewise in the Bible, Jesus is portrayed as Living Water, and the Spirit of God is compared to water flowing freely from a spring. God will do a mighty work in us if we allow his Spirit to flow through us. The question is, Will the Spirit set the flow? Or will we restrict the flow by our own fears and insecurities or by submitting ourselves to religious controls?

Fruits of Freedom

> Now, the Lord is the Spirit, and wherever the Spirit
> of the Lord is, he gives freedom.
> —II Corinthians 3:17–18

How we live in relation to the Water of Life determines the fruit that is produced from our life, just as the flow of water determines the health of a tree and its fruit. As David writes in the Psalms, "Oh, the joys of those who . . . delight in doing everything the Lord wants. . . . They are like trees planted along the riverbank, bearing fruit each season without fail. Their leaves never wither, and in all they do, they prosper" (Psalm 1:1–3).

Fruit can be enjoyed as the reward of labor, such as the fruit of the vine that produces a fine wine. Where the Spirit is Lord, we experience freedom from fear, guilt, expectations, depression, and anything that robs us from the fullness of Christ. The fruit of freedom is described in Galatians 5:22–23: "But when the Holy Spirit controls our lives, he will produce this kind of fruit in us: love, joy, peace, patience, kindness, goodness, faithfulness, gentleness, and self-control."

If we are not centered in Christ, the wellspring of life, it's easy to grow discouraged and spiritually dry. It reminds us of the story of Peter walking on water. He stepped out of the boat with a childlike faith and enthusiasm but was soon distracted by the storm raging around him. As soon as he took his eyes off Jesus, he began to sink.

As we hold on to Jesus amid distractions, the more we will learn to hear his voice and develop a deeper trust in him. In his book *Ruthless Trust*, Brennan Manning captures the essence of trust that leads to a life of freedom: "The way of trust is a movement into obscurity, into the undefined, into ambiguity, not into some predetermined, clearly delineated plan for the future. . . . The reality of naked trust is the life of a pilgrim who leaves what is nailed down, obvious, and secure, and walks into the unknown without any rational explanation to justify the decision or guarantee the future. Why? Because God has signaled the movement and offered it his presence and his promise."[1]

> We have been called to be fruitful—not successful, not productive, not accomplished.
>
> Success comes from strength, stress, and human effort.
>
> Fruitfulness comes from vulnerability and the admission of our own weakness.
>
> —Henri J. M. Nouwen (1932–1996), Dutch Catholic priest and writer (public address at Yale University)

As we journey in freedom, trusting in the all-sufficiency of Christ, we experience the wise pruning of the Father, and this allows the Holy Spirit to produce his fruit from within us. We see the importance of pruning illustrated in the making of a fine wine. Our family visited a vineyard in South Africa and learned of a wine that requires extreme pruning of the vines. This is done so that all the nutrients from the soil go into the few remaining grapes; when the grapes are pressed and wine is made the result is a more interesting wine with a more complex character. It is the same for us. As we submit to pruning, the Spirit works in our life in such a way that the core of our very character is affected, and so we reap the fruit of freedom.

> *I am the Real Vine and my Father is the Farmer. He cuts off every branch of me that doesn't bear grapes. And every branch that is grape-bearing he prunes back so it will bear even more. You are already pruned back by the message I have spoken. Live in me. Make your home in me just as I do in you. In the same way that a branch can't bear grapes by itself but only by being joined to the vine, you can't bear fruit unless you are joined with me. I am the Vine, you are the branches. When you're joined with me and I with you, the relation is intimate and organic, the harvest is sure to be abundant.*
>
> —John 15:1–5, *The Message*

✥ Reflection and Discussion ✥

Jesus loves you and invites you to love him and experience him. Find a quiet place where you can sit and listen.

- What hinders you from experiencing the fullness of his love and joy? Ask him. Listen.
- Simply confess any hindrances that come to mind. As the Spirit leads you, seek forgiveness, give forgiveness, pray for healing, and receive the love of Jesus.
- Reflect on the labor of Hercules and read the Psalm of David in 139:23–24. How do you need the Spirit to bring cleansing to your life?

19

LIVING INTO BEING

Forget the former things;
do not dwell on the past.
See, I am doing a new thing!
Now it springs up; do you not perceive it?
I am making a way in the desert and streams in
the wasteland.
            —*Isaiah, Hebrew prophet, Isaiah 43:18–19*

One evening as I walked onto the ferry bound for Bainbridge Island, I saw a friend I hadn't seen in several weeks. Hal, a creative media consultant and producer, is of Jewish heritage and describes himself as "Buddhist at heart." When he spotted me, he came right over with his arms open wide and embraced me. We sat together in a booth and started talking. Hal explained he was going home later than usual because he had stopped to get a tune-up from his acupuncturist and guidance from his psychic. "I was delivered from a bad spirit through acupuncture. I feel a lot better. . . . In fact my wife, Sarah, visits another acupuncturist on the Olympic Peninsula who kicks out negative spirits on a regular basis—almost every time she goes in for therapy."

Hal told me he pays his psychic $90 per visit to channel her "intuition" through tarot cards. "It really helps to give me a sense of confidence in moving forward." Hal paused and, with a laugh, said, "The Northwest is sure full of 'extraterrestrials.'"

I just smiled. I wasn't sure if he was referring to himself or the variety of spiritual practitioners he frequents.

As the ferry docked, I offered Hal a ride home, and he accepted. We kept talking as we drove the winding roads on the Island. He said he thought that many people, especially Christians, would not understand and might even freak out at what he did. Knowing that I believe in Jesus, Hal asked, "So what do you think of these practices? Do you believe in them?"

"I don't believe in any practice, but I believe *you*, Hal. I myself have seen the power of the Holy Spirit and have experienced his comfort and guidance. I have witnessed healings from sickness, disease, and addiction. And I've received spiritual direction at just the right time to bring comfort to me and others around me. But I don't believe in any practice; I focus on the source of the power. Two key questions for me are, Where does this power come from? and What is the fruit? I don't have to pay $90 to someone each time I want to tap into power, because I am a channel of the very Spirit of Jesus. The power comes from my relationship with Jesus."

"I thought maybe you'd think I was nuts. But my path to spirituality and wholeness is through health and body work," Hal interjected.

I answered: "I also value health and wholeness. But how do you know when a spiritual or healing practice is actually bringing freedom or further enslavement to the practice—and corresponding fees? You place a lot of faith in them. How do you know you're truly being healed? What if you're being subjected to a process that creates spiritual codependency, where you're never weaned of the 'therapy' because the practitioners need you for building their reputation and fattening their wallet?"

"Good question. It's hard to know what really works and what doesn't—and it does get expensive."

As we turned down the road to his home, I said, "Hal, just listening to all the things you're doing to ensure wholeness and healing in your life makes me weary."

With a quirky smile, Hal replied, "Well . . . I think you've got something there. What do you mean?"

"Hal, you're a deeply spiritual person and you value living a holistic life. You hold an eclectic mix of Jewish and Buddhist beliefs along with a variety of other spiritual practices, hoping to find physical healing and spiritual wholeness. You have your daughter in the Waldorf School for a sense of community. You grow much of your own organic foods. You visit acupuncturists for healing. You pay the psychic for spiritual direction, and you follow several Eastern spiritual practices. You're working hard at life. Have you ever recognized that despite all your efforts, you're often sick? You seem to be expending a great deal of energy and money to hold your life together with these disparate strands, but the goal remains elusive."

Hal turned to me and said, "I can tell the Spirit is very real for you, Jonathan. And I can see that you're instructing your children in this way of life. You are

> The path I walk, Christ walks it.
> —St. Columba, Abbot of Iona
> (512-597)

one of the most integrated guys I know. You live in the moment. It takes a certain kind of courage and faith to live the way you do. Like you, I want wholeness, healing, and fulfillment. But where do I begin, and how do I maintain it?"

I thought a moment, then looked at Hal. "I sure haven't arrived, but I have a sense of wholeness. I believe that my wholeness is related directly to my center and source. I can't hold it all together, but in Jesus I'm both fulfilled and in the process of being fulfilled. I'm both enlightened and being enlightened. I am saved and being saved. I've already been made whole, and one day I will be made whole." I shared with Hal the promise from the New Testament book of Philippians, "that God, who began a good work within you, will continue his work until it is finally finished on that day when Christ Jesus comes back again" (1:6).

"It's a work of the Spirit, Hal. *And* it's a work of mine. My part is to submit to Christ and let him work his pleasure in my life. Now, it's not always that easy and does involve pain at times. But it is always satisfying. Only recently is all this coming into organic sync for me and my family."

We sat in the dark, with my truck idling in his driveway. Hal said, "I can tell you're enlightened. What you say sounds good, but I just don't know what else to do. I don't believe I can have wholeness on this side. I don't think I'll be enlightened in this lifetime." He stopped short. "Hey, Sarah's waiting with dinner for me, so I'd better go. We'll have to continue this another time."

We exchanged good-byes and greetings to our families before I drove off. But that was not the end of our conversation. Over the next few days, we exchanged e-mails. Here's one e-mail I wrote Hal:

> Hal, I've been reflecting on our conversation from the other night. Over the past year, I've been finding another way that transcends these many paths that I have tried and you are trying. One major realization for me is though I am now becoming more centered, I am not the center. I am whole and becoming whole. I am holy and becoming holy. But this is not because of me. I've found this life in Jesus. Jesus is the Way. He is the eternal Tao. He is Life. He is the way into Life. Jesus is beyond metaphysical. He is both personal and transcendent. Now and eternal. Just and loving. Compassionate and powerful.
>
> That's why I believe the pathway to enlightenment begins with enlightenment. We live in the same way we begin—by coming into the light. I must get out of the center position and yield absolute control to the Creator—to the one who knows me better than I know myself. As I empty myself, there is room to receive what he has for me. I turn over my self-reliance and position myself to humbly receive.
>
> Why do I believe this? A big reason among many is that the Spirit of Jesus is radically transforming my life. Jesus has not just improved my life—he is my life. Though I lived much of my life as though I was in control, I now realize I never was. I've discovered that you and I were created in the image of God, as spiritual, eternal beings. We have been invited and enabled to experience God directly through our life in Jesus. We need no medium or mediator.

We were created to experience communion with God through his Spirit who is within us. Jesus has invited us and enabled us to live in peace with our Creator and creation. He did what we could never do for ourselves. He became flesh and dwelt among us, reconciling us to God through his life, death, and resurrection.

I have the Spirit inside me. I am one with God. He is my life. If you'd like to read some Scriptures that give some background on my experience, check out Psalm 139; Acts 17; Colossians 3:1–4. The very Spirit of God is always with me to comfort me, guide me, heal me, and empower me.

We are a living and continuous creation of the Creator. As the Scriptures say, "For we are God's masterpiece. He has created us anew in Christ Jesus, so that we can do the good thing he planned for us to do" (Ephesians 2:10). This word "masterpiece" in the original Greek is "poiema" (unique or workmanship) from which we get "poem." As his living poetry, God will use all our experiences to write us into a masterpiece. Contrary to some Eastern understandings of Enlightenment, which leads to losing oneself and blending into everything, I am experiencing both the realization of self and communion with God. And this is just the beginning.

Your friend and fellow pilgrim,

Jonathan

Our friendship and conversation continues . . .

Christ as Center: A New Way of Life

Our relation to God is not a "religious" relationship
to the highest, most powerful, and best Being
imaginable—that is not authentic transcendence—
but our relation to God is a new life in "existence
for others," through participation in the being
of Jesus.

—*Dietrich Bonhoeffer (1906–1945),*
Lutheran pastor, activist against Hitler

After an afternoon of kayaking, my friend Erik and I went to his house for a glass of wine and conversation. We discussed the commonalities and differences between the teachings of Buddha and Jesus. He said to me, "Unlike many I know, you embody what you believe. I was raised Jewish, but with no real understanding of God. I follow Buddhist teachings but do not consider myself Buddhist because I do not understand the deeper levels of Buddhism. I like the meditation, compassion, mindfulness, and the Buddhist way of looking at life. I've never experienced Jesus like you. It really comes down to 'What do I believe?' and 'How do I live?'"

The Earth is the center of
the universe
The house is the center of
the Earth
The family is the center of
the house
The person is the center of
the family.
–Traditional Basque song

"Well, it's been a process," I said. "And for me it's becoming more, 'Who do I believe?' From our journey, Jennifer and I see three questions that have been emerging throughout our last twelve years of leaving religion and embracing Jesus: What is the Way of Jesus? What is the Spirit saying to us? and How will we live this way with one another?"

Erik responded enthusiastically, "These questions are simple, but have huge ramifications."

"Yes. Jesus is our integrating reality. As we believe in Jesus, then we will listen to his voice, trust his direction, and join with others in following him in all spheres of life."

Erik continued, "This is moving and experiential. And so it can be threatening to many people. They either want to move or it scares them to death. But you don't remain the same after encountering this."

"Yes, there is a difference between *knowing* the Way and *living* the Way. It is Jesus' life lived in us and out from us. This is a life shaped from the inside out. The best way to picture this is as a spiral with Christ at the very center."

Spiral

Jesus, who is within his followers, is at the heart of all life and then becomes the center of our marriage, extending out with our children, and continuing out to other relationships. It means that Jennifer and I are joined together by our common life in Christ. From this place of centeredness, we are then free to connect and move with others. As a family, we are experiencing the joy of journeying with others who are also centered in Jesus and who value the convergence of marriage, family, mission, and work.[1]

Our trip to South Africa in the fall of 2004 emerged out of these convictions and marked the beginning of a new season. I had only known Brett and Lyn for a few hours before they invited me and my family to join them on a one-month mission to South Africa. (It doesn't take long to recognize those with whom you already share Life!)

As I told Jennifer and the children about these new friends and the opportunities in South Africa, David and Lauren interrupted, "When do we go?" I had never mentioned us going as a family. They just assumed we would. And it didn't make any sense financially, since I was rather underemployed at the time, but we trusted in the Spirit's leading and provision.

As the trip approached, the realities of the finances loomed large. We questioned again if we should go, but we still had the conviction that our family needed to go as a team. About this time, Brett called and asked if we could arrange a time to talk with the rest of the team on speakerphone so they could say hello to the kids. At the end of the conversation, the team shared that they had raised more than $7,000 for our children to go! We were humbled by and grateful for their generosity.

South Africa was a powerful experience for us as a family. With a team from the United States and South Africa, we saw leaders from the townships and greater Cape Town catch a vision to repurpose their companies to become Christ-centered agents of societal transformation in postapartheid South Africa. It enlarged our kids' hearts as they were moved to compassion while working with the children in the poor townships. Nathan, who was six at the time, explained it well when he said, "I like giving better than getting." Rachael realized that "a lot of people need things and we don't need a lot of stuff." David's eyes were opened to see that "the world is a lot bigger than America." Lauren's sense of justice questioned why the politicians had built a luxury mall instead of low-income housing. There were many seeds planted in our children's hearts that we will continue to nurture in the future. Our trip reinforced our journey together as a family seeking to work together as a team and to follow the leading of Jesus in all that we do.

Restoring Our Connections

> We are all caught up in an inescapable network
> of mutuality.
> —*Martin Luther King Jr.* (1929–1968),
> *Baptist pastor, civil rights activist, Nobel laureate*

In reaction to the inherent fragmentation of Western culture, there is a growing awareness of the interconnectedness of the universe. Such awareness brings with it a longing for meaningful connections. Meaning is determined not so much by function but by relationships, by a sense of the interdependence of all things.

The reality is that whether we realize it or not, we are in touch with God every moment that we live. It is impossible not to be con-

nected to God for the simple reason that God is the source of all life
and is life itself. So God's open invitation is to experience the reality of Jesus in all of life. To be aware of Jesus working in us is the
beginning of enlightenment.

Not too long ago, I was hanging out with my boys before they
went to sleep. We had been lying side by side on the bunk without
speaking for several minutes when David, who was nine at the time,
broke the silence and said, "We are in Jesus, aren't we, Daddy?"

Wow, I thought. After a brief pause, I responded, "Yes, we are."
Then I thought, *What a powerfully simple truth*. "How did you come
up with that thought?"

He answered, "I don't know, I just know it."

Oh, that I would live with the realization of this truth in my
life—twenty-four hours a day! The Way of Jesus is Jesus himself—
his very life in me, not just my idea of him or my modeling of him.

There is great danger in separating what God never intended to
separate. In modern Western culture, we're becoming more and more
disconnected from ourselves, from one another, from the earth, and
from our Creator. But there is a way to regain our connectedness.

Everything becomes simpler with Jesus as the integrating reality. The barriers are broken down and our connections are restored.
Paradoxically, in Christ we witness the beauty of complexity as we
see all things in a web of relationships held together personally by
the cosmic Christ.[2] "Christ is the visible image of the invisible God.
He existed before God made anything at all and is supreme over all
creation. . . . He existed before everything else began, and he holds
all creation together" (Colossians 1:15, 17).

In Christ, "all things hold together." The "all things" is just that.
His Spirit is at work everywhere. There is no place or culture or religion outside the ongoing influence of Christ's reach. The deeper we
unite in Christ, the more we will see the connection of all things,
physical and spiritual. In Christ everything is brought together,
establishing harmony with self, one another, and the world. We find
our fulfillment and we affect our spheres of influence when we are
fully aware and integrated in the reality of the living Christ.

Our neighbors John and Barb were transformed as Christ became the center of their lives and family. They lived just four houses down, on the corner. Our friendship began around our children and then grew as we went camping together and John got me hooked on fly fishing. Soon we were talking about our relationships and the role of spirituality in all of life. John and Barb experienced a spiritual rebirth that transformed their lives from the inside out. Evidence of their new life was seen first by their children, who embraced Jesus because of the reality of Christ they saw in their parents.

I'll never forget the Sunday afternoon a group of family and friends gathered at the neighbors' pool. John and Barb shared their story of meeting Jesus before Jennifer and I baptized them as a couple. Being immersed in the water symbolized dying to their old self, and coming up from the water celebrated their resurrection into a new life and lifestyle in Jesus. Then, while we were all still in the water, John and Barb baptized their two children in the same way. Within a couple of weeks, we were coleading a neighborhood fellowship that met in our homes. Basically, the presence and power of Jesus spread from John and Barb's life to their marriage, to their family, to their neighbors, then to their extended family, and eventually to their relationships at work. Neighbors began opening up to them about their troubled relationships. When John was promoted to general manager of a large outlet center, employees and tenants also saw this new Life in him. Soon, they were coming to him for spiritual counsel.

> As you start on the Way, the Way happens.
>
> —Rumi (1207-1273), Persian poet and Sufi mystic

It's only as we submit all of who we are—spiritual, physical, emotional, tribal, financial—that we experience this kind of holistic transformation. We are healthiest when we center in Jesus and enjoy wholesome relationships. The word *health* comes from the same root as the word for *whole*. And *whole* is from the same root as *holy*. Spiritual integration is manifest as we are centered in Jesus. As Paul writes, "Since you have been raised to new life with

Christ, set your sights on the realities of heaven, where Christ sits at God's right hand in the place of honor and power. Let heaven fill your thoughts. Do not think only about things down here on earth. For you died when Christ died, and your real life is hidden with Christ in God. And when Christ, who is your real life, is revealed to the whole world, you will share in all his glory" (Colossians 3:1–4).

Nothing exists in isolation. If we look at creation as an ecosystem, we'll see the absolute necessity of the interconnectedness of every part. As any one part changes, the whole is changed. It is the same way in the realm of human life. Though we may be separate and moving away from each other, we haven't lost the need to be together. Most indigenous peoples understand this. The Native American worldview is based on the ever-changing web of relationships among all things, whereas the European worldview is a linear perspective that focuses on cause and effect.

Perhaps the most well known Native American prayer is *Mitakuye Oyasin*. My friend Ray explained that this Lakota phrase, which means "All my relations," begins and ends all their ceremonies. Everything being related to everything else is the foundation of all tribal cultures and life. It defines and unites all people wherever they are; "It is how we all join hands here on Turtle Island." For Ray, family isn't just people who share a blood relationship: "Family includes the greater circle of the community, of the tribe, and of the world. And it has the potential to include all of the people who touch my life in some way."

Celtic tradition is also rooted in a worldview of interconnectedness. The *everlasting pattern* of Celtic artwork suggests the eternal interweaving of spiritual and material, heaven and earth, time and eternity. The Celtic followers of the Way recognized Christ in the whole of life and understood that all living things are dependent upon the Creator. Christ is not only over all but also in all, and the source of all life. God's presence and power fills all of creation. The ancient Celtic poem known as "Saint Patrick's Breastplate" captures the reality of Christ's presence within and everywhere:

Christ with me, Christ before me, Christ behind me,
Christ in me, Christ beneath me, Christ above me,
Christ on my right, Christ on my left,
Christ when I lie down, Christ when I sit down,
    Christ when I arise,
Christ in the heart of every man who thinks of me,
Christ in the mouth of everyone who speaks of me,
Christ in every eye that sees me,
Christ in every ear that hears me.

Jesus invites us to enjoy the same life he lived on earth. It's all about our life emulating him, and his life energizing us. Even when religious leaders asked Jesus, "What must we do to do the works God requires?" Jesus answered, "The work of God is this: to believe in the one he has sent" (John 6:28–29). How simple. And how freeing! It is not based on our abilities. In the Way of Jesus, less is more. That's why "God blesses those who realize their need for him, for the Kingdom of Heaven is given to them" (Matthew 5:2); and the religion-bound slogan of "God helps those who help themselves" is nowhere found in the Bible.

The choice is ours: work hard at integrating everything around us, or live from the center out. It reminds me of another conversation I had with my friend Hal at our local swimming complex. While the kids were playing on the water slide, we wandered off to the Jacuzzi, where we could keep an eye on the kids and still have a conversation. Hal briefed me on his latest round of efforts to keep up his spiritual and physical health. He was still juggling multiple practitioners and streams of spirituality. As I listened, I felt his exhaustion, just as before. And I felt a sadness, just as before. Like a bicycle wheel, Hal was the center hub, trying to keep all the necessary elements of his physical and spiritual health in balance. I shared that Jesus wanted to be center and he would hold together all of the spokes of our lives. As the source of wholeness and health, Jesus promises, "Come to me, all of you who are weary and carry heavy burdens, and I will give you rest" (Matthew 11:28).

As we live from the center, we become aware of our interconnectedness with all of life. We recognize that nothing is separate from Christ. We can move in the light of God's revelation, for the revelation is in us; we are in Jesus and Jesus is in us. As we turn away from the natural patterns of this world, we are then able to make room for the Holy Spirit to transform us into the likeness of Jesus.

Are we living what we believe, or just talking about it? It is one thing to abide in Jesus, but quite another to continue to live amid the push and pull of family, work, and school. We can tell when we're off center and lose our connection to Jesus. The signs are clear: when we're anxious about everything and nothing in particular, when we're impatient with our children, when we become self-absorbed with our own problems and shortcomings. Then we must go back to center, to the integrating reality and source of our identity (who we are), our reason for being (why we live), and our values (how we live). Through a daily practice of centering, we can grow in our awareness of Jesus' presence and walk in the way that Jesus walked.

> *And now, just as you accepted Christ Jesus as your Lord,*
> *you must continue to live in obedience to him.*
> *Let your roots grow down into him*
> *and draw up nourishment from him,*
> *so you will grow in faith,*
> *strong and vigorous in the truth you were taught.*
> *Let your lives overflow with thanksgiving for all he has done. . . .*
> *For in Christ the fullness of God lives in a human body,*
> *and you are complete through your union with Christ.*
>
> —Colossians 2:6–10

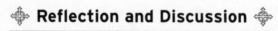

Reflection and Discussion

Read the parable Jesus told of the wise and foolish builders in the Gospel of Matthew 7:24–29.

- What are the differences and similarities between the two builders? Who are you most like?
- Are you living out what you believe? Where are the gaps?
- How can you bridge the gaps?
- Where do you need to trust the Spirit in order to move forward?

20

REALIZING CHRIST
IN COMMUNITY

> I have community with others and I shall continue
> to have it only through Jesus Christ. The more
> genuine and the deeper our community becomes,
> the more will everything else between us recede,
> the more clearly and purely will Jesus Christ and his
> work become the one and only thing that is vital
> between us. We have one another only through
> Christ, but through Christ we do have one another,
> wholly, and for all eternity.
>
> —*Dietrich Bonhoeffer (1906–1945),*
> *Lutheran pastor, activist against Hitler*

How many people does it take to be a Body of Christ? Jesus said, "For where two or three gather together because they are mine, I am there among them" (Matthew 18:20). This may be the closest there is to a definition for *church* in the Bible. Jesus is embodied in any group of people who live in loving relationship with him and one another. Jesus is saying in effect, "You (plural) are here on my behalf."[1] What set the early believers apart was the deep experience of Jesus in their midst. They had no "artificial" means by which they would experience God. None of the cultural understandings or structures of being "church" or community that we have today had yet been initiated. Their identity was in Jesus alone. Jesus continued to be enfleshed in and through them.

The depth of relationship that we can experience in community is determined by the depth of our communion with Christ. Our ability to give God's love and therefore experience community is dependent on our willingness to receive God's love. This is a key principle of Christ-centered community: "Give as freely as you have received!" (Matthew 10:8). We receive God's love, healing, and forgiveness in order to give God's love, healing, and forgiveness. And the more we give, the more we receive.

In our current cultural crisis, the most powerful demonstration of the reality of the gospel is a community embodying the *way*, the *truth*, and the *life* of Jesus. Healthy community is the life of Jesus living in us and through us. For community to last, our love for one another must be surpassed only by our love for Jesus. If the relationships are grounded upon anything other than Jesus, the community will fall—and the sooner the better!

Living in the Tensions of This World

> The pains of community are situated between the
> joy of this communion and friendship with Jesus
> and the joy of giving life to others.
> —Jean Vanier, *founder, L'Arche Community, France*

Tension is a sign of vitality and life. Anytime we have two opposing forces in proximity to one another, we have tension. Our bodies are in tension throughout the day as they respond to the force of gravity. Without our resistance to gravity, our muscles atrophy; they lose their tone and eventually we lose our ability to walk, run, and play. So it is with the Body of Christ. We are a living organism living in the tensions of culture. This is in contrast to the Body of Christ being extracted from culture to live in a zero-gravity atmosphere without any tension (that is, isolationism), or to completely give into the tension and lose all semblance of purpose and movement in the culture (syncretism). Both extremes have the resulting effect of losing mobility.

It is natural—even consistent with its nature—for the disciples of Jesus to struggle ceaselessly in the tension of being in, but not of,

Ekklesia (The Body of Christ . . .)	*Apostolos* (. . . in the World)
Tensions of Being: Living in the Sacred	
Called out of the World . . .	*. . . and Sent into the World*
Gathered church	Scattered church
Local communities (modality)	Itinerant bands (sodality)
Holiness, alternative	Worldliness, apostolic
Tensions of Action: Living out the Sacramental	
Blessed Abundantly . . .	*. . . in Order to Be a Blessing*
In community	On commission
Growth and maturity	Reproduction and movement
Attraction (centripetal)	Permeation (centrifugal)
Consolidate; stability	Stretch; flexibility
Unity, convergence, and integration	Diversity, divergence, and interpenetration

the world. We must guard against settling into the comfortable position of either extreme. Like Jesus himself, our identity is found in the midst of this tension. Believers gather in order to experience Christ together, build one another up, and disperse as "salt and light" in the world.

Only by living in this dynamic tension can we live out who we already are, embracing both reality (what is) and destiny (what is called to be). The church is at the same time called out of the world (*ekklesia*) only to be sent back into the world (*apostolos*) to call out others to be and do the same. We are the Body of Christ to the extent we embrace the tension of what it means both to be blessed by God and to be a blessing to the world around us.

Our friends Ben and Mike started a band several years ago in Los Angeles. As followers of Jesus they chose not to open for a well-known Christian band, because they'd be labeled as a "Christian band" and lose their voice in the world they wanted to be a light in.

This made for a longer road to earning well-paying gigs. But now after countless concerts, several CDs, and increased radio play, they are a mobile Body of Christ, traveling with their wives and friends to places that don't normally encounter Jesus. They've built a positive reputation among fans and the music industry. They often have members of other bands over for a barbecue and jam session. They are different and separate from the world, yet in the world so they can be a blessing in subcultures of society.

Deep Listening for Deeper Legacy

> Devote yourselves to prayer with an alert mind and
> a thankful heart.
> —Paul's Letter to the Colossians (4:2)

Sometimes we must fight for our freedom.

Have you ever sought to enter into a time of rest, of listening meditation, only to be barraged by the noise of things to be done, or an unexpected interruption suddenly showing up? I recall once when I escaped to a friend's cabin for a time of solitude. It was a serene place on Butter Creek, in the shadow of Mount Rainier. I just wanted to pray, listen, and write. But I found that it took me a few days to get rid of the noise—not from the outside but from inside my head. I had to fight through the thoughts that came to distract and discourage me. Basically, I had to get my mind off myself so that I could be free to listen and receive from the Spirit.

> Human opposition only
> enhances your glory.
> –Psalm 76:10

One of the greatest skills for navigating this Aquarian age is to learn to listen deeply. Listening is three-dimensional: to Jesus, to the inner longings of the heart, and to the world around us. If we but listen, we will hear the Spirit speaking to us. Deep listening calls for us to be in the culture and among the people. As agents of reconciliation, we stand between God and the world with a clear invitation to listen to both. George MacLeod, founder of the Iona Community in Scotland, lived with the conviction that "God is the life of the world and not merely some religious aspect of it. To listen to God is to listen deep within ourselves, including deep within the collective life and consciousness of the world."[2]

We experience the presence of Jesus on earth when we live in loving obedience to Jesus, in fellowship with one another, and in active participation in the world. It is in such an environment that religious refugees and spiritual sojourners can find a genuine answer to their longing for security, belonging, love, hope, and empowerment.

Listening with a readiness to love helps uncover the needs and feelings of those who live around us. We should learn to eavesdrop on the world at large with ears to hear the voice of the Spirit above the din. As we listen with deep compassion, the Comforter grants us wisdom to be the Good News and to share the Good News. Listen to the pains of the lonely, the disenfranchised, the poor, the alienated, the oppressed, even the ones who oppose us. Listen. What are you listening for? Who are you listening to? What is the Spirit saying?

Learning to Walk Again

> There is a difference between knowing the path
> and walking the path.
>
> —*Morpheus, speaking to Neo,* The Matrix

Having been raised in the West, we know how to go to church (or not). But we don't know how to be spiritual. Many of us have looked to religion to guide us in spiritual matters, or abandoned it because we do not think it can. As my friend Gary says, "Isn't it easier just to go to church than to try to figure out spiritual things and make sure the kids get what they need?"

Some of us, though, know there's got to be something more, but we don't know how to get it. It's hard to realize one is in bondage until one has tasted freedom. When some do get it, it often scares them because then they must make a choice between living free or remaining bound—psychologically, relationally, or structurally. In any case, they realize they are not really growing as they could and they don't see any way out. We know many who have labored in Western churches and suffered withdrawal as they moved out of the institutional system in order to move with Jesus and others as the living Body of Christ.

Sometimes we need someone to come alongside us and say, "You're not crazy; just follow how the Spirit is leading you. Keep on the path. Hold on to Jesus." Jennifer and I are grateful for the many who encouraged us at critical times along our journey.

When some good friends were wrestling with the chasm between Jesus and the church, we tried to encourage them as we had been encouraged. After a conversation with Dan, I searched my files and found a set of blank ordination certificates I had from when I was a professional pastor. Even though no certificate was needed, Jennifer and I thought it would be a humorous way to illustrate the truth of their authority in Jesus. So we sent a letter to Dan and his family and included an official ordination certificate, with all their names filled in and signed by our family to "authorize" them to minister to one another and their friends as disciples of Jesus.

A few months after the "ordination," Dan and I were enjoying fish and chips at his favorite seafood place. We talked about business and also about their transition out of a popular church so as to begin meeting together as a family. I said, "You've been out of religion for six months now. How are you and Robin adjusting?"

> The true well-being of the church: when she cannot count on anything anymore but God's promises.
> –Johannes Hoekendijk (1912–1975), Dutch theologian

He replied, "It's freeing, but it's not as easy as I thought it would be. . . . It's like someone adjusting to life outside slavery or prison after years of living under strict controls. Like in the movie *The Shawshank Redemption*: it's one thing to get the prisoner out of the prison, but quite another to get the prison out of the prisoner. You're clearly out of religion, but when do you know that religion is out of you?"

I cut him short: "When the guilt is gone . . . when you stop having the shakes on Sunday morning because you're not in a church service."

He chuckled and continued. "I know there's something in us that must come out. It's something that curbs our joy and freedom."

I asked, "What's the 'it' that has to get out of you?"

He thought for a moment. "Well, it's really not that we need human approval from a religious

> If people can't see what God is doing, they stumble all over themselves; but when they attend to what he reveals, they are most blessed.
> —Proverbs 29:18,
> *The Message*

official, but sometimes it's just hard to discern if we're moving in the right direction. We've always had others to follow."

I smiled in response. "You mean the ordination certificate we sent you wasn't enough?"

Dan laughed. "No, we all loved it! It's just that there's no safety net."

"What's the difference between a safety net and artificial life support?"

"Good question. I don't know. . . . But I know that we're becoming more deliberate about our faith. And I'm learning to shepherd my family. I didn't realize how much responsibility for my family I had given over to the church. . . . We're now reading the Bible and praying together."

I agreed: "Yes, both the greatest joy and the greatest challenge is living the Way at home with Jennifer and the children, but this is where life happens. It's real and sometimes a bit raw. And there's no safety net or artificial life support.[3] With regard to church, the artificial life support is anything that takes the place of our real life in Jesus. Usually it has to do with finances, programs, traditions, or professionals. They may feel good at the time, but it's detrimental to our long term health and movement. . . . We don't develop our own spiritual muscles. . . . When we want more than Jesus, we get less."

There is still nothing in the world more revolutionary than a people moving together by the Spirit of Jesus. The true well-being of community is when we cannot count on anything more than the presence of Jesus. Both the Spirit and the culture are calling us to embrace and live our Original Blessing. We need a new breed of spiritual community, one that is powerfully simple and free from the trappings of modern religion; capable of being planted in our age in such a way that our legacy of investment in all peoples can take root, grow, and reproduce freely as the Spirit directs.

> We are exiles in the far end of solitude, living as listeners,
> With hearts attending to the skies we cannot understand:
> Waiting upon the first far drums of Christ the Conqueror,
> Planted like sentinels upon the world's frontier.
>
> —Thomas Merton (1915–1968),
> Trappist monk and author[4]

✠ Reflection and Discussion ✠

The Way of Jesus is centered in Jesus and lived through community. You might want to discuss these questions with some friends or family members with whom you share similar spiritual questions.

- What does it mean for us to be in Christ? individually? as family? as community?
- What does it mean for us to be a healthy community? to be on mission together?
- What is the Spirit saying to me? to us as a family? to us as the Body of Christ?
- How will we then choose to live the Way of Jesus together?

21

LIVING A HOLISTIC SPIRITUALITY

Concerning our experience of Jesus . . . it is possible
that our borders can be enlarged considerably.
—*Daniel Hari, Swiss author,* Healing Like Jesus

Recently, I woke early in the morning with a strong impression that emerged from two dreams earlier in the night. I'd floated through a dreamland that did not operate by the rules of my familiar everyday world. I likened it to living in a black-and-white world and then waking up to Technicolor.

So too we need a similar awakening in our spirituality: more sunrise hues instead of dull, predawn drabs. There are natural laws, such as the law of gravity, with which we explain the world we live in; and there are supernatural laws that are above nature or not subject to natural explanation. Through our myopic way of seeing, we have compartmentalized our lives individually, as a society and as a global community. The intersection of the supernatural and daily life is all but absent in Western society and its corresponding religions. Our unexamined presuppositions box us into a materialistic, two-dimensional existence.

Our youngest child, Nathan, likes to ask, "How many people are here?" It might just be our family, so I will answer, "Six." He then breaks into a big grin as he announces triumphantly, "No! There are a thousand, because of all the angels!" Nathan's simple faith enables him to see a greater reality. Our children continue to confirm in experience the truth of Jesus when he took the children in his arms and said: "I assure you, unless you turn from your sins and become as little children, you will never get into the Kingdom of Heaven. Therefore, anyone who becomes as humble as this little child is the greatest in the Kingdom of Heaven" (Matthew 18:3–5).

We have inherited this *Flatland* worldview from the Greeks who saw the spiritual realm as essentially disconnected from the material and relational world. But this false distinction is a uniquely Western phenomenon, grounded in Plato's dualism of body and soul. In contrast, the Hebrew mind-set of the entire Bible sees the spiritual encompassing all of life. The unseen realm is one with the seen realm. It is not even another dimension, but the union of all life, both seen and unseen.

It makes little difference to add the supernatural perspective to our natural worldview as some mere supplement or an auxiliary dimension. Rather, we need to be transformed by the renewing of our mind to be free from the boundaries of the natural order and understand that the supernatural is not just beyond the natural; it is simultaneously in the natural *and* beyond the natural.

Getting the Big Picture

A recent visit to the Seattle Art Museum with my family offered an illustration of moving beyond the boundaries. The museum featured an exhibition of Vincent Van Gogh and other early Impressionists. But it was the works of Georges Seurat that caught my eye as we walked through the main hall. As I looked more closely at Seurat's *A Sunday on the Island of La Grande Jatte*, I could see that it was made up of tiny dots, a type of painting technique known as pointillism. Thousands of dabs of paint were arranged in such a way that the colors would merge into full solid forms when viewed from a distance. With remarkable contrast of colors and light, the scene came alive before my eyes. I never thought something so abstract could emit such life and emotion. It was not the parts that made the picture, but their interrelatedness. The picture was wholly different from the sum of the parts, as though it were creating a new reality.

This painting can be reduced to three elemental colors: red, yellow, and blue. However, it is the creative fusion of these three elements that brings forth the completeness and beauty—even a wholeness and holiness. It is not any *one* thing but the unity and the integration of the whole that exudes the depths of meaning.

The Way of Jesus is a lot like Seurat's painting. Over the years, we've come to discover from the Scriptures and from experience that there are three essential dimensions in our spiritual experience: love, truth, and power. The distinctiveness of our life in Jesus is marked by the creative integration of these dimensions. Though it is possible to experience one dimension at the neglect of the others, it gives a very different picture than it does in three dimensions. Can you really hear a Beethoven symphony if played with only one instrument? Or appreciate Van Gogh's *Starry Night*—if viewed only in monochrome? So it is with our spiritual life. Sure, we can hear great teaching but never have a personal encounter with Jesus. Or we can have loving community, but without integrating the truth of Jesus. Or we quench the power of the Holy Spirit through passivity and so experience only the best of what we can come up with on our own. Or we can experience all three dimensions but be hindered from moving freely by religious structures.

It is the interrelatedness of love, truth, and power that brings out the fullness in the Way of Jesus.

Celtic Triquetra

The Way of Love

For we know how dearly God loves us, because he
has given us the Holy Spirit to fill our hearts with
his love.

—*Paul's Letter to the Romans (5:5)*

The whole world is longing for love.

Love is the very nature of God and the distinguishing mark of
our life in Christ. To love is to reflect the nature of God to the
world. Jesus set the example and then passed it on to his followers,
promising joy as the fruit of his love. Jesus invites us to give and
receive the love of the Father: "I have loved you even as the Father
has loved me. Remain in my love. When you obey me, you remain
in my love, just as I obey my Father and remain in his love. I have
told you this so that you will be filled with my joy. Yes, your joy will
overflow! I command you to love each other in the same way that
I love you. And here is how to measure it—the greatest love is
shown when people lay down their lives for their friends" (John
15:9–13).

Growing out of the relational heart of God, we are the Body of
Christ *in the world*, called to live in communion with Christ and
healthy community with one another and the world around us.
Healthy spiritual community is not focused on community, but on
Jesus. Community is the fruit of abiding in the love of Jesus. As we
meet together, we see the interconnection of our lives with God,
one another, and the world around us. Community becomes an
environment where we give and receive the love of Jesus in tangible ways, to remind us that our grip on truth is fragile and incomplete, and to take off the masks that prevent us from truly being
known. True community is impossible without some degree of risk,
for the reality is that there can be no community without vulnerability, and no vulnerability without risk.

As the Body of Christ, we are called to make wrong relationships right: to reconcile people with God, one another, and the

earth. It is our love for Jesus that compels us to be a reconciling community. The heart of God's people will break over what breaks the heart of God, and join God's lament over our nations and cities, just as Jesus once cried over Jerusalem. Only by being *in* the world can we truly love the world. As my friend Charles Brock, a long-time missionary to the Philippines, says, "Out of love comes forth wisdom." Love is the greatest healer of all.[1]

When love waters and nurtures the seed of truth, walls of separation and rejection are knocked down. Love breaks through any and all of the social barriers needed for true peace making. Jesus strikes at the root of those influences that tear at peace and justice. Whether man or woman, black or white, urban or rural, old or young, rich or poor, Jesus is the unifying factor. It is our individual differences rather than our similarities that enable us to contribute significantly to both the church and the world.

The living Body of Christ is the Word "made flesh" as a tangible expression of God's love. Before many people will be open to receive the truth or power of Jesus, they must first see and feel (both spiritually and physically) the love of Jesus. Love is the great builder of trust. My friend Paul explains, "People will only have as much faith in God as they have in you." This statement reflects the two-part promise of Jesus: "Anyone who accepts your message is also accepting me. And anyone who rejects you is rejecting me. And anyone who rejects me is rejecting God who sent me" (Luke 10:16).

It is in and through community that relationships are built through which the gospel can spread freely across spiritual and structural barriers. The gospel is only fully realized in and through community. We cannot prove God. We cannot reason God. He has revealed himself to us through Jesus. Jesus reveals himself to the world through us—most powerfully, through us in community. Jesus himself declared, "So now I am giving you a new commandment: Love each other. Just as I have loved you, you should love each other. Your love for one another will prove to the world that you are my disciples" (John 13:34–35).

The Way of Truth

> . . . and you will hear a voice say, "This is the way;
> turn around and walk here."
> —*Isaiah, Hebrew prophet, Isaiah 30:21*

I believe God speaks today.

Even now as I write, I struggle with this reality. Not because I haven't heard God speak, but because I know he is speaking. My heart often struggles with hearing his voice over the noise of the reality of my daily life. God's voice should be the most familiar voice we hear. Through his life and teaching, Jesus opened the way for us to commune directly with God.

More than six hundred years before Christ, a prophet of Judah spoke of a promise that would come from God:

> I will pour out my Spirit upon all people.
> Your sons and daughters will prophesy.
> Your old men will dream dreams.
> Your young men will see visions.
> In those days,
> I will pour out my Spirit even on servants,
> men and women alike.[2]

Just as Joel predicted several centuries earlier, the Holy Spirit was poured out on all these early followers of Jesus who were gathered in Jerusalem on the Day of Pentecost (Acts 2:14–21). The gifts of the Spirit that began to flow that day are still available to all who believe in Jesus. God desires us to know him and promises to reveal himself.

God reveals himself in creation. The Celtic church was always seeking signs of God's presence in creation. They prayed that their eyes might be opened, that all their senses might be alert to the invisible. They lived in the expectation of meeting God in his creation, just as Paul wrote to the believers in Rome: "From the time the world was created, people have seen the earth and sky and all that God made. They can clearly see his invisible qualities—his eternal power

and divine nature. So they have
no excuse whatsoever for not
knowing God" (Romans 1:20).

God speaks through Scripture.
We gain understanding of Jesus
through the Bible, God's inspired
Word.[3] The Scriptures are not
merely reports about revelation;
they are revelation in written form.
The Bible is a guide for both what
we believe and how we live.

God speaks through the arts as a
language of culture. Since we are
made in God's image, it follows that we will reflect God's image
through our creativity, even if only in hazy ways. Throughout history, God has revealed himself through drawings, music, drama,
poetry, and stories. The early church often used symbols, pictures,
and other art forms to communicate the gospel visually across cultures to disciples, many of whom couldn't read.

> You Christians look after a document containing enough dynamite to blow all civilization to pieces, turn the world upside down, and bring peace to a battle-torn planet. But you treat it as though it is nothing more than a piece of good literature.
> —Mohandas Gandhi (1869-1948), peace activist, leader of India's independence

After weeks of the Holy Spirit revealing disparate images, our
friend Heidi stayed up late one night to paint a picture that had
been unfolding in her mind. The next morning she came with her
family to our home and presented the finished painting to Jennifer
and me in the kitchen. I took one look and was moved to tears,
even before Heidi could say a word of introduction. Through the
picture, the Holy Spirit addressed my heart's cry from that very
morning. The painting continues to speak forth the love and grace
of God to our family.

God speaks through community. The ability to listen to the Spirit
of God is not reserved for the few but freely available to all in the
Body of Christ: "Let love be your highest goal, but also desire the
special abilities the Spirit gives, especially the gift of prophecy. . . .
Well, my brothers and sisters, let's summarize what I am saying.
When you meet, one will sing, another will teach, another will tell
some special revelation God has given, one will speak in an

unknown language, while another will interpret what is said. But everything that is done must be useful to all and build them up in the Lord" (I Corinthians 14:1, 26–27).

Jesus predicted there would be an increase of spiritual activity and many voices competing with the voice of God. So, who do we listen to? The challenge is to turn down the noise of the world and religions, and listen to the quiet voice of God. The question is not whether or not God is revealing himself, but whether we are looking and listening for him. The Scriptures are full of promises of God speaking in a number of ways. If we don't believe we are going to hear the Sprit speak to us, we won't! Human plans, wisdom, and guidance must give way to the voice of the Holy Spirit. We must learn to dialogue with God. When God speaks, what we do next (not what we say or think) is what we really believe about God.

The Way of Power

> For the Kingdom of God is not just fancy talk; it is
> living by God's power.
> —*Paul, the apostle, I Corinthians 4:20*

God still moves. He still heals.

I have always believed this, but for many years my everyday experience did not match my belief. I was what our Swiss friend Daniel calls an "unbelieving believer," a person who believes a right theology about God but does not experience the power of God in everyday life. As with other areas of my life, God has used diverse people and circumstances to break me free from my overrationalized faith to experience the reality of his passion. My trip to East India in 1991 was the first of many experiences I couldn't explain away.

I'll never forget the train ride from Madras to Nellore. It wasn't just the natural beauty of the countryside that took my breath away, but the sea of people, animals, and vehicles filling the cities. *What am I doing here?!* I thought to myself. *I'm only here for three weeks. What difference can I possibly make in this country of a billion people?*

The more I saw, the more I became convinced of my powerlessness to make any difference. But I kept praying, asking God, "Why am I here?" and "What is your assignment for me?" Little did I realize it wasn't about what I could do for India, but how God would use India to begin transforming me and my worldview.

It was about dusk when the train approached the station in Nellore. An unusual peace came over me. I felt the calm assurance of the Lord inviting me to let him carry the burden for the country. I was reminded of the words of William Carey, an entrepreneur and pioneer missionary to India, who said, "Expect great things from God; attempt great things for God." *There must be some reason God has brought me here!* So I prayed with a heartfelt expectancy to give or receive as the Spirit directed.

A week later, I spoke in an old cathedral in Nellore, wearing the traditional dhoti that our hosts had given me as well as several strings of flower leis. The easy part was the message I gave. Speaking through a Telugu interpreter gave me time to pray and gather my thoughts for what I would say next. But the real challenge came when the gathering was over. Dozens of people remained, waiting for prayer.

I was led to the outside courtyard to a man lying on a straw mat with his wife and teenage son by his side. The man had been paralyzed from the waist down for three years. His body was showing signs of the progressive atrophy. With tears in her eyes, his wife told me, "We know God can heal." I prayed

> The genuine realist, if he is an unbeliever, will always find strength and ability to disbelieve in the miraculous, and if he is confronted with a miracle as an irrefutable fact he would rather disbelieve his own senses than admit the fact. Faith does not . . . spring from the miracle, but the miracle from faith.
>
> —Fyodor Dostoevsky
> (1821-1881), Russian writer

silently that God would grant me the faith to claim this man's healing. Then a few of us laid our hands on the man, and I prayed aloud for Jesus to heal him and bring peace to his family. They thanked us with genuine gladness, as if we had actually given them a gift.

Little did I know that Christ performed a miracle that afternoon. It would take me several weeks before I received a letter that included a family picture of the three of them standing in front of their home. The picture was taken just a week after I departed from India. With heartfelt gratitude, they shared their story that led up to the time I met them. They described the physical healing of the father and the spiritual transformation to them as a family. They were Muslims and had been key business leaders in the community until the man's health deteriorated. After God healed him, the family provided one of their buildings in the predominantly Muslim area to host regular gatherings of Jesus followers from the local community.

> A miracle cannot prove what is impossible; it is useful only to confirm what is possible.
> —Moses Maimonides (1135-1204), Jewish physician, rabbi, and philosopher

Jesus is more than an idea or ethic; he is the source of freedom to the prisoners, recovery of sight for the blind, and release for the oppressed. The Way of Jesus is the embodiment of power. Demonstrations of power often accompanied proclamation of the gospel in the first century. Luke records that "the apostles were performing many miraculous signs and wonders among the people" (Acts 5:12).[4] This was nothing new. Jesus performed many signs and wonders himself, and he gave his disciples authority to go in his name and do the same.[5]

The same power that raised Jesus from the grave is within us who believe in Jesus. In fact Jesus promised, "The truth is, anyone who believes in me will do the same works I have done, and even greater works" (John 14:12). When Jesus lives in us, we will love like Jesus and we will do the works of Jesus, not because we are special but because his Spirit lives through us. He can do everything and anything through us!

Though demonstrations of power are marks of the Holy Spirit, they are not *the* distinguishing mark, for even false teachers and dark spirits can demonstrate power.[6] On the other hand, we must also caution against underemphasizing the role of signs and wonders. Luke was a doctor who became one of Jesus' twelve disciples. Luke makes it a point to record in detail many miracles of Jesus in his Gospel account of Jesus' life and the Acts of the Apostles. He presents signs and wonders as a normal manifestation of our supernatural life in Jesus.

"Healing is necessary when teaching fails" is an East Indian saying that is true in the East and West. We've heard reports that more than 75 percent of the millions of emerging Chinese Jesus followers have experienced a miracle. Stories of healing in the Western context are on the rise. Signs and wonders open people's hearts to receive the good news of Jesus and authenticate both the message and the messenger.[7] Paul's prayer to the Ephesian believers interweaves God's great power and love: "I pray that Christ will be more and more at home in your hearts as you trust in him. May your roots go down deep into the soil of God's marvelous love. And may you have the power to understand, as all God's people should, how wide, how long, how high, and how deep his love really is. May you experience the love of Christ, though it is so great you will never fully understand it. Then you will be filled with the fullness of life and power that comes from God" (3:17–19).

Paul's prayer does not say that we are rooted and grounded in *power*, but rather in *love*.

God's power enables the believer to love after the pattern of Jesus. God's power is not conveyed indiscriminately, but *in divine relationship*. God listens to his people, feels their pain, and compassionately responds.

The New Testament writers made clear that the power resided not in the person but in the Spirit, who is freely given to all. This gives light to the paradoxical truth that God's power is manifest in our weakness. For example, after the apostle Paul prayed repeatedly for personal healing, Jesus finally answered, "My gracious favor is all you need. My power works best in your weakness" (II Corinthians 12:9). It reminds us that it is not *a power* that saves and heals, but *the person* of Jesus. Jesus commissioned his followers to continue with the same power and authority he demonstrated: "Go into all the world and preach the Good News to everyone, everywhere. Anyone who believes and is baptized will be saved. But anyone who refuses to believe will be condemned. These signs will accompany those who believe: They will cast out demons in my name, and they will speak new languages. They will be able to handle snakes with safety, and if they drink anything poisonous, it won't hurt them. They will be able to place their hands on the sick and heal them" (Mark 16:15–18).

God makes all things possible. We will not only heal other people, we will love other people and serve other people. Be patient with yourself. Stay in joyful expectation of what God wants to do for you, and through you. The more we are filled with the love of God, the more we trust him; it's then natural to expect him to reveal himself and demonstrate his power.

A Picture of the Whole

It was the beauty of the scene and the love that flowed so freely that brought an overwhelming joy to our hearts. The Swiss and Italian Alps surround the Lake of Lugano in southern Switzerland. We found a beach where a stream flowed into the lake and clusters of birch trees dotted the shoreline. The wind gave a fresh, invigorating feel even as it pulled up whitecaps on the lake. About thirty of us walked to the shore to celebrate the baptism of fourteen women and men. We quickly gathered branches and scraps of wood to warm ourselves by a bonfire.

We had all participated in a weeklong spiritual retreat on Christ-centered healing sponsored by our friends Daniel and Cornelia. People came to experience the *power* of Jesus. But it was the tangible expressions of God's *love* that enfolded them and drew them to a place they could embrace Jesus. This atmosphere of love and community, centered in Christ, allowed many to be set free from lies they believed and to experience healing, both of the soul and the body. The week had a spiraling effect of dealing with one layer at a time of people's physical problems, emotional wounds, and spiritual needs.

Longings were fulfilled. Eyesight was healed. Chronic pains were relieved. Several quit smoking. Deep emotional hurts were mended. Fears were relieved. Hope was restored.

By week's end, these new ones to the journey had already exercised their authority in Jesus by praying for one another's healing. It was nothing unusual, for their introduction to Jesus was through his healing touch. Gisela phoned home to pray for her mom, who was suffering with stomach pains. She prayed for her and then asked her mom to pass healing to her dad who was having problems hearing. When she called back later that day, her dad answered the phone. What joy she experienced when he said, "You are so far away, but I can hear you so clearly!"

Jennifer and I witnessed the life of Jesus take root in the hearts of these new pilgrims. Mind-sets and lifestyles began to shift. Tanya shared that she always enjoyed having people in her home, but hadn't wanted to open her home to her niece who struggled with drugs. But now she would, because her niece was the very one who needed to experience Jesus. We see these seeds that were planted that week growing and bearing fruit in our lives and the lives of others in several countries.

These stories and many others describe the essence of our pilgrimage to experience the reality of Jesus in the context of love, with the power of the Spirit, and centered in the truth of Jesus. As the wind blew across the top of the fire we had built on the lakeshore, it scattered embers of coals along the sand. What an appropriate picture of what is to come: the essence of the Way of Jesus caught as embers in the hearts of these new pilgrims, ready to be blown by the wind of the Spirit as they journey back to their communities.

Reflection and Discussion

In the Gospel of John 14:12, Jesus promised, "The person who trusts me will not only do what I'm doing but even greater things, because

I, on my way to the Father, am giving you the same work to do that I've been doing. You can count on it" (*The Message*). When Jesus lives in us, we will love like the Father and we will do the works of Jesus, not because we are special but because his Spirit lives through us. The Spirit can do everything and anything through us.

- Do you believe this promise? Why, or why not?
- Pray with a sincere love and simple trust: "Jesus, would you reveal yourself to me in a personal way? I want to hear your voice. Would you live through me and demonstrate your love and power in and through my life?"
- You can make it more complicated if you like. You don't need long prayers; just pray in faith, listen, trust Jesus, and walk as the Spirit leads you.

22

THE JOURNEY WILL
TAKE US THERE

Alone with none but Thee, my God,
I journey on my way;
What need I fear when Thou art near,
Oh King of night and day?
More safe am I within Thy hand
Than if a host did round me stand.
—*St. Columba (512–597), Abbot of Iona*

Solvitur ambulando [It is solved by walking].
—*St. Augustine (396–430* A.D.*),*
Bishop of Hippo

A friend from India recently asked me, "Are you living your life, or still preparing for life?"

I paused and answered, "Yes . . . I am *and* I am becoming."

The whole of life is a journey of ever becoming. Life is process. We resonate with a South African musician who describes our life in the Spirit as "God's poetry in motion." Just as each line of poetry flows to the next, unfolding its own rhyme and rhythm, so our lives unfold as we journey with Jesus. New views come into focus as we walk in God's grace and extend his grace to others along the Way.

Our new way of life is expressed in the Celtic word for pilgrimage, *Peregrinatio*, meaning more than a journey to a holy place, but a distinct way of living and relating. From the many stories, poems, songs, prayers, and blessings handed down orally from generation to generation, we see a people who lived in the present moment and moved with the rhythm of life. From the short daily journeys of the ordinary to the longer pilgrimages to far-off places, all of life is seen as an unfolding story and web of relationships. So the journey and life itself are one whole.[1]

The early Celtic believers were deeply moved by the presence and power of the Spirit. This may explain why they referred to the Holy Spirit as the "Wild Goose," a name rightly describing the unfettered, free, and wild nature of God. "*Amor non tenet ordinam*" (love does not concern itself with order) was what St. Columbanus once said in a letter defending his own spontaneous, free-flowing style. Yes, moving in the Spirit can often seem like a wild goose chase—especially to those watching from a distance.

The Bible is full of wild goose chases—stories of God doing extraordinary things with ordinary people. Pilgrimage is wandering forth as the Spirit leads and finding ourselves in the place of God's appointing. To those who have the courage to listen and trust, the Holy Spirit will lead forth. You may recall the story of God calling Abraham to leave his own country and go on toward a land that would be revealed only when he got there. He is promised that he would be blessed, and that he would be a blessing.

> Just as you can hear the wind but can't tell where it comes from or where it is going, so you can't explain how people are born of the Spirit.
>
> –Jesus of Nazareth, John 3:8

But he isn't told where he's going or what he's going to do when he gets there! The Spirit was calling him into the unknown.

Through this book, we have shared our pilgrimage of walking with Jesus . . . so far. Our writing has become a form of dialogue and prayer. Even after completing this book, we realize more than ever that we are just at the genesis of a lifetime journey. We know there are many adventures ahead that will bring challenges and questions we haven't yet faced, but from our experiences—both painful and joyful—we can continue to walk the Way with hope and joyful expectation.

We have sought to share pieces of our heart and truths Jesus has revealed to us. We hope our story has encouraged you along your journey. We borrow the words of Robert Francis, a Cherokee elder: "[We] ask that you take what you find here as you would a freshly cracked hickory nut. Gather all into your hand. Pick out the good to hold close to your heart. Blow the rest away with the breath of kindness. Know that whatever good you find is from Creator."

Our prayer is that you will be transformed by the love of God, experience the freedom of Jesus, and grow in the power of the Holy Spirit as you journey with others along the Way. We leave you with this prayer from the sixth-century Celtic monk and voyager Brendan the Navigator.[2]

> *I thank You for this, my God,*
> *I am a traveller and stranger*
> *in the world,*
> *like so many of Your people*
> *before me.*
> *There is a sense of adventure,*
> *of openness to possibilities,*
> *abandonment to God*
> *and expectation of fulfilling His will.*
> *I accept the responsibility,*
> *I'll hear and obey,*
> *and trust it is Your voice I hear,*
> *the call of the Spirit,*
> *the cry of the Bird of Heaven.*
> *It is a Yes to risky living.*
> *The sea takes me;*
> *where I do not know,*
> *but I gladly go.*
> *And I can only trust*
> *every word You say,*
> *and obey.*

✠ Reflection and Discussion ✠

There's no book that can do justice to describing what it means to experience Jesus and follow his ways. This may close the end of the book, but it is just the beginning of the rest of your journey.

- What is your next move? Are you ready to journey with others on the Way of Jesus?

- Just as Jesus prayed to his Father to reveal who he would walk with during his time on earth, take a few moments to pray and listen for Jesus to reveal to you who you should be sojourning with at this season of your life. You may be surprised how God answers your prayer.

- Read the prayer of Paul to the young gathering of disciples of Jesus in Ephesians 1:18–23. Then read the passage again, personalizing it as your own prayer for enlightenment. Ask Jesus to shine light on the next steps of your journey. Listen . . . and then move after him and continue to listen.

Notes

Preface

1. Peterson, E. H. *The Message: The Bible in Contemporary Language*. Colorado Springs, Colo.: NavPress, 2002.
2. De Waal, E. (ed.). *The Celtic Vision: Prayers, Blessings, Songs, and Invocations from Alexander Carmichael's Carmina Gadelica*. Liguori, Mo.: Liguori Publications, 1988, p. 251.

Chapter One

1. In using traditional male pronouns, we do not mean to imply that God is literally male. Traditional theologians, of course, did not mean to imply this either.

Chapter Two

1. Lewis, C. S. *The Voyage of the Dawn Treader*. New York: Macmillan, 1952, p. 184.

Chapter Three

1. Author's translation.
2. The modern worldview began in Europe during the late sixteenth century, with the intellectual genius of men such as Francis Bacon (1561–1626), René Descartes (1596–1650),

and Isaac Newton (1642–1727). The modern human can appropriately be characterized as Descartes's autonomous, rational animal encountering Newton's mechanistic world. Perhaps the simplest way to identify the modern era is as the two-hundred-year period between 1789 and 1989—between the storming of the Bastille, which marked the beginning of the French Revolution, and the breaking down of the Berlin wall, which marked the collapse of Communism.

3. Roof, W. C. *Spiritual Marketplace: Baby Boomers and the Remaking of American Religion*. Princeton, N.J.: Princeton University Press, 1999, pp. 9–10.

4. Drane, J. *What Is the New Age Still Saying to the Church?* London: Marshall Pickering, 1999, p. 187.

Chapter Four

1. "Number of Unchurched Adults Has Nearly Doubled Since 1991." May 4, 2004. Retrieved September 14, 2004. www.barna.org/FlexPage.aspx?Page=BarnaUpdate&Barna UpdateID=163.

2. "Number of Unchurched Adults Has Nearly Doubled Since 1991." May 4, 2004.

3. See the study by Andrew Strom (http://homepages.ihug.co.nz/~revival/00-Out-Of-Church.html).

4. Peck, M. S. *The Different Drum: Community-Making and Peace*. New York: Simon & Schuster, 1987, p. 297.

5. The word *bastard* is used to designate "something that is spurious, irregular, inferior, or of questionable origin," substandard, or "lacking genuineness or authority." Unless otherwise noted, all definitions are from the Web-based reference www.dictionary.com.

6. See Jesus' condemnation of religious pride and institutionalism in Matthew 15:1–20; 23:1–39; Mark 7:1–23; and Luke 11:37–53.

Chapter Five

1. As far back as 1949, Herbert Butterfield believed that the twentieth century was ushering in the most exhilarating period in the history of Christianity for fifteen hundred years: "We are back for the first time in something like the earliest centuries of Christianity, and those early centuries afford some relevant clues to the kind of attitude to adopt." Butterfield, H. *Christianity and History*. London: G. Bell and Sons, 1949, p. 135.
2. As quoted in Smith III, J. D. "Wordsmiths of Worship." *Christian History*, 1993, *12*(1), 30.

Chapter Six

1. Author's translation.
2. John 10:10; cf. John 6:35, 51, 63; 11:25; 15:11.
3. John 3:16; 17:3; I John 5:11, 20.
4. Guyon, Jeanne. *Experiencing the Depths of Jesus Christ*. Sargent, Ga.: Seedsowers, 1981, p. 41.
5. See also John 13:15; Acts 1; I Corinthians 11:1; Philippians 2:5, 8; Ephesians 5:2; I Peter 2:21; and I John 2:6.

Chapter Seven

1. The word *church* is used 115 times in the New Testament, mostly in the Acts of the Apostles and in the Epistles (or letters) to the Galatians, Colossians, Ephesians, and so on. In the four Gospels, the term is found only in Matthew 16:18 and 18:17.
2. I Corinthians 12; Ephesians 1:23 and 4:4–16; and Colossians 1:18, 24.
3. Capra, F. *The Web of Life: A New Scientific Understanding of Living Systems*. New York: Anchor, 1996, p. 17.

4. Capra (1996), p. 37.

5. The two cannot fully coexist. One must eventually give in to the other, and the institution rarely gives in.

6. Bosch, D. J. *Transforming Mission: Paradigm Shifts in Theology of Mission*. Maryknoll, N.Y.: Orbis Books, 1991, p. 374.

7. *Chaordic* refers to anything that may be characterized by both chaos and order at the same time. It is similar to the idea of "planned spontaneity."

8. I am grateful to anthropologist Paul Hiebert, who proposed a new way of understanding social groupings: centered sets and bounded sets. Hiebert, P. G. "Sets and Structures: A Study of Church Patterns." In D. J. Hesselgrave (ed.), *New Horizons in World Mission*. Grand Rapids, Mich.: Baker Book House, 1979.

9. See Ephesians 1:22; 3:10–21; 5:23–32; Hebrews 12:23; Revelation 21:1–22:21.

10. Romans 16:23; I Corinthians 1:11, 16; 16:15.

11. I Corinthians 1:2 and II Corinthians 1:1b.

12. The renowned Catholic theologian Hans Küng, who holds a strongly Christ-centered theology, observes how the process of boundary emphasis begins: "Finally, whenever the Church itself turned the Gospel into an infallible law (of teaching, dogma, morals, discipline), unspiritual force and bondage inevitably replaced Christian freedom and spiritual service. . . . The Church had to become a Grand Inquisitor and Jesus himself silently departed." Küng, H. *On Being a Christian*. New York: Doubleday, 1976, p. 559.

Chapter Eight

1. Wright, N. T. *The Challenge of Jesus: Rediscovering Who Jesus Was and Is*. Downers Grove, Ill.: InterVarsity Press, 1999.

2. Acts 9:2; 18:25–26; 19:9, 23; 22:4; 24:14, 22.

3. I Corinthians 12:13; Ephesians 2:14; Philippians 2:1–5; and Colossians 3:11.

4. Athenagoras. "A Plea for the Christian." In A. Roberts (ed.), *The Ante-Nicene Fathers* (10 vols.). New York: Christian Literature, 1885, p. 134. (Reprint by Scribner, n.d.)

5. Preserved in Eusebius, *Church History,* 7:22. Quoted in Chilton, D. *Power in the Blood: A Christian Response to AIDS.* Brentwood, Tenn.: Wolgemuth and Hyatt, 1987.

6. Many other New Testament passages give us a picture of how the followers of Jesus lived in the first century: Antioch (Acts 11:19–27; 13:1–4), Jerusalem (Acts 2), Colossae (Colossians 3:12–17), Berea (Acts 17:10–14), Ephesus (Acts 19:1–41; 20:13–38; Ephesians 1–5), Tyre (Acts 21:3–6), and the seven churches in Revelation 2:1–3:22. Each episode provides a picture and taste of the living Body of Christ.

7. We see many of these same essentials repeated in Romans 15:18–19 and Acts.

8. I Corinthians 2:1–5.

9. Romans 1:15–16; 15:16; I Corinthians 9:16; 15:1–8; Galatians 1:11–12; II Timothy 3:14–17; and Hebrews 4:12.

10. These apostolic teams included (1) Peter and John (Acts 3:1–11; 4:1–31; 8:14–25); (2) Peter and "six brothers" from Joppa (Acts 10:23f; 11:12); (3) Barnabas, Saul, and John Mark (Acts 12:25; 13:2–13; cf. 11:25–26); (4) Paul, Barnabas, and "companions" (Acts 13:13–15:12); (5) Paul, Barnabas, Judas, and Silas (Acts 15:22–35); (6) Barnabas and Mark (Acts 15:36–39); (7) Paul and Silas (Acts 15:40f; cf. 16:19–25; 17:4–10); (8) Paul, Silas, and Timothy (Acts 16:1–9; cf. II Corinthians 1:19; I Thessalonians 1:1; II Thessalonians 1:1; Philippians 1:1); (9) Paul, Silas, Timothy, and Luke (Acts 16:10f); (10) Silas and Timothy (Acts 17:14–18:5); (11) Paul, Silas, Timothy, Luke, Priscilla, and Aquila (Acts 18:2–19; cf. Romans 16:13); (12) Priscilla, Aquila, and Apollos (Acts 18:24–19:1); (13) Timothy and Erastus (Acts 19:21–22; cf. I Timothy 4:20); (14) Paul, Silas, Timothy, Luke, Gaius, and Aristarchus (Acts 19:29); (15) Paul and "Sopater son of

Pyrrhus from Beroea, Aristarchus and Secundus from Thessalonica, Gaius from Derbe, Timothy also, and Tychicus and Trophimus from the province of Asia" (Acts 20:4); and (16) Zenas "the lawyer" and Apollos (Titus 3:13).

11. I Timothy 4:15–16; II Timothy 2:2; 3:10–14; Titus 2:7–8.

12. Acts 1:8; II Corinthians 10:13–16; Philippians 1:13–16; and I Thessalonians 1:8–9.

13. See Acts 10, where God set in motion two convergent chains of "divine dominoes" that brought together Peter and the house of Cornelius in a most miraculous and spectacular way.

14. Throughout the book of Acts, we see the central role of the Holy Spirit in the growth and reproduction of churches: Acts 1:8; 2:4; 4:8, 31; 6:10; 8:29; 10:19; 11:15; 13:2, 9; 15:28; 16:6; 20:22–23; 21:4. There are also numerous references to believers being filled with the Holy Spirit, among them Acts 1:2, 5–8; 2:4; 3:8; 4:8, 31; 6:5, 8; 7:55; 8:15–25; 9:17; 10:44–46.

15. See Acts 5:17–18; 7:54–60; 8:1–3, 16; 17:13–15.

Chapter Nine

1. I recently heard a story on National Public Radio that reported Buddhist groups on the East Coast have been visiting Christian churches and church growth workshops to find ways of keeping their youth "in the faith."

2. Singh, S. S. *Wisdom of the Sadhu: Teachings of Sundar Singh* (K. Comer, ed.). Sussex, UK: Plough, 2003, p. 177. http://www.bruderhof.com/e-books/WisdomSadhu.htm).

3. Peck (1987), p. 293.

4. Kosomo, K. "Nande Culture: A Solid Ground for Theologizing In!" M.A. thesis, Fuller Theological Seminary (1994), p. 13.

5. Shenk, W. R. "Mission, Renewal, and the Future of the Church." *International Bulletin of Missionary Research*, 1997, *21*(4), 154–159.

6. A wine will never go beyond the quality of the grapes. Bad fruit cannot be improved with age.

7. See Psalm 40:3; 96:1; 98:1; Jeremiah 31:31; Matthew 26:28; Luke 22:20–21; II Corinthians 5:17; Hebrews 9:15.

8. Note, however, Peter's ongoing struggle in Galatians 2:11–16.

9. To fully receive the new wine, our battle is against *sin* and anything that separates us from God. But in acquiring the new wineskin, our battle is against *religious traditions* that oppose the grace of God. It is far more difficult for many to break free from human traditions than it is for them to break free from sin! Remember, Jesus was crucified not because he spoke against sin but because he exposed the hypocrisy of religious leaders and preached against their religious traditions. We must come to see what to release in order to hold on to the deeper, more essential truth of the Way of Jesus.

Chapter Ten

1. Romans 1:16–17; cf. Ephesians 3:8–9.

2. Shenk (1997), pp. 154–159.

3. The connection between death and rebirth is a central theme throughout the Bible; see I Samuel 17; Jeremiah 1:10; Luke 8:14; 9:23; Ephesians 4:22–24; and Hebrews 12:1.

4. I Corinthians 6:12; 8:13; 10:23–33; Hebrews 12:1–3.

5. I Corinthians 6:12; 8:13; 10:23–33; Hebrews 12:1–3.

6. As quoted by John GrosVenor in "Our Daily Frybread," an e-mail newsletter published by www.newgatherings.com. June 2, 2004.

7. For a great book on traveling light, read *Beyond Backpacking: Ray Jardine's Guide to Lightweight Hiking*. La Pine, Oreg.: AdventureLore Press, 2000.

Chapter Eleven

1. Jackson, K. (ed. and trans.). *A Celtic Miscellany*. New York: Penguin, 1971, p. 261.

2. MacEowen, F. *The Mist-Filled Path: Celtic Wisdom for Exiles, Wanderers, and Seekers.* Novato, Calif.: New World Library, 2002, pp. 47–48.

3. Peck (1987), p. 17.

4. Jung, C. G. *The Collected Works*, vol. 16, *The Practice of Psychotherapy.* Bollingen Series XX (R.F.C. Hull, trans.). Princeton, N.J.: Princeton University Press, 1954, p. 454.

5. As quoted by Matthew Fox in *The Coming of the Cosmic Christ.* San Francisco: HarperSanFrancisco, 1988, p. 11.

6. See also Genesis 1–2; Leviticus 25:23; Psalm 65:9ff; 115:16; and Matthew 5:45; 6:26–30.

7. Burks, P. "NACCE Congress, the Crisis, and the Church." *Earthlight*, 1996, *24*(1), 18–19.

8. Genesis 4:10; II Chronicles 7:14; Psalm 106:38; Ezra 9:11; Jeremiah 3:1; 16:18.

9. Cf. II Corinthians 5:18; Ephesians 1:10, 22; and Philippians 2:10–11.

10. Newell, J. P. *Listening for the Heartbeat of God: A Celtic Spirituality.* New York: Paulist Press, 1997, p. 64. See also Hebrews 1:1–3.

11. Newell (1997).

12. Hitt, J. "This Is Your Brain on God." *Wired*, Nov. 1999, issue 7.11.

13. Lesser, E. *The New American Spirituality: A Seeker's Guide.* New York: Random House, 1999, p. 37.

Chapter Twelve

1. For more on Christ-centered healing, see the book *Healing Like Jesus*, by our friend Daniel Hari (www.omegalive.ch).

2. Jeremiah 29:13–14.

3. Genesis 2:7; Job 32:8.

4. Meister Eckhart. *Meister Eckhart* (R. Blakney, trans.). New York: HarperCollins, 1946. See also the message of Jesus in John 10:34–35 (cf. Psalm 82:6).

5. See Jesus' parable in Matthew 25:37–46.
6. The root *eco* is from the Greek word *oikos*, which also is the root of both *economy* ("to manage a household")—and *ecology*—(the study of our household or the environment in which we live); cf. Genesis 1:26; Psalm 8:6.
7. Buber, M. *I and Thou* (W. A. Kaufmann, trans.). New York: Scribner, 1970), p. 55.

Chapter Thirteen

1. It was the early Celtic church's emphasis on the presence of God at the heart of all life and within all people that moved the Roman church to crack down on the Celtic Way. (The Roman church emphasized the truth of the original separation of humanity from God, which we look at later in this chapter.)
2. Wheatley, M. J. *Turning to One Another: Simple Conversations to Restore Hope to the Future*. San Francisco: Berrett-Koehler, 2002, p. 114.
3. In Old English, Lucifer means "the morning star," as in Isaiah 14:12; cf. II Corinthians 11:14–15.
4. See II Peter 2:1–3 and I John 2:18–29.
5. John 1:12; 3:16; II Peter 3:9.
6. Lewis, C. S. *The Problem of Pain*. New York: Macmillan, 1962), p. 34.
7. Singh (2003), pp. 51–52.
8. See also Jeremiah 12:11; 23:10.
9. Fox, M. *Creation Spirituality*. San Francisco: HarperSanFrancisco, 1991, p. 9.

Chapter Fourteen

1. I Corinthians 1:29–31; Ephesians 2:8–9; II Timothy 1:8–11.
2. Singh (2003), p. 67.
3. II Samuel 14:14; I Corinthians 15:45.

4. Romans 5:8–10; Colossians 3:10.
5. Matthew 5:48; I Peter 1:15–16; Leviticus 19:2.
6. Newell (1997), p. 103.
7. Romans 8:15–17 (cf. Galatians 4:6–7; Ephesians 1:3–5; 2:10; and Psalm 8:5, 139).

Chapter Fifteen

1. II Timothy 4:6; Philippians 2:17.
2. Bonhoeffer, D. *Christ the Center* (J. Bowden, trans.). New York: HarperCollins, 1960, p. 17.
3. Mark 8:27–29; cf. Matthew 16:13–17:1.

Chapter Sixteen

1. Some readers may be disturbed by our use of *(re)incarnate*. We use this spelling to refer to the equivalent of being "born again" in Jesus, which is a spiritual transformation that happens this side of death. The word *reincarnation* is derived from the Latin, meaning "taking on flesh again," which signifies being "born again." For purposes of this book, we use *(re)incarnation* to speak of being born again in Jesus and *reincarnation* to mean a central belief of Hinduism that refers to the incessant cycle of physical birth and death.
2. Muggeridge, M. *The End of Christendom*. Grand Rapids, Michigan: Wm. B. Eerdmans, 1980, p. 56.

Chapter Seventeen

1. In his book *Owning Your Own Shadow,* the Jungian analyst Robert Johnson describes this as one of Jung's favorite stories (San Francisco: HarperSanFrancisco, 1991).
2. After twenty years, I am beginning to understand Karl Marx's famous statement: "Religion is the sigh of the oppressed creature, the heart of a heartless world, and the soul of soulless

conditions. It is the opium of the people." Such an inflammatory statement by a Russian Jew, turned Lutheran, who later became the father of Marxist communism!

Chapter Eighteen

1. Manning, B. *Ruthless Trust: The Ragamuffin's Path to God*. San Francisco: HarperSanFrancisco, 2000), pp. 12–13.

Chapter Nineteen

1. We highly recommend a book by our friend Brett Johnson, *Convergence*, published by Indaba (www.inst.net).
2. As my friend Brad notes: "Acknowledging the breathtaking complexity of the universe doesn't mean I think everything is complicated, any more than by acknowledging that from the peace-bringing simplicity that unifies life I think everything is simplistic. There can be elegance of process and yet enormousness of personhood. So, to refuse comprehensivity and complexity is ridiculous. To refuse systems and simplicity is reductionist. To hold both in paradox biblically is righteous."

Chapter Twenty

1. See Jesus' words in John 14:12–14; 15:14–17; and 20:21.
2. Newell (1997), pp. 4–5.
3. Artificial life support is any system that uses technology to aid, support, or replace a vital function of the body.
4. Merton, T. *Collected Poems*. New York: New Directions, 1977, p. 201.

Chapter Twenty-One

1. John 3:16; II Corinthians 5:14.
2. Joel 2:28–29.

3. John 8:31–32; Matthew 22:29; Colossians 3:15; II Timothy 3:16–17; Hebrews 4:12.
4. Acts 2:43; 3:6–8; 4:30, 33; 5:12; 8:6–7; 9:33, 40; 14:3, 8–10; 16:18; 19:11. See also Romans 15:19 and II Corinthians 12:12.
5. Matthew 10:1; Mark 9:38–39; Luke 9:49–50; 10:1, 9; John 14:12.
6. Deuteronomy 13:1–3; Matthew 7:22; 24:24; Acts 8:9–11; II Thessalonians 2:9; Revelation 16:14; 19:20.
7. Acts 14:8–20; 15:12; II Corinthians 12:12; Galatians 3:5.

Chapter Twenty-Two

1. De Waal, E. *The Celtic Way of Prayer: The Recovery of the Religious Imagination*. New York: Image Books, 1997, p. 9.
2. St. Brendan (484–577 A.D.) became well known for his sea voyages in a traditional boat made of skin and wood. He and his band of brothers explored from Scandinavia to Africa and may have been the first Europeans to land on America, a thousand years before Columbus ever set sail.

Acknowledgments:
A Word of Thanks

This is not the book we began to write. Six weeks before the manuscript was due to the editor, Jennifer and I escaped to a beach house at the mouth of Washington's Hood Canal to bring the book together. We didn't do all that much writing. God had other plans; he ended up rewriting us. The book took another shift and became a story we write together. It now reflects *our* journey with Jesus.

We owe much to so many people everywhere who have encouraged us along the Way. Some have been with us from the beginning; some walked with us during critical seasons of our journey; and some have given us vital counsel, comfort, and even correction along the path. Any value from this book we share with all those we have walked with, while any criticisms belong to us alone.

We are grateful for our parents, Chuck and Louise Simpson and Robert and Elizabeth Campbell, for planting within us the desire to experience God and giving us the freedom to explore in our own way. Special thanks to Jennifer's mom, who generously gave her love and time to watch our children during the times we went away to reflect and write.

Thanks to the many friends and pilgrims who engaged in lively conversations along the Way, at Zeitgeist Café in Seattle, over e-mail, while kayaking in the Puget Sound, or around the fire with our families at a summer solstice party. Deep thanks to Neil Baker, Kim Coryell, Paul and Colleen Ziakin, and Howard Patlis. Our family friends, Tammy and Ross Hathaway, always had an encouraging word and came alongside us in so many practical ways.

We are especially thankful for those who have given us permission to include their stories here. Except where explicit permission was given, names and identifying information have been changed to protect confidentiality.

Thanks to all our friends who had the courage to explore the Way of Jesus when we began in Southern California, especially Chris and Tess Berry, Ramon and Theresa Covarrubias, Mike and Shannon O'Shields, Ben and Debbie Stewart, Beth and Jeff Kurtz, Hsieh and Teresa Sun, and Kasareka Kosomo, all of whom walked with us and encouraged us in those early days. We also appreciate L. E. Boydston, Robert and Julia Banks, Dave Palmer, Gene and Virginia Wilson, Jim Akins, Dick Scoggins, Jim and Patsy Frost, C. Peter Wagner, Charles Brock, Robert Fitts, and Nate Krupp, who believed in us and encouraged us at the beginning of our journey.

We are indebted to the many mentors who have shared with us so freely their wisdom and their lives: Salvatore Zambito, George Patterson, Thom Wolf, Carol Davis, John and Christine Noble, Wilbert and Juanita Shenk, Tony and Felicity Dale, Chris Daza, Dan and Jody Mayhew, Chuck Van Engen, and Wade Hankins. You have graciously encouraged us along the Way and exhorted us to continue on.

There are so many fellow sojourners we have learned from: James Russell, Paul and Keiva Kaak, Wolfgang and Mercy Simson, Linda Bergquist, Jim and Liz Stephens, Rick Leatherwood, Lorenzo and Nadine Hernandez, Owen and Sandy Brock, Reed and Monette Grafke, Neil Cole, Mike Steele, Bruce Graham, Bill Robinson. Special thanks to the families of Joel and Heidi Butz, and Alan and Catherine Wertjes, for encouraging us during an especially difficult season.

We are grateful for all the folks of Leadership Network and Jossey-Bass who have served along the way, especially Sheryl Fullerton for her professionalism and passion in guiding us through each phase of this project. Thank you, Brian D. McLaren, for writing the Foreword. Thanks as well to Carol Childress for calling me out of exile to write our story. Deep thanks to Brad Sargent for the editorial work that helped to revive our souls in the final leg of this manuscript. Thank you Elaine Colvin for your timely counsel. For readers Marsha Gilliland, Ray and Liz Lévesque, and Patty Nowell for giving of their time and input into this book, our appreciation.

We are deeply grateful for those who walked alongside us during our most recent season, especially Daniel and Cornelia Hari, Stefan Driess, Helen Huegli, Marcel and Maria Pütter, and the Omega Live team in Switzerland for the renewal and refreshment you so lovingly gave us; for Brett and Lyn Johnson, Mike and Julie Bullock, Doug Johnson, and the rest of the Equip South Africa team, who befriended our family and loved our children so selflessly; and for Brian and Erin Campbell, for believing in us.

To our children, Lauren, David, Rachael, and Nathan: you bring such joy and love to our lives. Each of you has played an integral part in our journey. Thank you for walking with us so cheerfully and patiently as we have gone through the sometimes painstaking process of writing this book: Nathan, for your spontaneous hugs that encouraged us while we were working on the manuscript; Rachael, for your beautiful notes and cards and your prayers of faith for the completion of this project; David, for coming alongside us with understanding beyond your age and your thoughtful prayers; and Lauren, for your encouraging presence, deep convictions, and great meals. May each of you be strengthened to walk the Way of Jesus in your uniqueness and experience the fullness of freedom and joy.

Finally, we give all the praise and glory to Jesus, our Waymaker.

About the Authors

Jonathan and *Jennifer Campbell* have been pioneering spiritual communities together over their twenty years of friendship and marriage. They and their children are part of local and international teams that exist to encourage and equip new movements of Christ-centered spiritual communities in the Pacific Northwest and beyond.

During his twelve years of professional ministry, Jonathan served as pastor, church planter, trainer, and professor at several graduate schools. He earned his Ph.D. from Fuller School of Intercultural Studies. Jonathan has extensive experience in coaching and consulting with leaders of churches, organizations, and corporations throughout North America and parts of Asia, Africa, Europe, and Latin America.

When they moved to the Pacific Northwest, Jennifer began home schooling their four children and Jonathan started a technology company and consulting practice. As an entrepreneur, Jonathan has codeveloped several businesses in the United States and abroad. Jonathan and Jennifer coach and build teams to become marketplace leaders for societal transformation.

Jonathan and Jennifer enjoy exploring the outdoors with their four children from their home in the Pacific Northwest.

Resources for the Journey

If you wish to know more about how others are living the Way of Jesus across cultures, we encourage you to visit www.wayofjesus.com.